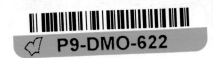

Praise for *The Fashion Designer Survival Guide*

"Lest fashion's neophytes get too dreamy, Gehlhar is there to ground them..."
—*Women's Wear Daily*

"Mary presents many expectations [new designers] will confront in the marketplace and provides excellent professional advice throughout the book."—Margaret Hayes, President, The Fashion Group International

"Must read...find out from a pro who has worked with up-and-coming designers."
—*New York Daily News*

"Every aspiring designer needs this book. Mary Gehlhar wrote an invaluable, step-by-step guide to succeeding on Seventh Avenue and beyond." —Nancy MacDonell, News Editor, Style.com, and author of *The Classic Ten: The True Story of the Little Black Dress and Nine Other Fashion Favorites*

"For anyone who's ever aspired to be an independent designer, this is the book to pick up." —*The Daily*

"Ms. Gehlhar to the rescue! Who better to school fashion young 'uns on the ins and outs of the business than the woman who does just that for a living?" —*Fashion Wire Daily*

"A must-read for anyone in the world of fashion. Gehlhar offers practical tips and strategies to increase chances of success." —*Soma Magazine*

"This book encourages all aspiring designers ready to embark on an independent career within the industry." —Rebecca Taylor, designer

The Fashion Designer Survival Guide

Revised and Expanded Edition

Start and Run Your Own Fashion Business

Mary Gehlhar

KAPLAN

PUBLISHING

New York

© 2008 by Mary Gehlhar

Published by Kaplan Publishing, a division of Kaplan, Inc.
1 Liberty Plaza, 24th Floor
New York, NY 10006

Printed in the United States of America

July 2008
10 9 8 7 6

ISBN-13: 978-1-4277-9710-0

Kaplan Publishing books are available at special quantity discounts to use for sales promotions, employee premiums, or educational purposes. Please email our Special Sales Department to order or for more information at kaplanpublishing@kaplan.com or write to Kaplan Publishing, 1 Liberty Plaza, 24th Floor, New York, NY 10006.

Contents

Foreword . ix
Preface . xi
One Piece of Advice . xiii

1 ■ Before You Start .1
 The Reality .2
 You Survived the Bad News .10

2 ■ The Fundamentals .13
 The Plan .13
 Elements of the Plan .15
 Setting up the Business, by Melanie Jones19

3 ■ The Money .33
 How Much Do You Need? .34
 Where to Find Money .39
 Factoring, by Tim Moore .47

4 ■ Product Development .59
 Know Your Customer .59
 Have a Point of View .60
 The Trends .63
 The Collection .64
 Signature Items .65
 The Quality Standard .65
 It Must Look the Price .66
 Commerciality and Show .66

5 ▪ Fabric and Materials .68
 Learn First .68
 The Challenges .69
 The Sources .74
 Once You Order .78

6 ▪ Production .84
 The Production Plan .84
 Sample Production .87
 Tips and Considerations When Hiring a Patternmaker,
 by Sally Beers .90
 Production Options .96
 Production Management .108
 Factory Management .114

7 ▪ Marketing and Branding Materials121
 Be Your Brand .122
 Logos .122
 Press and Sales Kits .122
 Other Marketing Materials .134

8 ▪ Sales .138
 The Financial Realities of Selling138
 Where to Sell .145
 Selling to the Stores .156
 Cold Calling, by Rachel Shechtman160
 The Appointment .164
 The Order .166
 Getting Paid .176
 Customer Service and Supporting Sales179
 Who Should Sell the Line? .186

Trade Shows .193
Making the Most of the Shows, by Barbara Kramer195

9 ■ Press and Public Relations .201
Good News/Bad News .201
The PR Strategy .203
Dressing Celebrities, by Roger Padilha212
Who Should Handle PR? .217

10 ■ The Runway .219
To Show or Not to Show .219
Producing a Runway Show .223
Sponsorship .239

11 ■ Copyrights and Knockoffs .242
Fashion Design and the Copyright Laws,
 by Jason Gabbard .242

12 ■ Expanding the Business .251
Licensing .252
A Second Line .254
Partnerships/Consulting .256
Creative Direction .259
Investors and Partners .260
Acknowledgments .261
Notes .263
Resources .271
Index .283

Foreword

When I began my business in 1972, I wish a book like *The Fashion Designer's Survival Guide* had existed that I could have turned to for advice on how to launch a fashion business. Fortunately, Mary Gehlhar has provided such an invaluable tool for today's generation of designers. Reading this guide brought me back to my first days as a designer and my own journey.

New designers often ask me what the key to success is when starting a business in fashion. My response is simple: you must first understand who or what you want to be. What is your vision? For whom are you designing clothes? It may take several months to figure this out, but once you do, the rest should come naturally.

Secondly, work with an experienced designer. Many of today's most successful designers worked as apprentices or assistants to established designers, which serves as a great opportunity for gaining exposure to the business of fashion and establishing industry contacts with suppliers, factories, editors, and retailers. I, myself, worked in a printing factory in Italy before I decided to design and launch my dresses.

Finally, never hesitate to seek help. Organizations such as the Council of Fashion Designers of America (CFDA) offer support and assistance, scholarships to design students, mentoring of emerging talent through the CFDA/Vogue Fashion Fund and other programs, and ongoing panels with industry experts on the business of fashion. The CFDA is committed to working hard on behalf of the fashion industry to help designers succeed. As president of the Council of Fashion Designers of America, I represent all designers, new and experienced, and believe in sharing all I have learned with emerging talent.

I leave you with this: a good designer must recognize that there will be ups and downs in one's career and must be prepared for constructive criticism by press, buyers, peers, and so on. Always remain confident yet grounded, embrace advice and criticism, learn from your mistakes, and do not hesitate to ask for help.

I did not know the mechanics of how to start a company, but I managed to do so because I was not afraid to ask. You should always ask and seek answers for what you do not know. Many of these answers lie within the pages of *The Fashion Designer's Survival Guide*, a great resource for new and established designers.

Fear is not an option…Go for it!

Sincerely,
Diane von Furstenberg

Preface

This book was originally published in 2005 and now, three years later, the proposition of being an independent fashion designer is as exhilarating as ever. Few industries move as fast as fashion, and opportunity abounds as the competition increases and the playing field changes daily.

Driven by celebrity obsession, fashion television, and the Internet, fashion is in hot demand. New designers are benefiting from an increased interest by retailers, editors, stylists, and even investors wanting to discover fashion's greatest new hidden talent and offer shoppers a diverse selection. Consumers are more interested in what's new than in big brands.

Economic forces are also at play. The deflation of the dollar against the euro is leading American buyers to cut their European purchases and seek new, U.S.-based sources, and Europe is becoming a viable market. Accessories are booming as consumers willingly invest in high-end bags and shoes that don't fluctuate with their weight. New markets are available to designers as mass marketing and low-end design gigs at large chains, such as Gap and Target, have gained acceptability.

At the same time, the market is more saturated, more sophisticated, and more challenging. Fashion's increasing role as part of pop culture has put more pressure on designers to be a personality or star and to differentiate their products to compete against the inexpensive, trend-driven fast fashion from chains such as H&M. More celebrities are launching their own labels, scooping up shelf space and licensing opportunities. Stores are less loyal to their designers as they look over their shoulder to welcome the next new name with buzz. The jaded say that starting your own label is really just a short-term strategy to getting a high-profile design job at an established label.

At the end of day, there is still a great need and desire for true innovation and creativity mixed with strong business acumen.

Few resources are available to help prepare designers for having their own labels. Fashion school will teach you about patterns, draping, and trend forecasts. It can prepare you for a successful career as head designer and even offer classes on bookkeeping and business plans. But running your own business is another matter.

This book is designed to help new designers successfully set up and run a business, benefiting from the pitfalls, mistakes, and triumphs of other designers who are doing it themselves. This second edition includes new sections on financing and private equity, sales and cold calling, and partnerships and consulting opportunities; an update on the extensive efforts to protect fashion designs legally; photo examples for branding and product development; as well as extended sections of quotes from entrepreneurial designers who are in the trenches facing these challenges every day. Through the course of writing the book, I've spoken with more than 100 designers and industry professionals about their specific areas of expertise. I have gained valuable insight from the innovative thinkers and great business minds who have generously shared their experiences. Among the buying offices, editorial departments, fabric mills, factories, and financial institutions, there is a passionate crowd rooting for the next generation of designers.

These pages will demystify the world of young designers and reveal the tough parts while providing the knowledge and tools to carry on. It is a collective summary of what it takes to survive. The advice is not sugar coated, and it's not always what you want to hear. But knowledge is power and should not discourage you.

The book is intended to help designers in their first few years and lend guidance to those who have been operating for much longer. It was written to increase the odds of success. Here's to the next generation.

One Piece of Advice

If you could give today's young designers one piece of advice what would it be?

John Bartlett

"If you want to start your own line I would do one of two things . . . I would commit myself to working for another designer company for at least four years to really learn from their mistakes . . . or I would concentrate on one product category, like t-shirts or shoes, and focus all of my energy developing the best possible product. Too many designers get caught up in doing a whole collection and doing shows. Shows are for ego, product is for survival."

Tommy Hilfiger

"Being a successful fashion designer is about more than just making great clothes. It's about running a business, and that means having a combination of diverse skills—you need creativity, business acumen, social skills, management skills, and most importantly, you need dedication. I started out in this business with $150 and a dream. There were many years, challenges, and lessons learned before getting to where I am today. The best piece of advice I'd give to a young designer is to first dream big and believe in yourself, and then approach fashion from a holistic point of view. You have to start with a great product, but you also need the right vehicle to get that great product into your customer's hands. That means planning, researching, merchandising, building great relationships, having a great marketing plan, and being able to execute all of those things in a carefully thought out way."

Donna Karan

"There are three things you absolutely must keep in mind: Realize that in the end, it's all about the customer—your customer. You need to decide who she is and then really get to know what she's about. That single-minded focus is the way you create a strong, consistent message. Make sure the people behind you are better than you and that you're all on the same page. Lastly, never believe the good press because that means you have to believe the bad. Be true to yourself."

Richard Lambertson of Lambertson Truex

"Stay true to your design ethics and try to be different, but don't follow the trends. You can't be everything to everybody. I also can't stress enough that the more practical experience you have the better. Everyone wants to work for the big names but you can get even more experience working for a small house."

Christian Louboutin

"As a supposedly established designer, I regret to say that I have very few words of advice to give to the emerging talent. The reality is that I continue to learn every day about my work. But, if I may give one word of advice, it would be this: leave, and always leave, your imagination above everything else; technique should always serve imagination, and not the opposite. To be a good technician is only a help, but should never be a priority. Why? Because technique can shrink your creation, and creation is everything, and the rest should gravitate around this. The more you are free, the more your design will reflect this sense of liberty, which is after all, one of the essences of fashion. Fashion tends to represent different points of view and meaning, and at its best should reflect individuality, eccentricity, and wit."

Cynthia Rowley

"Coming from a free-thinking art school that encouraged creativity, I very quickly learned about the constant battle between art and commerce and had to find the balance to survive. There are many ways to find your own balance and to learn both sides of the business. Once you learn the rules, I think it is very important to take chances and push the envelope as a designer—sometimes ideas work; sometimes they don't, but the most important thing is that you roll the dice. The fashion industry is forever evolving and so much of being successful is changing and adapting while remaining true to your vision and maintaining your integrity."

Richard Tyler

"I started when I was 18 by opening my own store. There's nothing like it for finding your own niche and it ensures your survival. You show your clothing to the world the way you envision it. It's healthy to see what people admire and what they can truly wear. When you get to know your client, they keep you balanced between designing what drives and interests you and designing for the person who is wearing your clothes."

Diane Von Furstenberg

"The important thing is to believe in what you do. Have a big dream and take small steps."

"One piece of advice from the up and coming labels."

"Be passionate and have a vision that you stick to. Always be humble—In fashion, success can be short-lived."—Jane Ko, Nervenkitt, jewelry

"Start with a very focused niche, just one product such as a very special jacket or shirt, and offer just 10 styles. Use just one fabric, one factory, do it from home, and with as little cost as possible to maintain a 30 percent margin. Then grow slowly, very slowly."—Robert Geller, menswear

"Be true to yourself—you will get a thousands comments on what you should do—if you take them all into account you will be too scattered."—Kristen Lee, shoes

"Be ready to work—A LOT! Build a good team around yourself."—Tina Hernaiz and Nike Clausing, Ingwa; Melero, womenswear

"Do it however you can. There are many different ways to start and they all can work. It's important that you do it in a way that suits you, or you may never do it at all."—Lily Raskind, Sunshine and Shadow, womenswear

"Focus on what you really love to do—not what you see in the street or in the industry"—Gustavo Cadile, eveningwear

"Know exactly what you are doing and who you are doing it for."—Ana Beatriz, Lerario Beatriz, womenswear

"Learn how to run a business, whether you partner up with someone who has the know-how, or you learn yourself. Make sure you have a very solid foundation beneath you; a high-quality product, a unique sales pitch, and most importantly, funds to cover production, the upcoming season, and the myriad of mishaps which may happen along the way."—Alison Kelly, womenswear

"Learn your market. Analyze your product. Be clear in your brand, perform to your best, and reach for the sky."—Diego Binetti, womenswear

"Learn patternmaking. You can save a lot of money"—Annie Lewis and Helen Cho, Lewis Cho, womenswear

"Never lose site of you! No matter what successes or downfalls come your way stay true to yourself."—Jessica Alpert-Goldman, World According to Jess, accessories

"Planning is the most important thing for anyone starting a clothing line. Specifically, I would focus on design and vision, sales and financial planning. Problems in any one of these areas will inevitably lead to problems in the other areas as well. Although you can't avoid all problems, you will save yourself a lot of headaches down the road by doing your homework in the beginning."—Romain Kapadia, menswear

"Work in the industry, network, gain experience and knowledge. When you decide to establish your company partner up with someone who has a strong background in business."—Brian Wood, menswear

"Use amazing fabrics. There are a lot of fantastic, gorgeous fabrics out there and it's important that your clothing feels great on and off."—Chloe, Samantha and Caillianne Beckerman, womenswear

"Be humble. The fashion world is very small and you should treat everybody nicely and equally with respect."—Grace Sun, womenswear

"Surround yourself with smart, dedicated people, they make all of the difference. Oh, and if you have a partner, make sure and have a partnership agreement!"—Jada Simons, Marie Marie, womenswear

"It doesn't happen overnight. You have to love it enough to keep going when it's not glamour and designer-y all the time. You have to have tenacity and patience of a doorknob. Like fishing, you have to work hard and throw as many hooks out as possible and some of them will work out. It's a process and the one that sticks around will see results sooner or later. Hopefully sooner."—Jane Ivanov, Eve Alexander, maternity lingerie

"Make a business plan. Try and create as much of an infrastructure before you begin to build your company."—Cheyenne Morris, Tashkent, shoes

"Surround yourself in business with people you trust"—Corinne Grassini, Society for Rational Dress, womenswear

"This isn't really fair for me to say since I didn't do it this way, but work for someone else first, make your mistakes on someone else's dollar and learn as much as you possibly can about the industry. Build your name and your resume. When you've worked for nota-

ble designers before you launch, you have a huge amount of credibility behind you. Let's say you do it like me. Then make sure you know what you're doing, do as much research as you can, know your product and how to produce it. Having an education in design. Knowing pattern making and sewing has been crucial. I made all of my product the first year, so when I grew, I knew exactly how it needed to be manufactured. If you're more business based and you have the ideas but not these skills, make sure you hire someone who does."—Lara Miller, womenswear

"Expect long working hours, requiring endless dedication, many degrees of extreme satisfaction as well as compromise. Never let go of the dream because your desire will take you there."—Nicole Romano, womenswear, accessories

"Start now — design. Design like there is no tomorrow because once the business starts to roll, you'll find yourself dealing with contractors, stores and handling problems long before you have any time to be creative with your pencil and paper. Most of the creativity that follows in the business is how to survive."—Christine Alcalay, womenswear

1

Before You Start

Now is the time. People are eager for young designers. Each year, there is growing interest, buzz, and support for new talent. Stores and magazines compete aggressively to discover the best new designer first. Around the world, industry organizations have created awards and financial assistance to recognize and support new names. Consumers are tired of the sameness offered by the big brands and seek something special to set them apart. The Internet has made new fashion accessible to all corners of the world, with many new sites dedicated to selling emerging labels and profiling the designers behind them. Even reality TV has jumped on the bandwagon to feed the curiosity about life as an aspiring fashion star.

All of this offers more opportunity to reach people and new ways to succeed. However, this is also one of the most challenging times for new designers. The competition is growing as more people are drawn to the perceived glamour and star power of the field. While the big brands are getting bigger, the department stores are consolidating, celebrities from Kate Moss and Victoria Beckham to Mary Kate and Ashley Olsen are continuing to jump on the designer bandwagon, and fast fashion—from H&M, Uniqlo, and Forever 21—is claiming chunks of the fashion-forward market. The press and buyers send mixed messages and put extraordinary pressure on designers to become instant household names. Ron Frasch, chief merchant at Saks Fifth Avenue, said, "Our industry does have a tendency to overhype the few who are the rising stars. We can destroy you probably faster than you can destroy yourself."[1]

It's tempting, but dangerous, to succumb to the hype and unrealistic expectations of the fashion world.

The Reality

To help you succeed, right up front we have to strip away the glamorous image of runway shows, celebrities on red carpets, and designers yachting in St. Barts. I don't want to rain on the parade, but fashion is a business. It's the business of making and selling clothing and accessories.

Aspiring designers enter the fashion world to be creative, but regardless of creative genius, fashion is nothing without commerce. Even designer Karl Lagerfeld has said, "Fashion is something you wear. It's not something you put on the runway to show how creative you are. There's nothing bad about selling dresses."[2]

Designer Isaac Mizrahi has said of his own career, "I used to think my job was about coming up with a new, bold, crazy look every six months, making something fabulous and pretty for my friends and the models." But as journalist Teri Agins wrote, "Now he gets giddy over how well his clothes sell to masses of ordinary women."[3]

Designers need to balance the business and creative sides—one allows the other to live. To say you are a creative person who can't do the other side is nonsense. Surviving day to day in business is creative in itself. Designers find unique ways to solve problems and promote their product without the proper resources or experience. Even Andy Warhol said, "Good business is the best art."

Where's the Glamour?

If you are doing this just to be famous, forget it. The fashion world requires hard work, discipline, perseverance, and passion. There is no magic formula or secret to success, and while designers can learn from others, they each must find their own path.

It's easy to romanticize the freedom of having your own business, but it's not as easy as it looks. According to the Small Business Administration, more than 50 percent of small businesses fail in their first year, and 95 percent are gone by the fifth. Gilbert Harrison, chairman of Financo, a New York invest-

ment bank, says starting a small fashion business is even harder and less than 1 percent make it. He compares fashion to acting: "How many people go to Hollywood to be a star and end up waitressing?"[4]

Several designers, including Darryl K, John Bartlett, and Isaac Mizrahi, who were considered established at one time, had to return to square one and restart their businesses. John Galliano and Michael Kors are two of many designers who have experienced bankruptcy.

Don't be discouraged but realize entrepreneurship is the hard road, not the easy one. When asked what surprised them the most about having their own businesses, designers Matthew Morgan and Allessandro Poddie replied "that it's so hard. Every bit from the fabric, production, and sales, to cash flow."[5] Be honest with yourself and assess whether self-employment is the right path for you. Not everyone is happy as an entrepreneur, and there are realities to brace yourself for up front.

It takes more money than you think. When asked, "What is the hardest part of running your own business?" the majority of designers answered "the money." In fact, designer Keanan Duffty says, "No matter how much you think it will cost, multiply that by ten."[6] Up front, you must determine if you can afford to start your own business and whether you are willing and able to work potentially for several years, stretching cash and struggling, to pay everyone but yourself.

You will live, eat, and breathe your business. Designers work 7 days a week, 12 or more hours per day, and have little time for friends, exercise, or vacation. Designer Daniel Silver of Duckie Brown confirms, "It has to become a lifestyle."[7] A designer needs physical and mental stamina and must be absolutely, passionately in love with what she is doing. Designer Micheal Spaulding of Gunmetal shoes says, "The hardest part is the endless hours you put into it. You are always tired and every morning you have to get up, and not be tired, and do your work."[8]

It could take years. Getting your business on its feet can easily take five or more years. Many designers who get significant press attention, grow their sales

each season, and are cited as models of success are in fact still not making money. Ralph Lauren did not go from tie salesman to fashion emperor overnight.

You will design less than 10 percent of the time. A designer takes on many roles and spends significant time on paperwork, managing people, shipping, spending time in factories, servicing customers, mailing lookbooks, sourcing, and chasing money. Most young designers do everything themselves, and while many learn to love the other aspects of the business, they generally spend only 5 to 10 percent of their time designing.

It demands militant self-discipline. When you work for yourself, no one is there to make you get out of bed each morning, meet your deadlines, or prioritize your time. An entrepreneur must create his own structure and set daily goals to stay focused and ensure everything is organized and on schedule. The buck stops with you, and when problems arise, you can't run and hide.

You need to be tough and assertive. This is business, and a designer can't be timid or take it personally. Designer Louis Verdad says, "The hardest part of being an entrepreneur is having a split personality. When running your business, you have to be hard, but the creative mind has to remain emotional and sensitive."[9] Business owners must deal aggressively with factory supervisors, store owners, and collections people who bully, intimidate, and try to rip them off. You will have to call people who owe you money, make tough decisions that can upset others, and learn to say no.

You are on your own. Being independent means facing the daily stress of not having a steady income, benefits, or any guarantees. Despite how nice it sounds to not have a boss, working alone can be lonely. Independent designers spend hours by themselves and often feel isolated.

Business can be shady. People will steal from you, stores won't pay, and others will copy your designs. One well-known young designer recently saw his $1,500 dress in a store next to the store's own $300 polyester knock-off. Unfortunately, this is part of the business. At times, you have to fight for yourself, but at other times, you have to just make the best of it, like the designer who walked into the offices of a large, well-known clothing brand and saw photos of his collection on their design board. Rather than explode with anger, he offered

to consult for them and ended up making enough money to fund his next runway show.

Or You Could Be Tom Ford

Having your own business is not the only way to go. Too many designers get hung up on the idea of being independent and lose sight of other amazing opportunities. Tom Ford, Nicolas Ghesquiere, and Hedi Slimane each made their name designing for another label without having to manage the business issues. Even Karl Lagerfeld, though he has his own label, is famous for designing at Chanel.

 Paige's Story

Paige Novick had a handbag line for ten years called Frou. She sold her product into the stores she wanted and created a well-known, respected brand. But despite landing the success many hope to achieve, Paige closed her business to become the creative director of a multibrand licensing firm, where she was responsible for two well-known fashion brands. She says the hardest part of being an independent designer is the financial pressure. Even with ten years in the business, she broke even some seasons—and didn't in others. "The burden is so great when it's your company because when you wear so many hats, design becomes an afterthought" she said. "In this new position, I am able to focus my efforts and attention on the creative without the outside distractions, and my design skills have flourished."[10]

While she admits there are times when it's hard to have a boss, the imposed structure has its good points. She can design a lot more product and do it quickly, whereas with Frou, she would labor over tiny details. "I was a prisoner before," she says. "With Frou I had so much anxiety about the other aspects of the business that I often played it safe. Psychologically, it has been very liberating to design under someone else's label and ultimately more creatively fulfilling."

There Is No Rush

Many young designers start their own businesses too soon without the resources to survive their mistakes or the experience to avoid them. Be patient and realize there is no rush. Showroom owner Denise Williamson said, "Too many designers want immediate gratification. You have to build it over time and be smart about it."[11]

Favors are a limited resource that you don't want to use up too soon. Putting yourself out there too early, building up debt, and making mistakes will slow you down rather than get you there faster. Don't strike until you are ready. Build your resume and put in the time. If you aren't ready now, you can be later. If you are talented, that will never leave you.

Realize that you have more than just one shot. Designers do take time off and come back stronger. They survive bad experiences with the stores and magazines. Everyone makes mistakes, and the industry will still be there when you come back, if you have the product, energy, and drive.

The Most Important Advice in This Book

Work for someone else first. Regardless of how many times I say it, or quote others who agree, it won't be said enough. Designers need to work for other designers, and work for them for a few years, before heading out on their own. This is the single most consistent advice I was given for designers from experts and veterans in all areas of the industry. The fashion business has a history of apprenticeship, and solid experience attained while working for someone else is critical to survive. Peter Arnold, the former executive director of the Council of Fashion Designers of America (CFDA), now president and CEO of Cynthia Rowley, says, "Virtually all of today's successful designers have worked for someone else, learned or at least learned to appreciate all of the elements of running a business, and then embarked on a venture themselves."[12]

Donna Karan worked for Anne Klein; Marc Jacobs for Perry Ellis; Narciso Rodriguez at Donna Karan and Calvin Klein; Karl Lagerfeld at Balmain, House of Patou, Chloe, and Fendi; and Richard Lambertson of Lambertson Truex for Geoffrey Beene and Gucci. Alexander McQueen learned tailoring on Savile Row before designing for Romeo Gigli.

At the *Teen Vogue* Fashion U event in October 2007, designer Vera Wang advised attendees to "Get a job! When you get a job you are getting paid to learn." She spent 16 years at Ralph Lauren before launching her own bridal line.[13]

Although you are anxious to get out on your own, if you fail, you will end up working for someone else anyway. Do it now and increase your chance of success. As a fabric manufacturer observed, designers used to work for an established house for 10 or 20 years before launching their own label for the rest of their career. Today, too many designers are going backwards, starting on their own and ending up three or four years later at J. Crew.

"Young designer" generally refers more to the age of the company, not the person. The Zac Posens and Proenza Schoulers, exceptions to this rule, are few and far between. Take time to reap the multiple benefits of working for someone else.

Knowledge. When working for someone else, don't just sit there and bang out sweater sets. Take advantage of opportunities to visit factories, attend fabric shows, and work with sample and patternmakers. This is an important time to acquire technique and perfect your skills. Be an active spectator and witness what makes your employer a success. Designer Derek Lam has said of his four years as vice president of design for Michael Kors, "Michael taught me the importance of identifying with your customer, the importance of quality fabrics, and above all else, to enjoy the business and have fun with it."[14] Even a bad experience is a great education and shows you what not to do.

Money. Working for someone else helps build the start-up capital you need. Too many people start without enough funds and burn out too soon. Kathryn Jones of Palmer Jones worked for 12 years at Ralph Lauren, and her sister Lindy spent 18 years with major corporations. They saved money and waited until they felt they knew enough and were ready for their own thing. When you are new, you will make mistakes, and they can be very costly. Better to learn from them while working for someone else, who can pay the damages.

Connections. Working for another company will lead you to important resources, help you determine whom to trust, and even unearth a potential business partner. You can travel to markets, factories, and fabric and trade shows. When Derek Lam worked for Michael Kors, the buyers, editors, and manufac-

turers knew him there. Those connections paid off when he set out on his own. The menswear label Greige Manufacturing receives support from the factories in China with whom the designers, Chris and Cory, created relationships while working for other companies. Their past jobs opened doors and gave the factory faith in them. Douglas Mandel, who designs the menswear label, Kamkyl, advises, "Spend ten years working in the industry to get to know exactly who and what you are, and to find a backer."[15] When he was 31, designer Joseph Abboud told Douglas he was still too young to start his own business and he should keep working for someone else and find a manufacturer with the dollars to support him.

Reputation. Designer Doo-Ri can't stress enough the importance of pedigree. No one knew who she was when she started, but the fact that she had worked for Geoffrey Beene for six years gave her credibility and *Vogue* came to her first show.[16] Cynthia Steffe was able to get an audience with all the top retailers when she first started because she had built a reputation designing a line for a large "dress for success" company that was very successful in the stores.[17]

This leads us to a few more important observations about the fashion industry.

It's all about relationships. The fashion industry is based on relationships. The interactions you have with financial people, factory owners, fabric suppliers, sales reps, buyers, and editors will largely determine your success. Fashion is a small industry. Everyone talks to everyone else, and word travels fast. In any interaction, there is opportunity.

It's best to be nice. The fashion diva is a fool—a boring stereotype in a busy and competitive field. Bad behavior will come back to haunt you. Fashionably late is also a misnomer. The shows run late because of crazy scheduling, but if you are late to meet a factory owner, buyer, or heel maker, you send a message of disrespect.

Listen to everyone. Many people, including patternmakers, salespeople, contractors, and buyers, have a wealth of valuable knowledge and experience, which

can help you. Listen to advice and criticism with an open mind and take every opportunity to learn.

Keep the door open. Learn to say no politely. If you aren't interested in working with someone now—a stylist, sponsor, magazine, or supplier—there is always a chance you will want to later. Young pride shuts doors that designers often wish they could reopen. Unfortunately, the most in-demand designer one season may find he is virtually forgotten the next. If you have a dispute or end a relationship, do it as professionally and amicably as possible. Be flexible and learn to compromise, but also be prudent on your own behalf. If someone asks for $10,000, come back and offer $5,000. The business demands constant negotiation.

Friend or foe? Obviously there is competition in the emerging designer community. If there are ten of you in a room, odds are several of you won't be in business in a year. But you are all struggling with the same issues, and no one will understand your highs and lows better than another designer. Take advantage of the plentiful opportunities to meet each other, such as when waiting in line at Galaxy for buttons or when buying fabric at Mood. Introduce yourself to the designers exhibiting across the aisle at trade shows. You don't need to give away your address book, and don't expect other designers to share all their resources either, but many designers do help each other, meet regularly to commiserate, and barter for each other's expertise and skills. You can work together to meet minimums, create selling opportunities, or just learn from each other's mistakes.

It's not a fair game. Some designers have strong advantages—socialite or celebrity friends, fluency in Mandarin, a family-owned factory, an influential husband, rich parents, or pull with Anna Wintour. Others have the looks or charm to melt icebergs. One young female designer noted, "Face it, Andre Leon Talley is not going to fall in love with me." Get over it. The success of others does not determine your failure. Insecurity is distracting, and bitterness is unproductive. Use the advantages you have, stay focused, and realize that in the end you make your own luck.

The ego. One designer told me the hardest part of the business is how it affects the ego. It hurts if the product doesn't sell or the press doesn't cover it, and it

hurts if you compromise your vision to make the buyers and editors happy. Make the product you believe in and realize that self-consciousness is a waste of time. Designers too often mistake people loving or disliking their designs for loving or disliking them.

You Survived the Bad News

If life as a design entrepreneur is right for you, don't be disheartened. Shoe designer Kristen Lee says, "At the end of the day it is extremely gratifying to do exactly what you set out to do despite the odds."[18] Designer Steven Cox from Duckie Brown says, "There are more highs than lows, and no matter the problem, there's always an answer."[19] If you are 100 percent committed, believe in yourself, and have a heavy dose of raw determination, it's time to move forward.

 "What was the biggest lesson you learned in your first year of running the business?"

"You never have enough money."—Alison Kelly, womenswear, Project Runway contestant

"Don't do everything yourself. If you can hire someone to do it well, do it! And the most important thing is the product, not the press or the marketing."—Jada Simons, Marie Marie, womenswear

"Not to trust retailers. I know this sounds harsh, but it is true. I sold shoes to stores that I thought were reputable because they carried brands like Prada and Giuzeppi Zanotti. However, to one of these stores I delivered a $22,000 order, and they never paid me. Now, I have a factor do credit checks on the stores, and I do not ship shoes to any store without good credit if they will not give me a credit card."—Ruthie Davis, shoes

"Many new designers think that it's mandatory to spend a lot of money on a public relations blitz or an expensive fashion show. In reality, when first starting out, your money is more effectively spent on developing quality samples and developing sales. Public relations is

only effective if customers are able to purchase product they see in magazines, on celebrities, etc. Build sales first and focus on promotion second."—Romain Kapadia, menswear

"You have to spend money to make money. Paying people to help you is not a luxury, it's a necessity. It's alright to learn as you go, but you can't do it alone."—Lily Raskind, Sunshine and Shadow, womenswear

"The importance of defining my customer. For example, what type of garment will I design, who will wear it, where will they wear it, and the appropriate price range for that garment?"—Nicole Romano, womenswear, accessories

"Enjoy the ride. I forgot to enjoy what I was doing while I was working on building the business. In the first year, I put so much emphasis on creating the perfect collection and having the best marketing plan … that I lost site of the adventure. I have learned to take a step back and appreciate all that I have created and pat myself on the back every so often. Owning your own business and having it run while making money is a huge accomplishment beyond any tear sheet in a magazine."—Jessica Alpert-Goldman, World According to Jess, accessories

"You can't do everything by yourself! Try to find help before it's too late."—Annie Lewis and Helen Cho, Lewis Cho, womenswear

"How to use QuickBooks, manage the cash flow, and have an effective business plan."—Chloe, Samantha and Caillianne Beckerman, womenswear

"It's extremely important to set up a solid foundation to run a proper business. Having insurance, finding a proper warehouse to ship, and great showrooms are very important for your growth."—Grace Sun, womenswear

"Our biggest lesson in our first year was to see that it really is possible to build a company without many resources or financial security, and that no matter what happens, there is usually some way everything works out in the end."—Tina Hernaiz and Nike Clausing, Ingwa/Melero, womenswear

"Mark-up—consider and include everything!"—Cheyenne Morris, Tashkent, shoes

"That I couldn't do everything myself."—Corinne for Society for Rational Dress, womenswear

"It only gets harder. It's flattering to have people love the line and buy the line. Once you start producing and having a demand, it becomes a totally different story. I started by making everything down to the fabric myself. Filling orders and keeping up with the demand when I'm doing everything myself with my own techniques—it's hard to find outsourcing that will work the way I am used to working. It becomes a puzzle to figure out which way is the best way. I became the salesperson, the PR, the face, the producer, the manufacturer, and graphic designer of the company. I had too many roles, which now I am happy to say is starting to change."—Karelle Levy, Krelwear, womenswear

"One of my biggest lessons was to learn to not take everything too personally. I see my designs and work as an extension of myself, and the first year, hearing from my clients and facing the issues dealing with fit hurt my ego. Grow thick skin for this business and take criticism as advice, not a threat to your self-dignity."—Christine Alcalay, womenswear

"A big lesson I learned was that fashion is a serious business and much more complex then it seems."—Hajnalka Mandula, womenswear

"The first year is the easiest in fashion—everyone wants you when you're new. The biggest lesson is timing, how to follow the calendar, work backwards in order to time the process of creating, sampling, and manufacturing. It does not have to be stressful—you just have to time it right."—Bliss Lau, accessories

2

The Fundamentals

The Plan

Before you even start your own fashion business, you need to know where you are going and how you will get there. Showroom owner Greg Mills says, "You really have to have passion and a plan. Think about what you are bringing to the game, and how to get from point A to B, then to K and Z."[1]

A plan keeps you focused in the face of fashion fantasy. It defines short-term and long-term goals along with the actionable steps to achieve them. It provides insight into the market opportunity, determines which resources you need, and proves the legitimacy of your business to potential suppliers, contractors, and investors.

Write It Yourself

In exchange for a few thousand dollars, there are people who will write your business plan for you. While it is extremely tempting to hand off what appears to be an overwhelming task—don't. No one can make a plan for your company better than you, and you will learn much in the process. Thinking through each element of the business is invaluable to creating the company you want and preparing it to succeed. The process is even more important than the final document. It will point out your strengths and weaknesses, helping you anticipate and avoid problems.

While you should not outsource the plan, you should avail yourself of resources that can help you. Classes are offered by the Small Business

Administration (SBA) and at a variety of schools, including fashion schools such as the Fashion Institute of Technology in New York. Designer Alice Roi took a business course at Parsons: The New School for Design that included writing a plan, and she says the process was really helpful.[2] Books, software, and templates are available online and at major bookstores. Websites, such as Entrepreneur.com (www.entrepreneur.com), offer guidance and resources.

Business plans average 15 to 20 pages, but they can be any length and as simple, formal, or involved as you want. Have someone review your plan once you are done. Bounce it off people in the fashion industry, as well as small business owners in nonfashion fields. The Service Corp of Retired Executives (SCORE), a division of the SBA, has 11,000 volunteers nationwide. SCORE advisors have decades of experience running businesses, and in New York, several were in the fashion and garment industry. The advisors counsel small business owners on a variety of business problems, review business plans, and help find funding. They have credibility and knowledge in the industry, and their assistance is free. The SCORE website (www.score.org) has free business plan templates as well as templates for sales projections, financial statements, bank loan requests, and more. Local economic development agencies also have resources and funding to encourage the growth of small area businesses.

Take Your Time

It's not all work. The business plan is part of the creative process, and the time you spend now will result in a plan that you will rely on and continue to evolve for years. Michael Spaulding of Gunmetal spent six months writing his 100-page business plan before starting his business.[3] At a Gen Art seminar, designer Sandy Dalal said he took a year to create his business plan, figure out the details, and anticipate hurdles before he launched his label.[4] Designer and showroom owner Ana Beatriz advises designers to go slowly and take a long time to plan before they start. "Think through the entire process as if you had a label already. Know how much you will spend, research and choose your patternmakers and factories, plan all the sales steps before you even launch so that when you get the moment to hit you will be ready."[5]

Review the Plan Often

The business plan is a working document and should be reviewed regularly as your business grows and changes. Spend time each quarter comparing your plan to your current situation to include unexpected opportunities as well as to stay focused and realistic about where you stand in respect to your goals.

Elements of the Business Plan

Executive Summary

The executive summary is the beginning of the plan, but you will probably write it last. It is a short summary of the entire plan and outlines your objectives for the next one to five years. The summary should refer to the major points in each section of the plan and clearly state any resources you need and how they would be used to make the business profitable. Make the summary as interesting and engaging as possible. This is the key section that potential investors read to gauge their initial interest in your business and decide whether they want to learn more.

Company Overview

The overview is a general explanation of your business and product. Start with some background on the fashion industry and the potential for your product in the market. Explain the structure of the business and how it fits into the industry as a wholesale, retail, or custom operation. Specifically describe what you design and whether it targets high-end, mass, or niche markets or fits an important lifestyle trend. Include the attributes that make your product unique and different from the competition. Describe your customers along with the strategy to reach them in terms of the stores in which you want to sell and the marketing and public relations efforts you plan to use. Finish this section with a top-line review of the money involved, the factors that will make you profitable, and the related time frame.

The Marketing and Sales Plan

This is one of the most interesting parts of the plan, because here you explore the market and opportunities for your product.

The market. Try to pinpoint the size of your market both in terms of number of customers and in dollars. If you design men's hats, research how much men spend annually on hats and what months of the year or geographic areas have the most sales. If you are starting a high-end women's shoe label, identify the number of shoes sold in the $300 to $500 price range, the number and locations of stores that buy them, and what percent of those sales you can expect to secure. The Internet offers a wealth of statistics on the apparel industry, but you may also need to clock some hours at your local library to find free market information.

Be realistic about your market potential. Too many designers want to design a high-fashion, high-priced line, which in reality appeals to a very small market. The consumers who are fashion-forward are often young and don't have the money for high-end designer clothes. Rather than focus on $1,200 dresses, you may have a better chance at success and profit designing for underserved markets, such as plus-size, maternity, or bridal. A designer can apply style to any of these markets and fill a need.

Each market is unique and evolving. For example, industry experts point out that in menswear, the high-end designer category is more difficult than women's because the number of stores that service this category is significantly smaller, there are fewer items to design, and it's more difficult to grow the business exponentially each season. However, in the past year, a new contemporary market for menswear has emerged, offering new opportunity for designers. The male mind-set is changing, and men are becoming more confident about style and less threatened by fashion. They are shopping more often and buying a more diverse selection of items, and new boutiques are opening to sell fashion-forward men's products at a slightly lower price than the designer category. Even the department stores are growing their independent and contemporary designer sections for men.

When researching any market, identify the broad lifestyle trends that relate to your product. The trend for stylish casual wear, the increase in low-priced

designer goods at Target and H&M, or the growing market for eco-friendly or fair-trade materials may be tied to the success of your line. Don't forget the other forces that influence demand for your product. The weather plays a major role in the success of a coat business, and swimwear designers should focus on the sunny states where a hat and glove business would be less active.

The target customer. This section should reveal a clear and detailed understanding of your customers. How old are they? What are their income levels, hobbies, and occupations? Where do they vacation? Include where they shop, how often, and whether they look for bargains or spend money freely. A customer may be influenced by trends or focused on the classics. A customer may be particular about fit, comfort, or glamour and might be motivated by brand, innovation, or luxury materials. Be able to picture your customer and keep that mental image with you at all times.

The unique selling proposition (USP). This statement defines the attributes that make your product unique and give it an advantage over your competition. What is different about the product you design, what will make it last, and why—among the hundreds of labels already out there—does yours stand out? Ask yourself what niche you can fill for both the customer and the retailer.

Sales strategy. The sales goals should outline the amount of product to be sold each season and to which accounts. Explain your pricing strategy and include actual numbers for expected sales and projected growth rate from season to season, as well as details on how you developed these projections.

Decide which accounts to focus on domestically and abroad and whether the product will be distributed in many stores nationwide or in a few select places. Outline your plan to hire a salesperson or showroom, to attend trade shows, or build a website. Include promotional plans to support sales with press kits, runway shows, travel for in-store appearances, and catalog buys.

Competitive Analysis

Name your top five to seven direct competitors. These are other new designers who make a similar product for the same market. Then name your top three

indirect competitors who own a large share of the market (such as Prada or Louis Vuitton). Research how long each has been in business, their annual sales, where they sell, who represents them, and how they market themselves. Compare the style, price, and quality of their product to yours and identify their business advantages and disadvantages. Observe the ways they serve customers well and where they do not meet customer needs.

Operations Plan

The operations plan covers the resources needed to run the business every day. It should outline details such as staffing requirements, the production plan, technology needs, and the support system for sales.

Include how many collections you will produce each year, a production time line for each, and a strategy for managing quality control. Cover as many specifics as possible regarding the contractors and suppliers you will use. Obviously this will take time and research, but it will be invaluable in helping you fully understand how to get your product made, which is vital to know before you begin sales.

Financial Analysis and Projections

Managing cash flow and planning finances is key to survival. The financial statements illustrate your ability to manage income and expenses and eventually earn a profit. They specify the amount of money you have, the amount you need, and where it will be spent. When creating the financials for your business plan, you may need an accountant or financial professional to help you. Actual numbers are difficult to pin down, but it's extremely important to use real figures to illustrate what it will take to set up your business and keep it going on a monthly basis. Several financial statements can be included in a business plan, but below are the big three.

1. **Income statement.** This is a summary of all projected income and expenses by month. Income includes sales and other revenue sources, such as consulting or commissions. Expenses include the fixed and variable costs of producing and selling your product. Fixed costs are those that do not vary depending on production or sales, such as equipment, licenses, and incorporation. Variable costs change based on sales and production quantities and

include fabric, samples, production, shipping, taxes, and sales expenses. The difference between income and expenses is the gross profit margin.

2. **Cash flow statement.** This statement is extremely important to a fashion business, because it shows exactly when and how cash will flow in and out of the business each month. The statement projects when specific expenses are due and where you will get the cash to cover them. The cash flow statement for your business plan should be created initially for an entire year, and when you start operating the business, you will create one for each month.

3. **Balance sheet.** This draws from the income and cash flow statements to report assets and liabilities at the end of a year. Assets include cash, accounts receivable (money owed to you), inventory and supplies on hand, and equipment. Liabilities include accounts payable (money you owe to suppliers, contractors, and rent), debt to banks, other loans, and taxes.

Setting Up the Business
by Melanie Jones, Esq.

There comes a time in every designer's life when he has to stop thinking of the work as only an expression of creativity and start thinking about it as a business. One of the first things that should be done is to contact a lawyer to form a legal entity. Every business owner, no matter what the size of the business, should make certain that the enterprise is operating as the proper legal business entity for its needs. Deciding which entity is best suited for your business is an important decision but not as complicated as it might seem.

- *Sole proprietorship and partnership.* The most common type of small business entity, a sole proprietorship is defined as "a business owned and controlled by one person who is solely liable for its obligations" *(Merriam-Webster's Dictionary of Law, 1996)*. If more than one person is involved, the business entity is a general partnership, and without an agreement to the contrary, its partners are each responsible for its obligations in full. This type of business does not provide protection of personal assets. If anyone sues your company, they would have the right to seek damages not only from the assets of the company but also from you personally.

- *Limited liability corporation (LLC).* This is one of the most common and popular types of formal business entities. Technically, it's a hybrid of a corporation (see below) and a partnership. The business can be informally structured like a sole proprietorship or partnership, but it affords protection from personal liability. There is also the limited liability partnership (LLP), but this is only allowed for certain types of businesses (usually legal, accounting, and architecture).

- *Corporation.* There are two types of corporations—the C corporation and the S corporation. Corporations must be properly formed and maintained. Annual filing fees (which vary from state to state) must be paid. A board of directors must be elected, annual meetings must take place, minutes must be kept, and stocks must be issued—all of which apply even if you are the only shareholder. If you don't keep up with all of these responsibilities, you run the risk of losing the benefits of the protection of a corporation. It is important to think of a corporation as having its own identity.

With C corporations, shareholders are double-taxed—the corporation is taxed on its income, and shareholders have to claim dividends as taxable income on their personal income tax returns. There are a few ways to avoid this. One way is to form an S corporation, which allows shareholders to claim their share of the corporation's income directly on their personal tax return, taking care of the double taxation problem. While an S corporation may cost a little more to form, it may suit your business needs. The best thing to do is discuss your options with a lawyer. In addition to the issues discussed above, your attorney will consider the following when counseling you on choosing the proper business entity:

- *Cost.* This is not only the cost of creating the business entity but also the cost of maintaining it. For some entities, annual fees must be paid so they continue to be recognized by the state in which they are registered.

- *Maintenance.* Some business entities require serious recordkeeping for compliance with state regulations. Consider whether this is something you are willing to spend time doing.

- *Tax liability.* It's possible to save money on your income taxes if the business entity you choose allows you to pass the income you make directly to you, the owner. This way, you avoid your money being taxed twice (once when paid to the company and again when paid to you through a paycheck).

- *Location.* Each state has its own regulations and fees. Some are more favorable than others.

Note that filing a business certificate with the state (also known as a DBA) is not a formal business registration; it simply reserves and makes known your business name. You also need to file with the IRS and your state's department of revenue for taxes, and depending on where you live and work, you may need certain business and manufacturing licenses and sales permits, including a resale number to buy wholesale.

Disclaimer: The information contained in this article is for informational purposes only and does not constitute legal advice. Nothing provided herein should be used as a substitute for the advice of competent counsel.

 ## A Business Structure Tip
from Charles Klein, a lawyer with Davidoff Malito & Hutcher LLP

Never operate your business as a sole proprietorship. If you operate your business under your own name, without forming a corporation or limited liability company, you will be personally liable for all the obligations of your business. Such liability should be avoided at all costs. Form a corporation or LLC to operate your business. Such an entity will "shield" you from personal liability on most issues. I recommend that you form an LLC; it is a more flexible business entity. The limited liability company can be typically formed for under $500. However, in New York, after the limited liability company is formed, a notice of formation must be published in two newspapers. In Manhattan, such publication typically costs around $1,500. Should you decide to form a corporation, which can usually be formed for under $500, consult your accountant concerning electing S corporation status, which may provide certain tax benefits to you.

Choosing the Company Name and Trademark

The company name should identify the label, support the image, and appeal to your target customer. This is a name that will last for years (hopefully!), so it should give an appropriate impression without being too confusing or niche. Choose a memorable and interesting word that reflects the attitude of the collection while setting you apart from others in the market. Don't choose a word that relates too specifically to a current trend or moment in time.

Using your own name for your business is a common and viable option but one you might want to avoid when first starting out. While most famous American and European brands are named for the designer who launched them, realize that you will make many mistakes in your first few seasons in business. As designer Nanette Lapore explained at a CFDA/Gen Art business seminar, there is a huge advantage to staying under the radar and not putting yourself out there too soon. She started her company and made her mistakes under another name and then was able to start fresh with her own name and identity.[6] Comme Des Garcons, Costume National, and Proenza Schouler are examples of well-known brands that are not named for their designers.

Designer Adam Lippes started his company under the name Adampluseve but then changed it to Adam Adam Lippes when his collection developed past just T-shirts and underwear to a full collection. In addition, he needed the change when his company received complaints after customers who heard about it on *The Oprah Winfrey Show* searched for "Adam Plus Eve" online and were led to a porn site.[7]

When choosing a company name, please don't use the word couture. Yes, Juicy Couture got away with it, but *couture* is the most commonly ill-used word in American fashion. For a design to be considered couture, it must meet a number of stringent requirements regarding the amount of work done by hand, the materials used, the number of employees in the atelier, and more as defined by the Chambre Syndicale de la Haute Couture in Paris. It doesn't just mean one-of-a-kind or made-to-measure garments.

Trademark Tips
from Charles Klein, a lawyer with Davidoff Malito & Hutcher LLP

Protect your trademark. A trademark comprises the word(s) and/or logo by which your goods are identified. Don't confuse your corporate or LLC name with a trademark. You still must register your trademark, even if your company name is the same. Before adopting a trademark, conduct a computer trademark search with the aid of a knowledgeable attorney. If your trademark is "confusingly similar" to another trademark previously registered, you should choose a different trademark. If the trademark is available, apply to register it both as a trademark with the U.S. Patent and Trademark Office and as an Internet domain name. If your brand starts to take off, register it in every country in which you might do business in the future. A European Economic Community registration will permit you to get coverage in all EEC countries at a very economical rate. International trademark pirates abroad read fashion magazines and will register your trademark in their country. If you don't register abroad early, you may have to buy your own trademark back from the pirate who registered it, assuming they're willing to sell it to you.

Shield your trademark from liabilities. Once you choose your trademark, apply for the registration in your personal name and then "license" your trademark to your company with a simple license agreement prepared by an experienced attorney. If your company goes under, your creditors will not be able to obtain your trademark, because it will be your property and not the property of your company.

Partnerships and Advisors

Both designers and industry professionals agree that some of the brightest young talents fail because they do not have a good business partner. Designers are often not good at the business aspects of running a fashion label, and even if they are, it's extremely difficult for one person to handle it all. In other creative industries, such as film and music, the artist is not expected or generally able to handle the business side. You need someone to create process and structure and who can focus on keeping things financially sound.

Most household designer names have a strong business partner behind the scenes. Yves Saint Laurent had Pierre Berge, Calvin Klein had Barry Schwartz, Marc Jacobs has Robert Duffy, and Betsey Johnson has Chantal Bacon. New labels, including Proenza Schouler, Peter Som, Zac Posen, Philip Lim, and Loeffler Randall, who are growing quickly and securing financial support, all have full-time business managers. Having a business partner is even becoming important to convince retailers and suppliers to work with you. Kimberly Grabel, Saks Fifth Avenue's senior vice president of marketing, says that when reviewing designers, the stores look for the combination of "a gifted, talented designer and a really good business partner."[8] The designer and the business partner are equally important to the success of a label. They should create a strategy together and have a strong working relationship.

To find a business partner, network in the industry and meet as many people as you can. Tell everyone from lawyers and accountants to suppliers and customers that you are looking for someone. Many former executives of established companies in the fashion and garment industry have an interest in partnering with a new line. They have established credibility in the community and look forward to a new challenge with a less-established name. Nicole Miller's first business partner was her boss from her old job. Someone who currently works for another label, a factory, or even fabric source may be an ideal partner who knows the business and can bring production expertise and contacts to your label. Another option to start out with is to find an MBA student or business school graduate who concentrated on fashion and may be interested in helping you out. You can contact MBA programs to ask for referrals.

A partner doesn't have to be a business professional. Many companies are started by two or more creative minds who pool their resources, share the workload and risk, motivate each other, and complement each other's skill sets. However, creative partners still need to work with external people for business expertise.

Be cautious when choosing a partner. You will need to give up some control and work with this person every day. Business pressure can ruin a good relationship with a friend or family member. The four friends who created the menswear line Trovata grew their retail accounts quickly, became press darlings, and

even won a coveted CFDA/Vogue Fashion Fund Award. However, despite their success, the partners soon parted ways due to creative differences.

Before entering any partnership, hire a lawyer to create a legal agreement to define the details. Most business managers want an ownership stake in the company, and you don't want to give away a percentage of your business without protecting yourself. Be specific about each person's role, who has the final word on which decisions, how profits will be shared, and what happens if one partner wants to leave. Even designer Michelle Smith and her husband Andy Oshrin, who manages the business side of their company Milly, have a formal contract that spells out their specific responsibilities and ownership in the company.[9]

Whether or not you have a partner, build a strong support group of people, both inside and outside the industry. Get to know other designers, business professionals, and entrepreneurs. Network your way into the industry and consult with manufacturing, PR, and showroom people. Ask established designers if you can meet with them for advice. Try to find a mentor and spend time with friends and family who support what you are doing. Search your area for professional networking organizations that are designed to help entrepreneurs make valuable business connections. The Athena Foundation's Powerlink program, for example, "links" a woman-owned business with a volunteer panel of advisors recruited from the local community.

You may also assemble a board of advisors who can bring knowledge and cachet to your business and make you more attractive to potential vendors, customers, and investors. Try to include someone who works in or is knowledgeable about the investment world, someone with fashion industry knowledge and experience, as well as a lawyer or accountant. The people whom you first add to your advisory group can help you find others.

Finding and Hiring Professional Services

At the root of a successful business is a good team, which includes key advisors with specific expertise. When hiring legal, accounting, or other services, referrals are best. Don't assume it's okay to work with a relative or friend. Your favorite uncle may have a law degree, but you need someone who, preferably, has fashion and small business experience and who may have

connections in the industry. Ask other designers, accountants, or bankers to recommend someone to you. Schedule a meeting and spend time with them. This initial meeting should be free. Ask about the professional's background and understanding of fashion. Make sure this person can explain things to you clearly in easy-to-understand language. You need someone with whom you feel comfortable and can communicate freely.

Shop around and compare rates. Most lawyers and consultants charge by the hour, and you should get an estimate up front of the time required for your issue. Ask them how to keep the costs down and see if they are open to barter. Product, seats at a runway show, and creative consulting can be enticing to business professionals. Many firms encourage their attorneys and accountants to do pro bono work for emerging designers and artists, and they enjoy the change from their daily routine.

Legal issues. Most people want to avoid hiring a lawyer at first because of the cost. Before you hire legal assistance, protect yourself by getting every agreement in writing and try to communicate important points via email. Keep all paperwork and records in case of disputes. Take notes on important conversations and meetings.

Read all agreements carefully and ask questions if there are terms that don't make sense. Designer Louis Verdad warns, "Be careful about what you sign when you are new. You are like a little chicken fresh out of the egg. You are too excited or afraid and later grow to regret it."[10] A contract should lay out all the responsibilities of both parties. Pay attention to details about dispute resolution and the length of the contract. Always try to resolve disputes without suing, because lawsuits are expensive and time consuming and there are no guarantees that you will win. Don't forget to use your intuition. If you have a bad feeling about any agreement, don't do the deal.

In many situations, legal advice up front can save you money and help you avoid mistakes in the long run. A lawyer can help you set up the business, negotiate leases, obtain licenses and permits, review contracts and agreements, deal with copyright issues, and help resolve disputes. Again, be sure to verify and monitor the fees for legal advice; it adds up quickly.

Bookkeeping and accounting. It's important to keep meticulous records of every financial transaction and to track expenses, cash flow, and inventory diligently. These records are needed for tax purposes, as well as to keep yourself on budget and to track the performance of your business.

Initially, designers should be able to handle the bookkeeping on their own, and plenty of good software is available to help. Many designers and small business owners use QuickBooks Pro, and the Fashion Institute of Technology (FIT) and other, nonfashion schools offer classes to teach designers how to use a variety of accounting software.

If you can't keep up, consider bringing in someone for a day or two each week to help. But even if you have a full-time bookkeeper, it's still your responsibility to stay constantly in tune with the finances of your business. The bookkeeper doesn't know what fabric came in and where it went. You have to help allocate each invoice. You should always sign your own checks to stay aware of the inflow and outflow of money. No one wants to experience unexpected cash flow surprises.

An accountant or bookkeeper should handle big issues such as taxes, payroll, and year-end financial statements. A good accountant can also be helpful with overall business development and planning, helping to check store credit, obtain financing, make deals, and position your business to appear legitimate to outsiders. Designer Marni Joy suggests getting an accountant who specializes in small business. She found hers through a women's organization and says he is involved in all aspects of her business.[11]

Insurance

Don't forget to obtain insurance to cover your property and inventory in case of fire, water damage, theft, or business interruption from blackouts or strikes. Liability insurance is also recommended in case your product or place of business causes injury or death.

Employees

Initially, most designers run the business and handle the major responsibilities themselves, but at some point, they need help. A good place to start is with

interns, who generally work for free in exchange for experience. Interns can be found by contacting fashion schools in your area, but remember that this should be a learning experience for the students and not just free/cheap labor for you. Make an effort to explain the reason and method for each task to help the interns gain valuable knowledge needed to land a job eventually. Keep in mind that an intern could become a valuable employee for your label after graduation, because that person is familiar with your brand and you've had ample opportunity to assess her strengths and skills.

Once the company can financially support part-time or full-time employees, you can expand your staff beyond interns. For most designers, their first employee is a general assistant to take on business responsibilities or a design assistant to help create the collection. The next hire is often a production manager to help source and traffic production materials and oversee the factory. It is often best to hire to compensate for your own limitations. Nanette Lepore hired a patternmaker first, as she knew that was not her strength.[12] Ideally, you want to hire people who are recommended by personal or professional acquaintances. When hiring anyone, review their experience and skills and check references. In a small company, chemistry is critical. Hire people you like and consider whether you can spend significant time with this person every day. Employees should have a similar work ethic to yours and understand your brand, vision, and business goals. Be wary of hiring friends because it can complicate decisions, as well as your authority, and result in the end of a good friendship.

As a small designer, offering a salary that is competitive with that offered by larger brands is often not realistic. Therefore, it's important to position a job with you as providing more opportunity, diversity, and hands-on experience than at a bigger label. Be sure to emphasize to potential hires that small companies offer diverse training, increased opportunity for input, and the prospect of building an exciting new business from the ground up.

If you are hiring a more senior or experienced person, it may be appropriate to offer profit sharing or even equity in the company.

When you do choose someone to hire, make sure you fully understand the legal issues, the financial impact on your business, and the importance of your commitment to the new hire.

 ## "If you could get any training or education to help you with your business, what would you want to learn?"

"I am finishing up my MBA right now, but had I not been doing that, I would go and get that MBA. Understanding business is almost more important than pretty product."—Jane Ivanov, Eve Alexander, maternity lingerie

"Perfecting the fit for your brand is the hardest thing to do if you are a new designer. I would love to get more education on that."—Grace Sun, womenswear

"I would want to learn more about licensing and private label contracts."—Corinne Grassini, Society for Rational Dress, womenswear

"I would go to business school and learn everything there is to know about running a business, or more realistically, take on someone who has gotten through business school who wants to team up with a designer."—Alison Kelly, womenswear, Project Runway finalist

"I do all of my designing by hand. I would like to better my education in graphic software like Photoshop, Illustrator, and all of the key software design programs."—Ruthie Davis, shoes

"One thing I'd like to improve on is financial planning and budgeting for my company. Although I work closely with my accountant, by the end of the season, I always wonder where all the money goes. There are smart ways to plan for each season, including setting up a line of credit, setting up factor, negotiating terms with stores, etc., all of which have helped me generate sufficient cash flow to support each season."—Romain Kapadia, menswear

"Business training and writing a business plan."—Bruno Grizzo, womenswear

"I wouldn't mind getting some training in CAD so I could apply it to my print designs and embroidery placements. For now, I like to do it freehand. I am still old-school since my major was in art. I love to feel my pencil in my hand."—Diego Binetti, womenswear

"We'd eventually like to add shoes and handbags into the collection, so we'd love to learn more about the production and design process for accessories."—Annie Lewis and Helen Cho, Lewis Cho, womenswear

"Accounting. Chinese, Italian, Spanish! Ideally, to learn how to properly understand the bookkeeping would be a wonderful gift. I also feel that communication is key—the ability to speak to a manufacturer in their native tongue is a huge advantage in any industry. Often the best craftsmen are from different cultures."—Bliss Lau, accessories

"What help do you need most? If you could hire just one employee or outsource one process, what would it be?"

"If you can only hire one person, it should be a production manager; then the second person should be a financial/accounting person."—Robert Geller, menswear

"A general assistant."—Ana Beatriz, Lerario Beatriz, womenswear

"A salesperson to handle accounts, acquire new accounts, and deal with client needs."—Cheyenne Morris, Tashkent, shoes

"I would love to find a knit house to make my full production line from yarn to finished garment."—Karelle Levy, Krelwear, womenswear

"I would hire production help—that's the biggest challenge."—Geren Ford, womenswear

"A production person."—Gustavo Cadile, eveningwear

"Ultimately, I would like to find a CEO—a business partner to help me continue to grow my brand internationally. If you look at all successful fashion designers, they have a right-hand person to run the business side of the company. However, I would not want a "numbers only" person. I would seek someone with vision, a design aesthetic, and product background. I think the designer and CEO should work together closely, like the left and right side of one's brain. There needs to be an overlap of skills and input. Right now, I set the business structure and do all of the designing and development. I will not be able to wear both hats for too much longer."—Ruthie Davis, shoes

"I would put my patternmaker on salary (instead of freelance) and hire a sample sewer in-house."—Jada Simons, Marie Marie, womenswear

"A top-notch sales representative who is established and respected in the industry."—Nicole Romano, womenswear, accessories

"A good office manager would be fantastic, and it would make things much easier."—Diego Binetti, womenswear

"I would hire a technical knitwear designer so we could expand our knitwear group."—Corinne Grassini, Society for Rational Dress, womenswear

"A production person."—Bruno Grizzo, womenswear

"A full-time sales manager. Sales are the most important part of any business and can also be the most time consuming. Cultivating relationships with stores is a year-round, full-time job in itself."—Romain Kapadia, menswear

"Shipping orders is the first thing we'd like to not do. It's a very important process, but it takes up a lot of time."—Annie Lewis and Helen Cho, Lewis Cho, womenswear

"Definitely a production employee. Hiring someone to take care of all of the production and shipping."—Chloe, Samantha, and Caillianne Beckerman, womenswear

"I would like to hire a salesperson/rep or a showroom."—Nina Valenti, NatureVsFuture, womenswear

"It's a tie. I would absolutely hire a business partner/manager. I am a designer, not a businessperson. So much of what I do is on the business end, which bogs me down creatively. I would also hire a production manager. As I grow, quality control becomes a bigger job, and it's such an important step in the process of making clothes. The logistics of production is overwhelming—so much problem solving!"—Lily Raskind, Sunshine and Shadow, womenswear

"Sales is the toughest division to find help. If you outsource and have a rep, nine times out of ten, the rep will be full force for your product for a few months and then lose stamina and move on to to the next new line in their showroom. It is hard to find a salesperson who loves the company and can sell the product as well as the person that created the company. My ultimate salesperson would be someone outgoing, fun loving,

and honest. I am not looking for a salesperson to "dupe" the customer into placing a huge order and then lose that customer months later when the product does not fly off the shelf. I need a salesperson who can relate to and really listen to the store owners' needs for their particular clientele, and then tailor the sale/product sold to fit the buyers' needs. This may not result in the huge initial numbers a salesperson is looking for, but it will help sell the line and build a trusting relationship with our company."—Jessica Alpert-Goldman, World According to Jess, accessories

"Sample maker. I currently make all my patterns but would love to have someone sitting beside me making the clothes with quality and speed. The art of tailoring and sewing is a skill and talent very hard to find."—Christine Alcalay, womenswear

"That individual would have to wear many hats and assume different job responsibilities. I would mainly utilize that person as a production manager—developing relationships with overseas factories, sourcing to get the best price on manufacturing the garments, overseeing production for the season (cutting, sewing, trim, pricing)."—Brian Wood, menswear

"An overall manager, but one that specializes in organizing and managing production. Someone who can oversee the process and ensure that what needs to get done for each order gets done so that I can focus on design for the next season. An adjunct job for the manager, once production and shipping is complete, would be contacting stores and being sure to get those checks!"—Lara Miller, womenswear

"Outsourcing a veteran industry professional/ambassador to link us into the world of editorial and sales would dramatically improve our position in the highly competitive industry of womenswear."—Jerry Tam, Form New York, womenswear

3

The Money

One of the realities of starting your own design business is that it takes money—money that can be hard to find. In fact, when asked what the hardest part of having your own business is, Andy Salzer of Yoko Devereaux replied, "Trying not to think about the money every day."[1] Unfortunately, thousands of good designs are never produced because there is not enough money behind them. On the other hand, millions of mediocre, even bad, designs are mass-produced and distributed around the world because the financing is there to back them up.

Once you start your label, you will probably lose money for the first couple of years. The break-even point, where you have enough income from the business to equal your expenses, will elude you because as the business grows, costs increase. For example, if a designer sells $100,000 worth of product and has a margin of 10 percent, he is making $10,000—not earning a salary, but making money. At $200,000 in sales, he is making a little more. But then at $300,000, he is suddenly losing money because he had to hire people and increase his costs to handle the increased business.

Unfortunately, the reality is that that many designers' fame far exceeds their finances. After five years in business, numerous industry awards, press attention, sales in more than 80 high-profile doors, including Barneys NY and Bergdorf Goodman, a resort collection and an eyewear license, Proenza Schouler—with wholesale volume estimated at more than $6 million—was not expected to break even for another two or three years.[2]

How Much Do You Need?

One of the biggest reasons designers fail is that they don't start with enough money. Too often, they financially overextend themselves and have to close the business after a season or two and start over, but this time under a burden of debt. You can, and should, delay the launch of your label until you are financially prepared.

How much you need is a difficult question to answer. The economics are different with each designer and depend on the designer's goals. The story of Calvin Klein's starting his business with $10,000 is a famous one, but that was in 1968. More recently in 1998, Tuleh started with $225,000,[3] and Gunmetal started its shoe label with $300,000.[4] Designer Derek Lam launched in 2002 with $380,000.[5] Although industry professionals suggest starting with as much as $1 to $5 million, don't despair; many start successfully with much less. Tim Moore, director of business development at Hilldun Corporation, suggests you can start with as little as $25,000 for womenswear.[6] Nanette Lepore started in 1992 with a $5,000 loan from her dad[7], Ingwa; Melero started with $10,000[8] in 2001, and Twinkle started with $900 in yarn and knitting needles in 2000.[9] If the response to your line is immediate, it may require more investment soon. Milly started "bare bones" in May 2000 with $100,000, but an additional investment of $350,000 was needed to fill the first year's orders of 10 monthly deliveries.[10] From that point on, the business financed itself.

A designer should plan enough funding to cover the initial outlay for setting up the company and for operating expenses such as production, materials, fabric, patterns, shipping, sales, and rent until cash is flowing back into the business. Creating a business plan should have resulted in a realistic cash flow statement that includes the cost to operate each season. While some advise having cash to last through the first six months, most recommend having enough to get you through the first three years. An article in WWD reported that new designers are "averaging an annual cost of $250,000 to create, show, promote, and sell their collection, not to mention actually making and distributing the clothes."[11]

As a worst-case scenario, when you start a business, it's good to know up front how much money you are willing to lose (just like going to Las Vegas). Many designers set a threshold for the amount they are willing to invest before

they throw in the towel. Designer Doo-Ri Chung says that she has always been very realistic about the business and decided when starting, "If I don't make a profit in five years, I'm out."[12]

Cash Flow: The Two Most Critical Words

Cash flow is cited by designers, financial consultants, and production experts as the major reason small design businesses fail. Each day, money flows out for equipment and supplies, rent and utilities, lookbooks, postage, and more. The cash flows in less frequently, primarily when retailers pay for goods or when the designer receives a loan, payment for a freelance project, or a sponsorship check. Obviously, the goal is to have more money flowing in than flowing out, but this is easier said than done.

To manage cash flow, you need not only to track the movement of money but regularly project the inflows and outflows several months in advance to know how much cash you need and where you will get it. Even at the large companies, only planning and constant monitoring can prevent crises. As designer Alicia Bell says, "You need access to money at all times."[13]

You Can Only Ship According to Cash Flow

In fashion, cash flow is particularly challenging, because designers must spend significant amounts of money on materials and sampling far in advance of getting paid by the store. As you can see in the following schedule, spending for Fall 2009 begins in late 2008, but payment for that collection isn't received until September 2009, a full nine months later. At this point, you have already spent money to create samples and selling materials for Spring 2010.

Example Cash Flow Schedule

October 2008	Begin designing and ordering fabrics for Fall 2009.
November/December 2008	Create patterns and begin sampling for Fall 2009.
January 2009	Finalize Fall 2009 collection, create look book, and begin sales.
April 2009	Finalize orders, buy fabric, and begin production for Fall 2009 orders.
May 2009	Buy sample fabric and materials for Spring 2010 Pay for grading, cutting, sewing, and finishing of Fall 2009.
July 2007	Begin patterns and samples for Spring 2010
August 2007	Finalize Spring 2010 collection.
September 2007	Begin shipping Fall 2009 to stores and receive cash on delivery COD payments. Ship September deliveries for Fall 2009. Begin to receive payment on net 30 terms.

Because of the cash flow delay, getting more money is not as simple as increasing your orders. Bigger orders require more money up front to produce. As a rule of thumb, you can generally take orders for twice what you have in capital. For example, if you have $50,000, you can take $100,000 in orders. You ship and then wait for the stores to pay before you can produce more. If you get $200,000 in orders, you have to prioritize them. Pick the top $100,000, which are the most important to produce first. Call the other stores and tell them you can't manage their order yet and ask if they will take the goods at a different delivery date or in a smaller quantity. Once you have the first batch of orders shipped, you can get the money (via factoring or COD terms) to start the next batch.

If you have confirmed orders, try to negotiate the payment terms with suppliers. Support from vendors and contractors can be a critical contribution to cash flow for a designer. If the mill or factory gives the designer "terms," then the designer has 30 or 60 days to pay for fabric or production instead of having to pay up front. It's like having an investor in the business. In fact, more designers are partnering with their factories, designing lines for them or even selling a portion of their company to their factory in exchange for investment, better

terms, and access to the materials sources and distribution that the factory can provide. If you have cash flow concerns, ask the factory if it can give you 30-day payment terms to help produce the product, even if you have to pay a fee or an interest percentage for that extra time.

Good credit opens doors. Pay fabric and production people on time, and they will help you with discounts, terms, and flexibility on minimums. One designer's secret: "Everyone is so busy screwing themselves and each other, if you pay on time, you stand out and the word will spread."

A designer's policy in collecting from stores also makes a big difference to cash flow. Asking for deposits or requiring COD from the stores brings the money in sooner and greatly affects the cash flow each season. Demand is power, and if a line receives press coverage or has a strong sell-through at a store, buyers will be more flexible with payment terms and may even support production of the collection with a deposit.

Stretch It Out and Make It Last

When creating the first line of samples, it is important to invest very little in yourself and keep expenses as low as possible. Controlling costs is key to making your resources last. Even a designer with $1 million in sales can be barely surviving if costs are high. All the money that comes in must go back into materials and production. A financial advisor told one menswear designer that he wouldn't really start to make any money until he had $10 million in sales. Of course, it is possible for a designer to make money with half a million in sales or less, but it's more likely to be a designer with low overhead, working from home, with no more than one employee. The designers who lose money tend to be the ones who had employees from day one, created big collections, had large inventory, rented studio or showroom space, and spent a significant amount of money on product development and design.

Discipline Now Pays Off Later

A designer explained to me that she is financially breaking even after only two years, but it took sacrifice. Depending on your resources, you need to have the discipline to avoid excess expense. For example, every designer wants to have

her own studio space, but most work out of tiny apartments for several seasons before putting money into studio rent. Even with sales of $1 million a year, $1,400 per month in studio rent adds a lot of extra pressure. Designer Doo-ri has a studio in the basement of her parents' dry cleaning business, and even Anna Sui worked from her apartment for most of the 1980s.

Wenlan Chia, the designer of Twinkle, moved into a studio space after four years in business. She had been working from her large Manhattan apartment, which she says her husband refers to as "an office with a bed."[14] When she shipped, the entire place was overrun with product, boxes, shipping materials, and paperwork. But it was still better than the two years they'd spent in a 650-square-foot apartment, where Wenlan needed every inch of space just to design. Fabric was draped everywhere, samples were on the bed, and if her husband needed a space to sit down, he went to Starbucks.

Samples can also turn into a money pit. Designer Doo-Ri says it is extremely important to stay disciplined. "If you have a budget of $8,000 to make samples, don't spend more."[15] Many designers easily spend $1,000 per new sample, resulting in at least $30,000 in cost per season, but others create a full line with $5,000 to $6,000. You can create a gorgeous sample line on a small budget, especially if you keep the collection small and don't order excess fabric or overcut.

Pay Yourself

Your own labor is an important cost factor, just like the cost for sample makers, accountants, and patternmakers. Up front, you should decide how much to charge your company for your own work. Even though you probably won't cut yourself a check for some time, the cost of your labor must be included in your cost charts and pricing strategy. Otherwise, they won't accurately reflect the work that went into the product, and down the road, when you decide to outsource some of these responsibilities, your margin will disappear. Obviously you can't pay yourself the high salary you would probably earn working for another company, but designers generally allocate a low hourly wage or annual salary to cover their labor in their financial projections.

Where to Find Money?

Personal Sources

The first option for financing a label is the designer's own personal resources. In fact, when starting out, this is often the only option, until the business has some sales and can get off the ground enough to attract outside financial support. Many designers and industry experts suggest using personal money as long as possible, not only because of the dangers and costs of outside sources but because the designers who run the most carefully planned and smart businesses generally are those with their own money at stake.

Personal savings. Your first option is to use savings you have personally built up over the years, hopefully while working for another designer and getting experience.

Don't quit your day job. Most designers, including those who have shipped for several seasons, cannot afford to devote themselves full-time to their new company. They continue to work full-time, or at least part-time, to support their label financially. Ideally, your other job will be at a fashion company where you can continue to learn, make connections, and benefit from the expertise of coworkers. Designer Behnaz Sarafpour worked full-time designing private label for Barneys NY while she got her own label on its feet.

While a design gig is ideal, any kind of work can help fund your own business. Designer entrepreneurs are funding their lines with graphic design work, writing, illustrating, bartending, set design, visual display, retail sales, decorating Christmas trees, costuming, and interior design. Designer Oliver Christian Herold supports his eveningwear line by moonlighting as a stockbroker at Fleet Securities.

If you do have a full-time design job in the fashion industry, keep in mind that your employer may or may not be supportive of your own venture. While some are very encouraging, like Geoffrey Beene who gave Doo-Ri two industrial sewing machines to start her company, others are threatened and will fire you if they find out you are working on your own label. Until you know how they feel about such situations, it's better to keep it quiet.

Freelance work. Freelance design work is an ideal way to support your line financially. It provides the flexible schedule you need to manage your own business and keeps you tapped in to the industry and its resources. Freelancing is extremely common and doesn't in any way mean you are less serious or dedicated to your own label. Even designers who have been shipping their own label for several years freelance regularly. In fact, several of them run into each other frequently in the design offices at The Gap.

Mass manufacturers and high-end labels increasingly seek young designers to design collections or to collaborate on product groups with them for a fee. They hear buzz about the designer's own line and prefer to cash in on that talent rather than hire their own in-house person. Some of these places want to credit the designer publicly and benefit from that person's cachet as a new talent. When Coach hired headwear designer Eugenia Kim to design a collection of hats for the brand, it brought expertise and buzz to Coach and provided cash and high-end recognition with a new set of customers to the smaller label.

Some freelance jobs pay very well, and you might be able to negotiate a percentage of their sales. In fact, although designers often complain about the fashion lines started by musicians and celebrities, designing for a company such as Sean John or L.A.M.B. can provide financial support for a designer's independent line.

The best way to find freelance work is through word of mouth. Let people in the industry know you are available. However, Bruno Grizzo, who calls his design job for Whim his "bread and butter," got it the old-fashioned way by answering an ad.

A variety of placement services are listed in the Resources section of this book.

Built by Wendy Meets Wrangler

When *Jane* magazine asked Wendy Mullin of Built by Wendy which organization, other than her own, she would want to design for, she answered Wrangler. After seing the article, Wrangler contacted Wendy and hired her as creative director for the Wrangler 47 line. She creates a collection each season and says it's great to have money to support her label and pay off her debt. In addition, now that she is with VF Corporation, which owns Wrangler, the suppliers and factories pay more attention to her than when she only had her own line.[16]

Private clients and sales. A loyal private clientele can provide reliable income that bypasses the retailer and pays up front. On occasion, private customers have even become financial backers. However, while helpful with cash flow, private clients can be time consuming and distract from wholesale. Some designers create excess samples for the purpose of selling at sample sales and shopping events when they need cash. If you can successfully spread the word about a private sale in your studio or showroom, you will receive payment for product on the spot that will help fuel the next season. Just be wary of tying up money on extra stock that may not sell.

Personal loans. If you don't have enough of your own money, the next most common source of funding is from friends and family. Mothers, fathers, husbands, wives, and close friends have invested a great deal of money in fashion. While it's wonderful to have the support of people you love, it's important to be aware of the emotional issues involved in taking money from family and friends. Designer Sandy Dalal, who funded his business with family support, said at a Gen Art seminar, "When you add money to a relationship, it changes everything."[17] In the end, even the closest friends expect to be repaid, and there is always a risk that you will fail and their money will be lost. Money from family and friends may come with strong opinions and regular doses of advice. Sometimes this can be helpful, but at other times it is a source of conflict. When you take money from people close to you, be up front with them regarding their role in the company. Unless you want them to be a major player in the business, let them know you will consider their advice but final decisions remain with you.

Credit cards. Credit card financing is another common route young designers take, but it is the most expensive and, therefore, dangerous. If you feel that you must use credit cards, be careful! Credit cards have extremely high interest rates, and it is easy to get caught in an expensive cycle of owing so much interest each month that you can't afford to pay off the principal. In fact, if you have credit card debt and are paying a typical interest rate of 15 percent, it would be better to take out a small bank loan at 7 percent to pay off the credit card immediately.

If credit cards are your only option, find a card with the lowest possible interest rate. Look for new cards with promotional offers such as "zero APR for six months"

to attract new cardholders, but be aware of when the promotional rate expires or you will be paying 18 percent before you know it. You can transfer balances from card to card to continue taking advantage of promotional rates, but this requires attention and time and, if you slip up, may result in a bad credit rating.

Outside Financing

At some point, as your business expands, you will probably need outside financing to support increased production. Before you seek outside funds, plan ahead to know how much you will need, when you will need it, and how it will be used. Searching for funding at the last minute is expensive and risky, and you may not make the best decisions when under pressure.

Understand that most of the financial world sees fashion as very high risk. It's a creative industry subject to trends, consumer whims, and even unpredictable forces such as weather. It will take significant effort to convince anyone to hand money over to you—especially if you have little experience and limited personal finances. Anyone who gives money wants something (generally a lot more money) in return.

Don't hesitate to tell people if you are looking for money. If you don't tell people, they may assume that you are financially set. And you never know who can help you find funding. It's possible to meet potential investors at parties, meetings, in the factory, on an airplane, or even in the grocery store. While your business plan will include extensive information about your company and goals, you need to be ready to describe your company and its potential in person quickly and concisely—in 30 seconds—at any time. The financial world calls this the "elevator pitch." It's what you would say if you met a potential investor in the elevator at the top floor and only had until you arrived at the first floor to gain the individual's interest in your company. The purpose of this pitch is to attract a person's interest enough to want to see a full business plan or set up a meeting to learn more about your label and its potential.

A sample elevator pitch may sound like this:

I design a line of high-end women's dresses that currently sell to Barneys New York as well as 14 high-profile boutiques on the East Coast. The line has been featured in publications including Elle and has been photographed on Cameron Diaz

and Christina Ricci. The label is drawing great interest from buyers from other key national chains, and I'm seeking finances to expand both my distribution and production to service these stores, as well as to develop the product range further to include separates and coats per the request of my current and prospective accounts.

What lenders and investors want. Whether it's a loan officer or a potential investor, no one will look at your design portfolio, declare you a genius, and write a big fat check. People invest based on the belief that you can sell your product in increasing quantity over time while managing your cash flow well enough to make money. Marty Staff, president and CEO of the Joseph Abboud Group, stated, "Lenders don't care if it's clothing or toothpaste. They don't care about your potential; they don't care about your book. A bank will not lend money against potential; the bank will only lend money against orders."[18]

Most investors are looking for early-stage businesses, a few years past start-up, that already have a solid, growing wholesale distribution with potential to expand to multiple global markets. They want to hear that you understand your market, that your product is in a growing category, and that you have a proven product concept featuring a unique quality that differentiates it from other products in the market. Store orders or proof of interest from stores are key.

New businesses don't have a long track record. Therefore, investors and bankers look at a multitude of factors to decide whether or not the business is a good investment or just a big risk. This is where the business plan becomes essential. Potential lenders and investors want to see a strong, realistic plan and the facts and data to back it up. They need to see projected cash flow, growth plans, and a realistic ability to repay them on time. They look closely at your personal track record with money—where you stand with other lenders, your credit history, payment history, and current debts and assets. A designer must get used to opening the books and showing everyone the finances. While it may be uncomfortable, it comes with the territory. Josh Patner, cofounder of the line Tuleh, compares this part of the process to "dropping your pants at a checkup."[19]

Before sharing your financial information with anyone, you may want them to sign a nondisclosure agreement (NDA) to stop them from sharing your information with anyone else. While some say this step is unnecessary, it will give

you peace of mind and may help you to appear more professional. You can find a basic NDA form on the Internet or get one from a lawyer. If you are headed down the road to outside investment, you will need a good finance lawyer to make sure that you are protected and that any deal is in your best interest.

A potential investor ideally wants to see a strong management team, which preferably includes a savvy business manager who works well with the designer. The investor will also judge your character, professionalism, and maturity and will ask for references. Tell them about your industry training and experience and ability to manage people, budgets, and processes.

Include a strong list of references from high-level people in the fashion industry, your suppliers, factory, and anyone in the finance and business world who believes that you will be successful and will add to your credibility.

As you seek funding, be sure to ask questions, and if you are turned down, find out why and what would change it. Don't forget the Golden Rule: Everything is negotiable.

Read the fine print. With any financial arrangement, a designer should make sure he thoroughly understands all the terms. Read the fine print: understand the interest rate, the length of the loan or partnership, back-out clauses, the repayment terms and deadlines, the payment amounts, and any additional fees or requirements.

Small amounts of money are easier to get, but with small amounts, it is even more important to evaluate whether the loan is worth the risk and cost. Before you accept any deal, plug the numbers into a cash flow statement to see when the money will come in, when you will pay it back, and if it will really be enough to help you grow and make a profit.

Generally in terms of expense, bank loans are the cheapest method of financing, followed by factoring, invoice or purchase financing, and finally equity financing, which usually costs a percentage of ownership in the company.

Bank loans. Bank loans are the most common type of outside financing and, while loans can be the least expensive option, they are often the hardest to get. When you take out a loan, you receive a certain amount of money and then pay it back, with interest, over a set period of time. Banks offer loans with both fixed

and variable rates of interest. With a fixed rate, you pay the same percentage of interest throughout the life of the loan. A variable rate will fluctuate as federal interest rates change.

Shop around and compare loan rates and fees at several banks. Some designers have had success with small banks that deal with small customers and small loans, yet others find that the big banks can be the easiest places to get a loan of up to $50,000, because it is such a small amount of money to them.

Banks don't like risk, and some insist a business be at least two years old or more before they will work with it. Banks carefully check creditworthiness of the business owner before granting a loan, and many require security—something of value that will become theirs if the owner defaults on the loan payments. The bank could ask for business collateral, such as equipment, inventory, or accounts receivable, or it might require personal collateral, such as your condo. While you should try to avoid giving personal guarantees for a loan, often this is the only choice you have.

A bank may require a cosigner for the loan. A cosigner is held liable if the person with the loan fails to pay. The lender can go after the cosigner and her assets to recover the loan amount. Consider this seriously. You don't want Grandma to lose her house because you didn't manage your cash flow.

When you choose a bank, find someone there whom you like and who understands small business and even fashion. Your lender should be someone with whom you can readily communicate and who could become an important resource and advocate for your business.

Other loans. Some other types of loans for small business owners are worth exploring.

> **U.S. Small Business Administration (SBA).** The SBA will not only direct business owners to numerous loans but can often guarantee a loan for them, if they don't qualify on their own at a bank. The SBA can help prepare a business plan, fill out loan applications, and shop business owners around to different lenders. Some SBA-acquired loans are expensive, but they may offer a longer maturity, providing you more time to pay them back. Check out the SBA's website (www.sba.gov/financing/).

Minority and women business owner loans. Associations such as the National Federation of Business and Professional Women's Clubs and the Association of Black Women Entrepreneurs direct small business owners to financial resources and loans. Accion is another good source of microloans for minority and female small business owners.

Local economic development organizations. These organizations often offer loans for entrepreneurs in their area. Some provide tax incentives or grants to businesses that support the area by increasing jobs, restoring old buildings, or moving into challenged neighborhoods. Several of these groups offer additional support for small businesses. For example, the Brooklyn Economic Development Corporation has held fashion-specific entrepreneur seminars. Seedco Financial is a national nonprofit organization that provides loans for small business owners and neighborhood entrepreneurs in several different states. Designer Andy Salzer of Yoko Deveareux says that securing a Seedco loan was key to the growth of his business.[20]

Online lending marketplaces. Prosper.com is an online lending marketplace, where people list and bid on loans using an online auction platform. Designer Lara Miller's third loan, from Prosper.com, provided $10,000 to put toward production and sample costs.[21]

It takes time and effort to track down and sort through these potential sources, but it is time well spent as you never know where you might find a little pot of gold.

Factoring
by Tim Moore, Hilldun Corporation

Factoring is a simple and effective tool used by designers to grow faster and more efficiently. Factors provide a cash advance once goods are shipped and invoiced, so companies do not have to wait for the customers to pay. By receiving this advance, a designer can pay his suppliers and contractors, enabling him to ship more product in the same period of time. If a designer comes up with the money required for his first shipment, he will be in business. However, he will begin to feel a cash crunch when he has multiple deliveries in a row and has not been paid for his first delivery but must begin production for his second and third deliveries.

1. Without factoring. Designer has $150,000 in orders to ship over a three-month period—$50,000 in June, $50,000 in July, $50,000 in August. She only has the money to pay for the June production of $25,000 (assuming the cost of fabric and production is 50 percent of the wholesale amount). She will have to wait to get paid from the stores before she can go back into production for her July and August deliveries.

2. With factoring. Designer has $150,000 in orders to ship during a three-month period—$50,000 in June, $50,000 in July, $50,000 in August. He only has the money to pay for the June production of $25,000. Upon shipping the June delivery, he forwards a copy of the invoice to his factor and receives a payment advance; for example, 70 percent or $35,000. This money will allow the designer to go back into production immediately for the July and August deliveries.

Factoring exists because suppliers and factories need to get paid before the designer is paid by the store. Also, due to the seasonality of fashion, designers ship heavily during certain months, and their need for cash rises quickly during peak seasons.

Designers should understand that the factor's advance should (as much as possible) only be used to pay for the production of goods or anything that is directly related to goods being shipped to stores, such as fabrics, production, trade shows, and sales reps. If designers use the factor's money to produce a fashion show, buy bigger office space, or new computer systems, their current cash flow will suffer, and they may not have the funds to fill their next orders.

The main advantage of factoring is that designers get their money before being paid by the stores. This improves their cash flow while putting relatively inexpensive systems in place to deal with stores or outsourcing the management of receivables. Besides providing advances to help cash flow, many factors provide designers with good credit advice and effective collection efforts and lower their risk of not getting paid by stores.

Factors save companies time and protect them from risk by checking credit and handling their collections to get their money faster. Collections are generally done in a professional, strategic manner that will only enhance a company's relationship with its customers. Who wants to ask for an order one day and call regarding past-due invoices the next? Customers know that if they do not pay the factors, they will damage their credit, and their other suppliers will stop extending credit to them. Even though factors may save designers from having to check credit and collect from their stores, the designers still need to have someone act as a liaison between the factor and the stores.

The factoring cost of 2 to 3 percent of sales is usually not costly, considering companies will be outsourcing a good portion of their receivables management and will have access to additional funds to grow their business. However, factoring costs money, and companies should always be aware of their expenses.

What makes you factorable? Many factors work with start-ups as well as well-established companies. Generally, before you can be considered by a factor, you need to be able to ship up to $75,000 to $100,000 of goods. Some require $1 million per year, yet others will start at much smaller levels, such as $25,000. You can get a factor at any size, but be careful if your sales volume is small because the arrangement can be extremely expensive. The cost of factoring, and the way a factor structures its deals, can vary greatly. The cost can range from 1.5 to 7 percent of sales, depending on the size of your business, how long you have been in business, the risky attributes of the company, the capital in the business, extenuating circumstances, customer makeup, and the nature of the business. Generally the higher your sales volume, the lower your factoring commission.

When choosing a factor make sure you understand how the factor structures its deal, that it knows your business, and that it has quality systems. Try not to pay more than 3 percent for nonrecourse factoring, which means the factor takes the credit risk and pays its client, even when a store defaults on payment. Factoring is not

a regulated industry and can provide funding when banks are unable to do so. Some factors are set up for very aggressive lending and charge more for it.

Working with a factor does not end all your problems. You are still responsible for handling disputes with the stores. If a store calls and complains that the merchandise does not fit or is not what it ordered, designers cannot say, "Oh well, deal with my factor." These situations are generally considered a "charge back," which is when a store disputes an invoice and refuses to pay because of a problem with the goods.

Basically, when a business decides to look into financing, it will decide whether to work with a bank or asset-based financier. Banks generally look for established companies that can provide a financial statement showing that the company is profitable and has solid net worth. Because most new companies do not live up to these standards, asset-based financing/factoring is usually the way to go. However, many companies, which have been around for a while and are in good financial condition, stay with factoring because of the service and flexibility factors provide.

There are different opinions on factoring. Some designers compare them to loan sharks, while others swear that factoring is critical, not only for cash flow but for protecting yourself from the stores. It's easy to see the advantages. Factors provide money when you need it most. They eliminate risk by handling credit checks and pay you if a store they approve doesn't pay. When you factor, the stores tend to pay faster, and it is easier to negotiate terms with your suppliers.

The downside really arises from the rates and fees. Be wary of incremental fees for specific services and small volumes as well as contractual commitments. Most factors want to lock you into a contract for a certain amount of sales volume and charge the commission for that volume, whether or not you actually reach it. For example, if you commit to $1 million in sales and you pay a 1 percent commission, even if you only hit $500,000 in sales, you still have to pay the 1 percent on $1 million. You shouldn't commit to a specific sales volume unless you are certain that you will hit it. It is better to pay a higher percent on a lower sales volume if you are unsure.

One other reality of factoring is that factors only cover orders from stores that they approve, and designers have recently complained that factors are

becoming more conservative, often denying approval of small boutiques, which are most supportive of new designers.

In the end, many different companies offer factoring services, and each has different agreements and terms, some more favorable than others. You need to do due diligence and calculate the net cost to you before making an agreement.

Purchase order financing. Purchase order financing lends money based on confirmed orders from stores. These are expensive loans because of the risk involved. The order doesn't guarantee that a retailer will accept the goods on delivery and pay. It's very difficult to obtain purchase order financing when you only have a small amount of sales. Some require as much as $1 million in purchase orders. For large orders, purchase order financing can be found at a variety of banks, factories, and companies that specialize in this type of financing.

Line of credit. A line of credit can be obtained from a bank, and unlike a lump sum loan, it lets you borrow with more flexibility. For example, if you have a $50,000 line of credit, you can borrow $1,000 or $5,000 simply by writing a check. You only pay interest on the amount you actually borrow. If you never tap in to the line of credit, you never owe anything.

Many designers use a combination of the above options just to get through each season. For example, designer Alicia Bell started with a bank loan and arranges purchase order financing to cover her until the clothes are shipped and the invoices are turned over to the factor. The factor gives her the money to pay back the purchase order financing—and she starts again.

Angels and Investors

Many experts say that looking for angels and investors in fashion is a complete waste of time that would be better spent buckling down and growing their business themselves. For investors, fashion is far from a sure thing, especially with a new, unknown name.

However, in the last few years, the investment world has opened up to providing opportunities for fashion designers, and there is growing interest in small to midrange fashion companies that are in the earlier stages of development. Strong consumer and retail interest in high-end design and new, smaller brands; increased

efficiency and access to overseas sourcing and production; and rising profits in luxury goods have helped attract the finance world and convinced investors that, despite the risky and unpredictable nature of fashion, they can make money.

Private equity companies and investment funds not related to the fashion world have recently purchased larger fashion companies, including Betsey Johnson and Jil Sander, and with the increased role of fashion as entertainment and designers as celebrities, entertainment moguls have jumped into the mix, too, with Miramix's Harvey Weinstein buying Halston and Britain's Simon Fuller partnering with Roland Mouret.

If you want to find an investor, whether an individual, company, or fund, focus on how investing works. People with money invest money to make more money. They seek opportunities with growth potential and then buy a percentage of the company to share in the profits. Generally they want some control over the business and the decision making to help ensure profitability.

How to Find Investors

At the end of one of his Spring runway shows, designer Miguel Adrover followed the last of his models onto the runway wearing a T-shirt that read: Anyone seen a backer? While this may not be the most effective way to find financial investment, it doesn't hurt to be creative in your approach.

A designer can search for "angel" in investor networks in her area that focus on specific areas of business; specific geographic areas; or specifically on businesses started by women, minorities, or other groups. But be warned that some angel networks and services, especially on the Internet, charge to review companies on behalf of investors. These investors are unlikely to invest in fashion, and the services often take your money and provide little result. *The majority of fashion backers come from within the industry.*

Funding is not just about money. The best deal is to find "smart money"—a strategic partner who will provide critical business advice, industry expertise, and strong connections with factories and suppliers and who can help make retail deals on your behalf. Fortunately, many of the new private equity funds that are focused on fashion have managers with extensive fashion industry expe-

rience who know how the industry works. They understand the value of a good designer and appreciate the realistic time frame for success and growth.

Investors who do not come from the fashion world can pose serious risks. They don't understand the industry or how to value to intellectual property of the designer. They expect returns in the short term, such as in three to five years, so they may push a company to expand too quickly. When things don't work out, they back out, leaving the designer with extensive debt, damaged supplier relationships, and a confusing, overextended brand.

The best way to meet a potential investor is through personal introductions from other business people, lawyers, accountants, or—ideally—your retail, editorial, or supplier contacts in the industry. Connections are vital, and you should cast the net wide. Industry associations can help you find executives who may be interested in supporting a designer with potential. Also, ask the buyers, editors, and contractors with whom you have good relationships which other fashion brands might be able to help you.

Big manufacturers and retailers. Big brands and department store chains occasionally invest in small brands that fit into their mix. For example, Sean John invested in Zac Posen, Neiman Marcus invested in Kate Spade, Liz Claiborne bought Juicy Couture, and Oxford Industries bought Ben Sherman.

A growing wave of fashion companies is investing in smaller labels. Liz Claiborne recently purchased a 50 percent stake in Narciso Rodriguez; in 2006, Kellwood Company purchased designer Holly Dunlap's company Hollywould Inc.; and in July 2007, Valentino Fashion Group SpA paid $3.7 million for a 45 percent stake in Proenza Schouler.[22]

Factories and suppliers. If there is a supplier or factory with which you conduct a lot of business, ask it to partner with you. Many designers who don't have an investor survive because of the support of their factory.

Leverage with the factories and fabric mills can mean receiving your fabric and production earlier, allowing earlier delivery to the stores and more time to sell at full price. Better pricing helps you control your costs, and a strong relationship that leads to terms and discounts can eventually lead to greater finan-

cial support. Ralph Lauren's first investment of $50,000 came from Norman Hilton, his suit manufacturer.

Wing Son Garments Ltd., a Canadian manufacturer and supplier of jersey and fleece garments, bought a 50 percent controlling interest in Andy Salzer's label Yoko Devereaux. Wing Son is a vertically integrated manufacturer that handles sourcing, cutting, sampling, screen printing and inspection. Andy was working with Wing Son for four years before he approached the firm with a formal presentation, asking it to become a full production partner to help with shipping, bookkeeping, and providing capital to grow. They adopted a shared resource model and created a new company, with Andy staying on as creative director while licensing his name to the new company. Although Andy gave up a controlling interest in his own company, it was worth it for him to turn over many of the time-consuming aspects of running a label and free himself up for new projects to grow the company to the next level. Andy had pitched many others outside of the industry for capital interest but says it was impossible to secure commitment from "suits" who didn't know him or the business. While it's very difficult to sell yourself to a group of strangers who want to know what guarantees your staying power in an industry where there is a new name every week, Wing Son knew him, had worked with him, had seen the growth of the business, and, therefore, believed in the investment.[23]

Similarly, fabric company CEO Wen Zhou put up $750,000 from her fabric business for designer Philip Lim to launch his label, 3.1 Phillip Lim, and now she is his business partner. The label was started in 2005, but by Summer 2007, the collection was already in 300 stores and had a recent season of $12 million wholesale.[24]

Private equity funds started by fashion industry executives. Many new private equity funds have been formed recently by fashion executives who seek to invest in small to midsized early-stage fashion labels.

- *The Atelier Fund.* Started by Marty Wikstrom, former CEO of Harrod's, and Dawn Mello, former fashion director at Bergdorf Goodman, this fund made its first investment of approximately $9 million for a 49 percent stake in adampluseve, now know as Adam Adam Lippes.[25]

- *TSM Capital.* Former Bloomingdale's CEO Marvin Traub partnered with Mortimer Singer and Aslaug Magnusdottir to invest in designer businesses

with revenues of between $5 million and $50 million. Their first investment was a 22 percent stake in Matthew Williamson Holdings Ltd. They seek active roles in the management of the companies in which they invest.[26]

- *The Fashion Enterprise Fund in England.* Formed by Harold Tillman, who owns fashion brand Jaeger and Jane Shepherdson and was the former brand director of Topshop, in conjunction with the Centre for Fashion Enterprise, this fund is seeking new designers with plausible business plans.[27]

- *Iceland's Baugur Banking.* This fund, which owns 8 percent of Saks Fifth Avenue along with stakes in All Saints, Danish label Day Birger et Mikkelsen, Steinunn, Matthew Williamson, and House of Fraser, is a private, family-owned company. It is willing to take minority stakes and work alongside the current management team.

- *NRDC Equity Partners LLC.* NRDC, which owns retailer Lord & Taylor, paid approximately $10 million for a two-thirds interest in Peter Som Inc., which has a wholesale volume of $7 million to $8 million and has been getting close to profitability.[28] In this case, the company has an expertise in retail distribution, which can bring significant growth to the brand.

Other funds interested in investing in early-stage labels are being formed by Jeffrey Aronsson, the former CEO of Donna Karan, and Robert Bensoussan, the former CEO of Jimmy Choo, who is working in conjunction with Towerbrook Capital.

As with any potential investor, these funds should be approached with a strong business plan; proof of your growing success and potential; and a concrete explanation of why you need funds, where they would be used, and how investing in your business would pay off for the fund. However, because these funds are run by experts from within the industry, they will be very interested in your connections and industry savvy. A personal introduction and references from respected industry executives are key in gaining their interest. Ask a well-known buyer, fashion director, editor, or business executive to make an introductory call on your behalf. Also, be prepared to discuss the experience of your team and to engage in an in-depth conversation about the production, sales, and distribution processes.

Former fashion executives. A few of the retired executives at the Service Corps of Retired Executives (SCORE) said that they would personally invest in a

designer if the right one came along. Former executives of more established companies in the fashion and garment industry often invest in young designers. For example, designer Katayone Adeli worked for Parallel, and the former president of Parallel partnered in her business. Fashion executives have credibility and knowledge in the industry. These types of investors usually want to be part of something and expect to be involved in the running of the business. They seek personal fulfillment in addition to the hope of making money. Even if they don't invest, they can often point you to other sources and become valuable mentors and advisors.

Vanity investors. "Vanity" investors are interested in the glamour and social industries of bars, clubs, restaurants, and fashion. They will put up $200,000 to $500,000 just for the thrill of being involved in the fashion world while generally asking for little involvement or control. Their goal is to feel important, sit in the front row at your show, wear designer clothing, and meet the models. If you can provide all that without giving up a percentage of the company, go ahead and consider it.

Losing Control

Giving up control can be dangerous. Lawyer Steven Hahn states, "An investor would most likely insist on receiving majority control of the entity with veto ability on any major (and sometimes any minor) business decisions. You should consider what this actually means. The designer is now relegated to the status of employee."[29]

The trade-off may be worthwhile if the investor brings other expertise to the table in addition to the equity investment. But be careful that the investor doesn't take advantage. Money to grow the business also adds the burden of greater expense. Investors may pressure you to do things that aren't part of your agreement, such as design their cheaper lines. Investment from a factory means you have to use that factory, even if you aren't happy with its production.

Tim Moore of Hilldun Corporation warns that "nine times out of ten investors don't understand your business, have expectations that are too high, and can cause your business harm."[30] Some large manufacturing companies buy small companies as a tax write-off against their successful businesses. They don't

really believe in the growth potential of the small line and are even counting on it to lose money.

Some designers—including Halston, Jil Sander, Darryl K, and Pamela Dennis—actually lost the use of their name for periods of time. Designers should try to keep control of their name by licensing rather than selling the name to a partner. In the case of both Andy Salzer's and Peter Soms's recent acquisitions, a new company was formed by the investors, and the designers licensed their name to that new company. If you can't license the name, partner with the investor under a new name to protect yourself.

A designer must believe that the investors have the business acumen and knowledge to make not just good business decisions but decisions that are in the designer's best interest. The investor should truly understand and believe in your vision before you partner with them.

Always Get Outside Counsel

Surround yourself with good advisors. Have a lawyer review the deal and help you to negotiate terms, percentages, control over your name, and other important issues before you sign. Solicit second opinions from both inside and outside of the industry to help you think clearly. Designers have been approached to give up 50 percent of their company in exchange for only $100,000. In a designer's desperation for cash, it takes a good friend or counselor to talk them out of it. When you are desperate to pay a contractor or supplier, $100,000 can sound like salvation, but that amount will only float you through a season or two, and when it's gone, you may not even own your own company.

Business involves calculated risk. Keep your head on straight, find out about other deals involving the investor, and check references. It's worth doing the homework if someone is interested in giving you a chance.

Back on Your Own

Often, investor situations don't work out because the business doesn't grow fast enough or there are creative differences about the direction of the line. Investors

may want to take the line to a mass market, changing the design and the quality of materials and production as they seek to cut costs.

Investors always build an exit strategy into their deals in case the company doesn't hit its goals and they want to get out before losing more money. Designers have lost backers in the middle of production and had to cancel their orders with stores. Chanel invested in Isaac Mizrahi, giving him the opportunity to grow and operate on a large scale, but when Chanel pulled out, he was out of business. Once a backer leaves, the designer may need to refocus and start over from the beginning.

"If you were given $10,000 to spend on your business right now, what would you do with it?"

Production

Hire a production person—Bruno Grizzo, womenswear

"Buy fabric and then put it into production."—Gustavo Cadile, eveningwear

"Use it toward this season's fabric costs. We order our fabrics from Italy, France, Greece, and Japan, and the cost to ship them over for sampling and production is expensive."—Chloe, Samantha, and Caillianne Beckerman, womenswear

"Invest into inventory is my number one knee-jerk reaction. We are very frugal, and I try to do it by keeping overhead low. Makes me sleep better at night knowing that I am not burning through cash and it's all sitting in the warehouse."—Jane Ivanov, Eve Alexander, maternity lingerie

"Sampling and fabric procurement—put the money where it counts, into the product and design that show your best efforts. We find that money spent on PR, sales, and marketing takes away from the initial goal: making fashion-forward original designs."—Jerry Tam, Form New York, womenswear

Tradeshows

"If I were given $10,000 to spend on my business, I would allocate it to the cost of trade shows for the upcoming season."—Brian Wood, menswear

"Can I get more? The fashion industry is so expensive that $10,000 would not last me very long. I would use it to go to trade shows to find sourcing for my techniques and production."—Karelle Levy, Krelwear, womenswear

"I would put the money towards more trade shows. Trade shows are the backbone of opening new accounts. Right now I only do ENK in NYC. I would try my hand with either a trade show or a showroom in California."—Jessica Alpert-Goldman, World According to Jess, accessories

"Do the Prêt-à-Porter trade show in Paris."—Annie Lewis and Helen Cho, Lewis Cho, womenswear

Hiring

"I would put it towards hiring a sales assistant."—Cheyenne Morris, Tashkent, shoes

"I would put $10,000 toward a business advisor who has a lot of experience in the fashion industry."—Hajnalka Mandula, womenswear

"Hire a part-time business assistant who can implement a productive system of operations and manage the business."—Bliss Lau, accessories

"I would hire a consultant to help me make my business more energy-efficient and environmentally friendly."—Corinne Grassini, Society for Rational Dress, womenswear

"I would spend it on further developing my corporate website. A designer's website has become one of the most powerful marketing tools in conveying their vision to the outside world. Furthermore, it greatly increases your exposure from a local audience to a global one. I would set-up an e-commerce store as well. An online store offers several benefits, including higher margins, inventory management, and most importantly, accessibility for potential customers to buy your product worldwide."—Romain Kapadia, menswear

"I would put it into a public relations department to help gain more exposure for the brand."—Diego Binetti, womenswear

"It would be a toss-up between paying off some debt and using it to improve customer service (via trunk shows, traveling to see stores, and merchandising the department stores)."—Jada Simons, Marie Marie, womenswear

4

Product Development

Product development is an integral and interesting part of design. It requires a careful balance between maintaining integrity and point of view as a designer on the one hand and selling clothes on the other. The two are not mutually exclusive. Successful designers stay aware of the marketplace as they develop each collection. They have a deep understanding of their target customer, as well as the motivation behind the decisions of editors and buyers. Designer Wenlan Chia of Twinkle says, "You can hit both the creative and the commercial. That can be the most interesting part."[1]

Know Your Customer

Have your specific target customer in mind as you develop the line. Stay focused on that person's lifestyle—what she eats, where he lives, what she drives, where he vacations, and how she spends her day. A designer should know how each item in the collection will fit into the customer's life and make that customer feel and look good. "Who is your customer?" is one of the first questions that any buyer or editor will ask a designer, and you need to be ready with a quick and concise answer. For example, in press releases, designer Michael Kors described his line MICHEAL by Michael Kors as "carpool couture." The line focuses on fashion-conscious "soccer moms" who spend much of their life in the car. The clothes are practical yet chic, and they're more affordable than his signature collection. Ana Beatriz, the designer of Lerario Beatriz, who also owns showroom FiftyTwo, says it is

critical to know exactly who you are designing for. She insists that each of the designers she represents completes an extensive questionnaire to define their customer.[2] Some designers are afraid that specifically designing for one customer will limit their market, but that is exactly what you need to do. You cannot offer something for everyone.

Famous designers often have a muse—Karl Lagerfeld and Amanda Harlech, Marc Jacobs and Sophia Coppola, Phillip Treacy and Isabella Blow. The muse inspires the designer and helps the designer stay focused when creating the line. A muse can be someone you know or perhaps a celebrity or society figure that represents the ideal customer for your line. Many designers are their own muse, inspired to create items that fit their lifestyle and taste. Keep photos or other visual reminders of your inspiration, your customer, and their lifestyle in your studio to help you stay focused.

Have a Point of View

A designer needs a signature point of view to differentiate his line from others and make it special. Each season, work to establish what the marketing world calls "the DNA of the brand." This is the overall style and aesthetic customers think of when they hear your name. It's what enables a shopper to say, "That looks like a Cynthia Steffe dress," or "She is so Prada."

Developing the point of view takes time. Reed Krakoff, president and executive creative director of Coach, said he spent "a year and a half or two years of really flailing around and being too contemporary or too European."[3] It took a lot of trial and error before landing on the acclaimed signature style of "accessible luxury" he created for Coach. He knew when he hit it. It doesn't happen overnight.

Once the point of view is defined, capture that essence and make it integral to all of the designs. The identity of a label can encompass the fit, fabrication, or its appeal to a particular lifestyle. Even among the dozens of brands of jeans, whether it's the weight of the denim, the amount of stretch, the low-rise waist, or signature pockets, each brand has defining characteristics.

Put the identity into words and test each item against that definition. If your signature is sexy, flirtatious, and fun, each product must meet those crite-

ria. At first blush, point of view may sound creatively limiting, but in reality, it refines and focuses your palette.

Be Consistent

Consistency is cited by buyers as one of the biggest problems with new lines. Each new collection has unique influences, but the point of view must remain consistent from season to season to meet the expectations of retailers, editors, and consumers. Look at designer collections and study the consistency from item to item and from season to season. Maintaining consistency across all collections will allow you to grow and extend your brand to new areas, such as shoes and housewares. Ralph Lauren has been the master of consistently telling the same story with each product for more than 40 years—whether it's a corduroy jacket, a polo shirt, sunglasses, sheets, or paint. He represents a specific all-American, upper-class lifestyle, and everything created, at every price level, fits that image.

Gustavo Cadile: Design What You Love

When Gustavo Cadile started his signature label, he decided to focus on the ready-to-wear market, as this seemed to be the most lucrative market with the most opportunity. Although his passion was for eveningwear, he observed that the eveningwear collections in the stores were very small, while ready-to-wear collections were huge and had the majority of the promotional support. However, each season, the buyers reviewed his ready-to-wear and were lukewarm, saying it wasn't special enough.

He continued to make the eveningwear he loved for private clients and soon designed a wedding dress that would change his career. The dress was worn on Friday, and on Sunday, he received a call from Joan Kaner, the fashion director of Neiman Marcus. Ms. Kaner's friend had attended the wedding and forwarded a photo of the dress to her. Joan met with Gustavo, loved his work, and pronounced him ready to sell in the eveningwear salon at Neiman Marcus. She said he had to have a showroom first and made several recommendations. Gustavo signed with

Michael Atchison, the well-respected eveningwear representative for brands including Monique L'huillier.

Now Gustavo is selling his exquisite beaded gowns to socialites and well-dressed women for $3,000 to $5,000 at Neiman Marcus. He creates special-order dresses sold at trunk shows at Saks Fifth Avenue and also retails at more than 25 high-end boutiques nationwide. Gustavo travels throughout the year for more than 30 personal appearance and trunk shows. His celebrity clientele includes Eva Longoria and Catherine Zeta Jones.

Gustavo plans to expand his line to include bridal and to add a less expensive secondary line of cocktail dresses catering to businesswomen. He says that you can start with higher-end, expensive product and later add a less expensive line, but you can't start with a cheaper product and add the higher end. He lives for the glamour of seeing women in his dresses, and his advice is that you must focus on what you really love to do—not what you see in the street or in the market.[4]

Design from the Gustavo
Cadile Resort 2008 collection.

The Trends

Many emerging designers say they don't look at fashion magazines or the big collections because they don't want to be influenced by others. But you can't have your head buried in the sand and ignore fashion or what is on the streets. Whether or not your line is trend driven, you need some sense of trends, because buyers, editors, and customers do think in those terms.

On the other hand, don't chase trends too heavily, or you will dilute your identity and make it difficult for buyers to know what to expect from you. Stay focused on your customer. Pink sequins might be dominating the magazines and flying out of the stores, but if your customer won't wear them, they shouldn't be in your line.

Approach trends from your unique point of view. Robert Burke, consultant and former senior vice president of the fashion office and public relations of Bergdorf Goodman, said that they picked up menwear designer Thom Brown because they noticed a trend in young men wanting to dress up and wear a jacket, but not look like their father. Thom had a line that fit that, was very specific, and yet unlike anything else they were seeing in the industry.[5]

Designer Alice Roi testified to the struggle of finding balance between being visionary and being relevant to the current fashion. She created a collection of pouf skirts several years ago, which were panned in the press and shunned by the stores. A few seasons later, when she had moved on, pouf skirts became huge. Although Alice was way ahead with the vision and could say she did it first, it didn't matter. She says, "In the cyclical world of fashion, it's more important to be timely than first. It's better to play the game and show your uniqueness in it, than to rebel and not get anywhere."[6]

In addition to seasonal fashion trends, overall lifestyle trends affect fashion. The trend toward comfort and loungewear drove the extraordinary success of Juicy Couture. Young girls are revolting against sexy bare midriffs, shoppers are increasingly interested in ecologically sound products, men are dressing up again for work, and there is a growing demand for plus-size maternity and children's wear. It helps to be at least aware of changing mind-sets and how they affect what people buy and wear. Staying in touch with what is going on around

you may open up new opportunities to grow your business to which you can respond in your own unique way.

The Collection

Donna Karan's first collection focused on "seven easy pieces"—a tight group of skirts, tops, and bodysuits that all worked together and communicated the same message of easy dressing, comfort, and style from day to night. The collection took the fashion world by storm. Here are a few principles to guide you in creating a tight, focused collection.

Edit. Too many ideas are confusing, and without careful editing, a line can look directionless and immature. Editing is often a difficult task for the designer. Ask professionals you trust, such as a stylist or sales representative, to help you merchandise the line and eliminate items that don't fit. The product needs to look good when displayed and have "hanger appeal" to make it attractive to the customer in the store. The goal is to leave in only the strongest pieces, resulting in a tight, balanced collection. Marc Jacobs handbags are some of the most talked-about and sought-after bags each season, but there are really very few styles. As Loeffler Randall COO Amanda Thomas says, "Too many styles confuse a brand."[7]

Start small. When you are new and have limited resources, it's best to start with a small number of pieces and grow over time. Micheal Fink, senior fashion director of Saks Fifth Avenue, looks for quality over quantity. "We don't want to see 20 pieces if only 10 are good."[8] Big collections cost money, and rather than spend all your resources on many pieces, create just enough looks to provide an overall sensibility. When shoe designer Kristen Lee launched her men's shoe line, she focused on just three variations on the classic loafer. Three groups—The Rustic, The Rocker, and The Gent—offered the loafer in three colors, along with a matching attaché and a larger bag.

Balance. A collection is not a random selection of great items. It must have an overall direction, and the pieces should work together as a group. Unless you focus on a single classification, carefully review the collection to identify gaps. There should be a range of tops and bottoms that tell the same color and fabric

story. The pieces should be able to be worn together or fit in as accent items that can be sold alone.

Focus. Designers often feel they have to be everything to everybody, but it's too much. You don't need to cover all the possible items from blouses, sweaters, pants, and skirts to dresses, shorts, and coats. It's better to do one thing well or shine in one or two categories. Shoe designer Kristen Lee says, "My customer is one girl. I need to give her a few options, but I don't need something for every girl." A focused collection is also more efficient and keeps down the costs of development and production.[9]

Signature Items

There is a saying in manufacturing that 99 percent of the product manufactured is wrong; you survive on 1 percent. Many labels have built their business on a strong demand for one particular item that they do really well. The Chaiken pant, the James Perse T-shirt, and the Diane Von Furstenberg wrap dress are all examples of signature items from successful designers. A simple nylon Kate Spade bag launched an entire brand.

The signature should lie in an attribute of the garment that is not subject to fast-moving trends. For example, regardless of the color and trims each season, Darryl K pants have a unique cut and fit that stays consistent from season to season.

Over time, certain best sellers might naturally evolve into signature items. They can be carried over from season to season by keeping them fresh through subtle changes in color, fabric, or design. Juicy Couture started with a velour tracksuit, then created a cashmere version and followed with one in terry cloth. However, be careful to not rely too heavily on just one item; have something else up your sleeve in case your signature item is knocked off.

The Quality Standard

I once stepped into a Los Angeles store where the owner was fuming about the skirts she had just unpacked in a shipment from a new designer. Touted as being made with the highest-quality "couture" technique, hand sewn, and very expensive, the skirts were a mess. The inside of each unlined skirt was a tangle

of loose threads, frayed edges, and crooked seams. It was a complete embarrassment, and the buyer, and anyone she knows, will never place an order with that designer again. Some new designers seem clueless about quality.

Quality is a combination of the craftsmanship, materials, and finishing of the product. New designers should study quality by looking at a wide range of garments from designers they admire. Also, study vintage garments from the 1940s and 1950s, when garments were made with great care, as well as mass-produced items. You'll learn that great fabric does not guarantee great quality. Beautiful leathers are often wasted on poorly constructed garments, and beautiful construction is wasted on cheap synthetic blends. Price is not an indicator. One can find $800 wool skirts that aren't lined and $25 white cotton shirts that are surprisingly well made.

When developing your line, aim for the highest quality possible for your price. Once you set this standard, it is vital to stay consistent from season to season to meet customer and buyer expectations. Successful brands, ranging from high-end Louis Vuitton to the less expensive Gap, carefully maintain the same quality standard from season to season.

It Must Look the Price

The price of each product must accurately reflect its value and quality and stay consistent from season to season. Price must be kept in mind throughout the design process, because it affects the materials you can use, how intricate the design can be, and who will be able to buy it. Part of the design puzzle is figuring out how to make the product great within its price point. Price is discussed more extensively in chapters 6 and 8.

Commerciality and Show

Designer Michelle Smith from Milly credits her sales success with having a product with mass appeal. It's wearable, pretty, and easy to understand. But she says one of her biggest challenges is finding a balance between commercial appeal and press-worthy pieces.[10] Most collections have a mix of best sellers and distinctive items to create buzz, tell the story, and add excitement. Retailers do buy some

show items to help sell the rest, and designers create pieces that aren't intended for sale but rather to attract the press. Miguel Adrover received enormous attention when he made a dress of ticking from Quentin Crisp's mattress.

Even the couture lines in Paris mostly lose money, but the buzz they draw and image they create sells thousands of dollars in ready-to-wear and perfume.

Don't go overboard when creating items for press. New designers sometimes try to be too unique or inventive and forgo reality. They need to rein it in to make it sellable. Items created for the press are often adjusted for the retailer. Menwear designer Thom Browne put himself on the fashion map by giving the silhouette of his suits a short, shrunken look. However, the men who work daily in his store wear their suit pants hemmed to fall well above the shoe while selling pants with unfinished hems so the customer can choose a more traditional length.

5

Fabric and Materials

Choosing the fabric, materials, and trim is an exciting and critical part of the design process. A certain ribbon or tweed can inspire an entire collection, and an item may require specific materials to communicate the full vision or function of the design.

Learn First

Before you source the materials, learn about fibers, textiles, trims, and finishes. This will help you with the entire production process. The content of the materials greatly affects the design results, and a designer should understand the behavior of different fibers and whether they stretch, whether the color or print is dyed or woven, the attributes of natural versus synthetic fibers, and how the weave and weight affect the shape and durability of the product. Ideally, a designer should be able to feel a fabric and know if it is suitable for the design.

The best way to learn about fabric is through hands-on experience. Working a stint at a fabric store such as Mood in New York is great training. You can also learn by visiting a fabric show. Approach the fabric representatives in booths when they aren't busy and ask questions. If they have the time, people love to share their expertise. A designer can volunteer to help a fabric rep in exchange for "fabric lessons." It's well worth packing up a booth or working a few days in an office to acquire this knowledge.

The Challenges

There are many sources of fabric, and researching and reviewing the options can be overwhelming at first. As a young designer, your options will be narrowed considerably once you consider price, minimums, and lead times. Choosing the right fabric becomes as much a business decision as an aesthetic one.

Minimums

Most suppliers of fabric and trim have a minimum amount of yardage (or meters in Europe) that designers are allowed to order. The minimums exist because for the supplier, servicing, shipping, and selling small quantities is less profitable. Each supplier has a different threshold of what quantities are worthwhile. Minimums can range from 15 to 5,000 yards, but generally for the designer fabric market, the average is around 300 yards. Certain fabrics from the same mill have different minimums, depending on the content of the fabric, the finishes, or the print.

When you are new to the market and your orders are small, meeting minimums can be difficult. New designers do not need, nor can they afford, to buy excess quantities of fabric. When approaching any source for fabric or trim, find out the minimums up front. Although this question will expose you as a little fish, possibly not worth the supplier's time, in my opinion, it's a waste of your time to discuss materials you can't have. You don't want to fall in love with a sample fabric that you can't get to produce your orders.

Not Meeting the Minimums

The reality is that new designers frequently cannot meet the minimums required by fabric suppliers. Don't despair—there are a few things you can do.

> **Buy sample yardage.** Generally, a supplier has two prices for fabric: the price for sample yardage, which is a higher price for a small amount of fabric that designers buy to create a test sample for the design, and the price for production yardage, which is the lower price charged for the larger quantities needed to produce store orders. Sample yardage is expensive, 20 to 50 percent more than production yardage, because the quantities are small. But if you can't meet the required quantity for the production price, you can purchase the entire amount needed at the sample price. However, the cost will be high, and there is a risk

that the mill won't work with you next season because you didn't return for a larger production quantity.

Pay more. Sometimes a source will make a minimum exception if you pay more per yard or pay a fee. This is generally a much better deal than paying the full sample yardage price. Many European mills have expensive "couture" lines of fabric. Because the fabric is expensive, the profit margin is higher for the mill, and it will sell that fabric in smaller quantities. You can also negotiate with the supplier to find other ways to get past minimums or keep your price down. Ask them if a major manufacturer is buying the fabric, providing the opportunity to tack your order on to the end of the larger one.

Buy stocked fabric. Ask the mill or supplier what fabric it has in stock. Most places house a selection of fabrics that require smaller minimums. If they don't stock exactly what you want, such as black lace, they may have white lace you can dye. They may also stock greige goods, which are unfinished goods that can be quickly dyed or treated. Ask whether they sell off leftover fabric at the end of the season. If you do buy stocked fabric, find out how much they have in total. If they run out, you may be back to facing a 300-yard minimum to fill orders.

Be creative. Designers find other clever ways to deal with minimums. For example, if you offer a shirt in four color ways and the orders don't meet the minimums to buy the fabric in each color, you could buy the fabric for all of the shirts in white and dye it yourself (just make sure the fabric can be dyed).

Lead Time

Another factor that can limit your fabric options is lead time. This is the time it takes to receive the materials once you place the order. Lead times vary. Some fabrics arrive in four weeks, but eight weeks is standard with mills and converters if the materials aren't in stock. The same applies to trims. Basic items such as zippers may be stocked, but a special button or ribbon can take several weeks to arrive. Large orders take precedence, and your small order may be pushed to the end of the queue, causing unanticipated production delays and late store delivery. In fact, Amanda Thomas, COO of Loeffler Randall, says the biggest challenge to delivering to the stores on time is the regular delays in receiving raw materials.[1]

Large, established fashion brands have spent massive budgets on "supply chain optimization" technology and systems to save time and money on production. Plan carefully to know exactly how much lead time your production schedule affords and make sure that you always build in a cushion in case of problems. Designer Gary Graham buys his fabric in Italy now, but when starting out, he only bought domestic fabrics. He says, "Delivery is so important when you are new, and you just can't be too much of a fabric snob."[2]

Sit down with the sales agent and ask what you can receive in the least amount of time. Be sure to include shipping time in the schedule. It can take a week or more to get the fabric from the mill once it's ready.

Cost Considerations

Know your budget and stay within it! Fabric ranges widely in cost, and expenses can escalate quickly if you let your creative side off the leash. Fabric can account for as much as 30 percent of each season's costs, and the cost of each material also affects the final product price. Know in advance what you can spend while keeping your profit margin and creating items shoppers can afford to buy.

The fabric expense must make sense for the garment. Designer Nicole Miller explained the importance of fabric quality and price making sense to the end consumer. "It has to look like the money. You can buy a plain linen for $25 per yard, or you can buy a beautiful evening fabric for $25 per yard. You can get the money for the evening dress, but you won't for the linen, because no one can tell a nice linen from an average linen."[3]

If you use an expensive fabric on an intricate garment with complicated construction, tailoring, or pleating, the high fabric cost will add to the high production cost, potentially resulting in a market price too high to sell. To keep the cost of the final garment reasonable, expensive fabric should be used for simple designs that cost less to cut and sew. Designer Gary Graham offers an option to buyers when using expensive materials. If he is using a $21-per-yard jersey for a dress, he will offer the dress in a $3.50-per-yard cotton ribbing as well. The quality of material must also be consistent throughout the

product. Don't make the mistake of the eveningwear designer who lined a silk charmeuse gown with polyester.

Limit yourself to fewer fabrics. For the first few seasons, this will help you keep down expenses and meet minimums. A fabric can be used in multiple designs and still look fresh to the buyer and customer. For example, the same silk chiffon will look completely different in an evening dress versus a playful tank top. It can be lined or unlined; crinkled, pleated, flat, or bias cut; and mixed with different trims.

Don't order excess fabric. Overordering wastes money and results in inventory that the designer needs to sell at a discount or throw away. In fact, menswear designer Robert Geller recommends that new designers focus on buying only piece goods versus placing fabric orders. Excess fabric eats up so much money, and you are left with fabric you can't use. Even if a fabric is only $2.50 a yard and you buy 20 yards, you may only get enough orders to use 10 yards, which means your fabric really cost you $5 per yard because you must factor the cost of the excess into your overall expense.[4] Unfortunately, when you do resell leftover fabric to a jobber, you often receive as little as 1/30th of the price you paid. Of course if you have a strong season and have to repeatedly reorder small quantities of fabric at the higher price to fill reorders from the stores, you will also be wasting time and money. With experience, you will learn to anticipate reorders for certain items and order the fabric in advance. But when starting out with limited funds, it's not worth the risk.

Don't order fabric until you are sure. Wenlan Chia, who designs Twinkle, makes her fabric decision early in the design process. She looks at swatches and doesn't sample fabric until she knows it will definitely be in the collection. Michelle Smith of Milly designs her entire collection off the swatches and even finalizes her silhouettes before ordering fabric.

Always confirm price and payment terms. When you are ready to order, clarify the price for sample fabric, a full roll (generally 60 to 80 yards), and production quantities. Make sure you get the best price available for the quantity you need and don't be afraid to negotiate. Read the fine print and work out delivery

details and payment terms up front. Most fabric suppliers require prepayment or cash before delivery (CBD), payment in full on a credit card, or at least a deposit with the balance due cash on delivery (COD). Once you establish credit or build a relationship with the vendor, you can ask for net 30 terms, which give you 30 days from when the fabric is shipped before you have to pay. When buying imported fabrics, confirm the price currency. There is a big difference between US$8 per yard and €8 per yard. (Note: Fabric from Europe is sold by the meter, adding yet another variable.) When the U.S. dollar declines in value, U.S. designers should keep an eye on the exchange rate. If the dollar falls by 5 percent, the fabric cost increases that much, and it may be necessary to source your materials elsewhere. Designing your own prints is very expensive. If you do create a custom print, understand that each color adds to the cost. To save expense, keep the number of colors per print down and then create the print again in different colors to get more use from it.

Don't forget shipping cost. Too often, designers are shocked when they receive the final fabric bill because of the shipping and duty cost to bring fabric into the country. When choosing fabric, find out whether the price includes shipping and insurance and try to anticipate the total cost before you order. You don't want to end up like the menwear designer who had suiting from Italy sitting in customs for weeks as he tried to find cash to pay unexpectedly high shipping and duty fees. His production was delayed by each day his fabric sat in port, and to add insult to injury, U.S. Customs charged a daily storage fee for the goods.

Pricing terms specify which party covers the different costs of shipping. If the price is free on board (FOB), it includes only the transportation to the shipping port, not the shipping, duty, or other costs from that point on. Cost, insurance, freight (CIF) includes shipping but not duty. To avoid surprises, you should ask for landed duty paid (LDP) in which the shipping and all duty is included in the quoted price. However, many places won't ship fabric LDP, and the difficult task of calculating duty is left to you.

According to the Harmonized Duty Tariff Code, there is a different duty charge for each type of fabric and garment imported. Whereas linen might be charged 3 percent, the wool duty could be 30 percent, radically affecting the

total cost. A designer who shipped 600 meters of white cotton from Italy, which cost $1,100, says he had to pay $1,500 including shipping and duty, an increase of about 36 percent. A fabric agent recently shipped fabric that was $7 a yard FOB but $13.50 per yard LDP. The duty charge almost doubled the price of the fabric. Duty is also affected by country of origin and the fabric's planned use.

A customs broker or freight forwarder can help accurately estimate the shipping and duty. Brokers are paid a percentage of your total order. Although expensive, UPS or DHL can be used for shipping small quantities under tight time frames. These companies will handle customs, and it shouldn't take more than two to three days to receive fabric from Europe shipped by air.

The Sources

Finding the mills and suppliers who have the product you need and who will help you get good fabric on time, in good condition, and for a fair price is challenging. One strong tip from Howard Silver, president of Jasco Fabrics, is to "go beyond the fabric."[5] Don't just choose a supplier that has goods you like. Get a sense of the person and her control over the entire process. Know that the agent or sales representative across the table can pick up the phone and get the job done.

It takes time to find reliable sources and develop relationships with them. There are several avenues to explore.

Trade Shows

Textile and fabric trade shows take place around the world on a set schedule. At the shows, dozens of mills and textile manufacturers display their new fabrics each season. The shows feature fabrics one year in advance. For example, the shows in early March 2008 show fabric for Spring/Summer 2009.

In addition to fabric, the shows are a great source for suppliers of buttons and trims and even factories that offer production packages. Some shows Preview specializes in high-end European fabric and is probably the most popular New York show for small designers. However, it takes place earlier than Première Vision, when many mills are still taking immediate orders and may not

yet have all of their new fabrics. The Los Angeles International Textile Show is a good option for designers on the West Coast.

Regardless of which show you attend, it's worthwhile to visit a fabric show at least once. Designers should register in advance to attend and must show a business card or other proof of being part of a legitimate business. If you place an order at the show, suppliers will ask you to fill out an application detailing how long you have been in business, your resale or tax number, and references to verify activity and creditworthiness.

Mills and Agents

The mills are the actual manufacturers of the fabric or textile. They own the goods and control the flow of the beginning yarn through each of the weaving, dyeing, and finishing processes. This "vertical" structure involves fewer outside entities and, therefore, should be very reliable. However, even the mills outsource some products, generally to suit the trends. Find out the mill's in-house specialty, as these fabrics are more likely to arrive on time and in good condition.

Working directly with the mill generally entails very high minimums and long lead times. But most mills have salespeople around the world who know where the goods are at all times and can help supervise the process to control quality and stay on time.

Independent sales agents often represent one or several mills. They don't own the goods and take a commission on their sales. When you meet with an agent, ask how long the agent has been with the mill. This will indicate the strength of his relationship with the mill and ability to help you receive the goods on time.

Converters

Converters buy unfinished fabric or greige goods from mills and finish the material themselves by printing, treating, and/or dyeing it for resale. Converters generally have lower minimums than the mills and offer a wide selection. However, they have less control over the goods, because they didn't actually create them. When working with a converter, ask if it stocks any of the fabrics or yarn or if it waits for all of the goods to come from a mill. Get a sense of how closely it works

with the mill and what level of control or influence it has over the yarn used, the flow of process, and the lead time.

The Secondary Market

Jobbers in the secondary market don't actually produce or treat fabric. Instead, they buy unsold and leftover finished goods at great reductions from mills, manufacturers, and designers. They offer a potentially ideal place to find small amounts of a large variety of unique fabrics without worrying about minimums, lead time, and quality. The fabric is at the store where the designer can look it over and take it immediately. Mood Fabrics, B&J Fabrics, the fabric stores on the Lower East Side of Manhattan, S. Rimmon & Co. in Los Angeles, and the small fabric stores and warehouses across the country are examples of the secondary market.

Some jobbers offer wholesale and may be willing to purchase fabric from a mill on your behalf and help you reach the minimum if you pay for the majority of the order and they believe they can sell the rest at the store. When buying from a jobber, there are two key issues to keep in mind:

1. **Quantity.** Because the fabric is left over, the risk is whether you can get enough for production. If sales are strong for a particular item, the fabric quantity needed may be high. Unlike a mill or a converter, a jobber can't make it for you. Some jobbers may help you find out which mill originally made the fabric and call to see if there is any more. Most often, you have to try to source it yourself or find a similar fabric as a replacement. To eliminate some of the risk when you buy sample fabric from a jobber, ask the jobber to hold the remaining stock for a few weeks until you have the sample and know if you need more. Ask up front what can and can't be reordered. Often the fabric is "dead," and no one makes it anymore.

2. **Consistency.** Because jobbers buy goods from all over the world in a wide range of styles and quality, the goods are inconsistent. They don't know the fabric content, making it difficult to estimate shrinkage and fabric functionality. The law requires the fiber content of a garment be included on the label when sold, along with the care instructions. If you don't know the content, a burn test can help determine it. For more information, visit the Federal Trade Commission website (www.ftc.gov/os/statutes/textilejump.htm).

The Internet

There are hundreds of fabric websites, and you can search them by fabric type. When ordering materials online, request swatches before you buy, because a computer screen cannot accurately show color, pattern, texture, or quality. Several online resources direct designers to fabric sources with small minimums. Fashiondex Inc. (www.fashiondex.com) publishes a book called *The Small Design Company's Guide to Wholesale Fabrics and Trims*, which specifically lists fabric and trim suppliers that work with small manufacturers. Infomat (www.infomat.com) also lists fabric and trim suppliers and their minimums.

International Sourcing

There is a wide variety of fabric to choose from overseas. European mills are known for high-end quality fabrics, such as Italian cashmeres, as well as innovative and luxurious fabrics and prints. Japan has high-tech fabric, Korea has outerwear and synthetics, India has beading and silk, and China offers a large variety of inexpensive goods. Most designers work with at least some imported goods. However, extra shipping and duty cost, shipping delays, customs, and vacation times are issues to consider when working with overseas sources. Italian mills are closed for the entire month of August, and Asia has several holidays, some of which result in mills being closed for more than a week at a time. Long lead times can jeopardize delivery and the ability to fill reorders from the stores. For your first few seasons, buying overseas might not be worth the additional stress.

Vertical Manufacturing

Increasingly, factories and manufacturers have "vertical" operations and will source your raw materials for you. The factory can obtain discounts and demand quick and reliable delivery, because it orders for multiple clients representing a large amount of business for the mill. The designer may meet with the factory early in the development process to review options for fabric, trims, and even hardware such as zippers and buttons. Many overseas factories, such as the knitwear manufacturers in China, send packages of yarn options in various colors, fibers, and blends. For many designers, it is extremely convenient to have their choices laid out before them, knowing that all the options are accessible and they don't have to

worry about chasing the raw goods or taking up additional time in shipping them from supplier to factory. Of course the downside of this is that each factory has limited options. Many designers love the process of researching fabrics and sourcing each button as well as creating their own colors and prints.

Sewn Goods

Many growing labels, especially in menswear, have started out as T-shirt brands or graphic-based labels with screen printing on sweatshirts or Henleys. Many of these new designers start out using already-sewn product, such as T-shirts from American Apparel. This can be a great place to start and a way to avoid sourcing raw materials and production facilities as you start to establish your brand. However, at some point, you will need to step up to a better quality and lose that American Apparel label to be taken more seriously and to justify the more expensive cost of your designer product.

Once You Order

Convincing Suppliers to Work with You

Mills and fabric agents are often hesitant to work with new designers. In fact, a designer told me she approached a supplier who was standing in front of a rack of black ribbon, and when she asked, "Do you have any black ribbon?" the supplier said no.

The relationships you develop over time with fabric, leather, and trim suppliers will be invaluable. Fabric company CEO Wen Zhou put up $750,000 from her business for designer Philip Lim to start his label.[6] It's not surprising that designers who speak fluent French or Italian often evade the minimums at European mills. A supplier of activewear fabrics at the IFFE told me that even though he has a 500-yard production minimum, if he enjoys speaking to a young designer and determines from the conversation that the designer is serious and smart, he may let that person buy small quantities with a credit card.

Some fabric suppliers enthusiastically support new designers. Erich Soldat of Textile Agency said, "Young designers bring energy and creativity to fashion and keep New York fashion from being boring."[7] Jasco Fabrics supports new

talent and allows new designers to order small quantities of its high-quality, American-made jersey.

To increase the odds of getting fabric from a new supplier, introduce yourself, demonstrate some knowledge of fabric, share your vision, and mention interest in your collection from press or stores. Let the supplier see the potential for increased business and convince it that you are able to pay.

If a rep does give you an appointment, be prepared and don't waste the rep's time. Agent Erich Soldat emphasizes, "No designing here!" If you start developing your concept in a supplier's office while looking at all the fabrics and asking for random swatches, you won't be invited back. Have your concept and direction for the collection before you meet the fabric agent. Tell the agent exactly what you need so she can help you find it quickly.

Sourcing fabric will get easier. Ingwa; Melero's fabric suppliers now stock some of its fabrics to help with reorders, and they bring previews of upcoming fabrics to see if the designers want special colors or details.

Exclusives

A new designer fell in love with a printed fabric she sampled at Première Vision so much so that she planned her entire collection around the print. Then the mill called to tell her the fabric was no longer available because a big brand had bought a large amount of it and demanded an exclusive. Unfortunately, this is one of the hazards of being the little guy. If it happens to you, ask the mill to send you alternatives to help you find a replacement.

Realize that exclusives tend to prevail with more recognizable things such as prints. Keep in mind that when you buy fabric, you do not have an exclusive. Large overseas mills often distribute their goods to many different agents, and they can end up everywhere. Ask the supplier if another designer or manufacturer has bought the same fabric to avoid having your luxury market coat in the same fabric as the hot new item at The Limited.

Replacing the Goods

Sometimes, you may need to replace fabric or supplies, even after you have shown your samples and taken orders. The jobber may run out of the goods, or the fabric may arrive too flawed to use.

When replacing materials, try to match the original as closely as possible in terms of quality, look, and feel. Once you find something, you should show it to the buyers who ordered the affected items for approval. There is a risk that they won't approve the replacement or will use the change as an excuse to cancel the order, but better that happen at this stage than later when the items are already produced and shipped. A menswear designer told me that he doesn't ask buyers if the replacement is "close enough" because they placed the order six months ago and won't remember exactly what it looked like. However, if they do remember, they could return the entire production.

When you replace goods, make sure the production bundles don't mix the original fabric with the replacement, or you may deliver a garment with one fabric on the body and another on the sleeves. Remember to include any cost differences resulting from replacement materials on the cost sheet.

Don't Let It Be Late

Once a fabric or trim is late, everything is off-schedule. The production will be delayed, and you will have to make up time to hit the retail delivery dates.

If the fabric is late, asking for money back from the supplier won't get your orders shipped on time. The key is not allowing it to be late in the first place. As Howard Silver at Jasco Fabrics says, "No news is no news."[8] Don't take anything for granted. Stay on top of the mill or agent at all times to ensure the goods are on schedule. Call and ask where the fabric is in the production process. Have they received the thread, has it been dyed, is it being woven, is it on the truck, and when will it get to the airport? If the person on the phone doesn't know, ask him to find out. Many things can push the fabric off schedule. For example, each mill has a set number of looms. If you need 300 yards of tweed and a rush order from Marc Jacobs comes in for 5,000 yards of tweed, your job may be removed from the looms to get them all working for Marc Jacobs. You must stay on top of your order or it will be continually swept aside. Obnoxious is not effective, so be polite

and professional when you check in. When you work with an agent, you can try to find out what mill is working on the fabric and contact it directly to ask questions and track the goods. It may annoy your agent, or she may be happy to not deal with it, but either way you could get answers more quickly.

Quality Control

Many things can go wrong with fabric production, and you cannot take anything for granted. A good mill should contact you in advance if there are problems and show you the fabric to make sure you still want it. Often, large manufacturers request a sample half yard from the production run of the fabric to check the quality before it even ships. The mills may refuse to do this for small customers, but it doesn't hurt to ask.

It is imperative to inspect all of the fabric and trim thoroughly immediately upon receipt. This probably means a trip to your production factory, assuming you ship the goods directly there versus transporting it yourself. Inspect everything carefully before it's cut. Once it's cut, you own it, and the supplier is not responsible. Technically, if you contract out the cutting, the contractor is responsible for spotting flaws, but check the goods yourself to be safe.

- Measure to make sure you received the correct yardage.
- Ensure that the fabric is the correct width. If you planned your cutting and quantities based on 60", everything will be off is the fabric is 58".
- Check for flaws or quality issues relating to the color or weave.
- Check the goods against your initial sales sample. If the product differs from what the stores ordered, they might send it back.

If you find a problem, call the supplier immediately to negotiate a solution or replace the fabric as quickly as possible. Be professional and say you found damage. If possible, the agent should come to look at it and make a settlement before it's cut. Ideally, the mill should replace the damaged goods or take them back and refund your money. More often, for the sake of time and shipping, they will offer you a discount on the goods if you keep them and work around the problem. This is generally the best option to keep production from being further delayed.

Keep in mind when negotiating a settlement that flawed fabric may cost more to cut because you have to work around the flaws, resulting in unusable fab-

ric. When you buy from a supplier, find out the policy for late or flawed fabric. If there is no recourse, you may want to reconsider working with that supplier.

At some point in the process of choosing fabric, test each fabric for color-fastness and shrinkage. Use sample fabric or cut a small piece of yardage from the bolt. Garments from new designers often are returned to the store because colors bleed or garments shrink when worn or cleaned. Suppliers should know the shrinkage factor of a fabric, but with a test you will be certain.

"Green" Is the New Black

For years, it's been common knowledge that Stella McCartney uses no leather or fur, Giorgio Armani makes jeans from organic cotton and hemp, and American Apparel manufactures locally with organic fibers. But recently, the buzz about "green" materials and demand for environmentally sound practices has made these options accessible to design companies of all sizes.

The business and consumer worlds are responding to cries for environmentally sound products, and wealthy consumers are choosing to pay more for organic food and socially or ecologically responsible materials and goods. Fashion savvy shoppers want designers to provide high-end luxury product in an area previously dominated by hippie skirts and Birkenstocks. Designers such as Linda Loudermilk have grown their brands based on their commitment to high-end products rooted in sustainability.

Luxury stores are responding to demand, with Barneys NY launching its "green" initiative with Loomstate, the New York–based organic apparel company, designed by Rogan Gregory of the Rogan jeans label and a partner of Edun, the socially conscious apparel brand created by Bono and his wife, Ali Hewson. Wholesale trade shows have jumped to support the cause as well. The official theme at the Pitti Immagine Filati in Fall 2007 was "Eco-Culture, Eco-Couture," featuring collections of ecological and organic yarns. Designers and agents in New York launched a "Go Green" initiative featuring an "eco-chic capsule" of curated fashion, lifestyle products, energy-efficient products, and educational materials promoting global sustainability. Even the fashion weeks in Los Angeles, Seattle, Portland, and London have all had "green" themes.

Because of this enthusiastic response, there is some concern that the "green" movement is just another trend being utilized to sell goods and gain press attention.

And some high-end luxury brands that are instilling socially conscious practices are not advertising them for fear of aligning their brand too directly with a "cause."

If organic product or sustainability is of interest to you, you will have to work a little harder to source your materials. Demand is still low, keeping costs high and product less accessible to smaller designers. However, many suppliers have yet to land very large orders for their "green" offerings and are open to working with smaller minimums. Jasco Eco, for example, has a stock service collection of certified organic and sustainable fabrics in vibrant colors created with eco-friendly dyes. There are no minimums on the stock service items, and a percentage of the proceeds are donated to Future Fashion Initiative.

Fabric mills are increasing their offerings of natural or sustainable materials, such as organic wool and cotton, hemp, bamboo, and recycled polyester and leather, while putting developmental efforts into new products, such as mud-dyed linen, vegan silk, and textiles made of wood pulp such as Tencel®, Ingeo™ (created from corn), Seacell® (created from seaweed), and recycled fiber fabrics such as Polartec® and POP (made from recycled soda bottles).

Several fabric trade shows have focused areas on sustainable fabrics. In 2007, both Material World and the Los Angeles International Textile show had "eco" areas and themes and featured fabrics including organic cotton, bamboo, soy, seaweed, and coconut. Interstoff Asia features environmentally friendly fibers, dyes, and fabrics with bamboo knits from Taiwan, organic cotton and flax from South Korea, biodegradable PLA from Japan, soy fabrics from China, and polyester made from recycled bottles in China and Taiwan. Some of the fabrics were dyed with oolong tea and persimmon.

Because "green" materials are often sourced internationally, like organic linen and bamboo from Turkey or cotton from Peru, some designers are deciding to keep their production in the same place where they source the fabric to lessen the time and natural resources spent in transporting the materials to another location.

Numerous organizations exist to help promote the use of sustainable materials and to help educate designers and assist them with sourcing. The Future Fashion Initiative by Earth Pledge promotes the use of sustainable materials and methods in the textile, apparel, and home furnishings industries. It recently sponsored press events featuring garments designed by Peter Som, AsFour, Lela Rose, and others made from eco-friendly materials donated by Earth Pledge. Several other helpful organizations are listed in the Resource section at the back of this book.

6

Production

∎ ∎ ∎

If you went to fashion school, you probably learned about the production process as it relates to big companies. But it is very challenging to navigate the world of production on your own. Many designers name production as the part of their job that is the most difficult, and some even say it's the only part they hate. But despite the frustration, production is where your brilliant ideas become reality.

A critical person in large fashion houses is the production manager. For most new designers, this means you. The designer must manage all the steps of production, from initial samples through final shipping, and plan carefully to stay on schedule, meet retail delivery dates, and keep track of every cost from start to finish. Don't take anything for granted—actively oversee it all.

The Production Plan

Fashion lives on a strictly set calendar with hard deadlines, and you must work within them. For each collection, you need a master production schedule. This includes each step of development from ordering fabric, first patterns, first samples, sales, and finalizing orders through the production processes of final patterns, cutting, sewing, and shipping. The schedule will track where each material is at all times.

To create a schedule, start with the shipping dates and work backward through all the steps. Schedule plenty of time for unexpected delays. Don't forget that the seasons overlap. At the same time designers ship fall orders,

they are sampling for spring and may be producing holiday. Manage your time well. Industry experts are quite serious when they recommend that a designer design her first two or three collections before even starting her business because she will never again have the luxury of that much time to design. As you see from the sample production schedule in Figure 6.1, production for your Spring collection, which takes place in the Fall and during the holidays, is much more crunched than production for Fall, and the seasons overlap significantly.

Fabric selection often starts even earlier, when the European preview trade show takes place in June and July, and sales may extend longer depending on the market. Menswear and accessories run on slightly different schedules: menswear sells primarily in early July and January and ships in early January and August, while accessories have five markets per year, which take place after the ready-to-wear markets. However, high-end accessories and shoe designers sell at the same time as ready-to-wear.

The Steps of Production

1. Research materials and concepts.
2. Develop silhouettes.
3. Select fabric and materials.
4. Order sample cuts of fabric.
5. Create first patterns.
6. Cut and sew sample garments.
7. Finalize collection of samples.
8. Sell collection and finalize orders.
9. Order production fabric and materials.
10. Finalize production pattern.
11. Finalize production prototypes.
12. Grade pattern for sizes.
13. Create marker for cutting fabric.
14. Cut, sew, and trim.
15. Pack and ship.

FIGURE 6.1 Sample Production Schedule

	Fall 2009	Spring 2010
September '08	Research fabrics. Start design.	
October '08	Select fabrics. Order fabrics.	
November'08	Create patterns. Begin samples.	
December '08	Develop collection. Review production strategy.	
January '09	Finalize collections. Begin sales.	
February '09	Show collection. Continue sales.	
March '09	Close sales.	Research Fabrics. Start design.
April '09	Order production materials. Create production samples.	Select fabrics. Order fabrics.
May '09	Begin production.	Create patterns. Begin samples.
June '09	Monitor production.	Develop collection.
July '09	Monitor production.	Review production strategy. Finalize collections.
August '09	Begin deliveries and collect COD.	Begin sales.
September '09	Continue deliveries. Collect payments.	Show collection. Continue sales.
October '09		Close sales.
November '09		Order production materials. Begin production.
December '09		Monitor production.
January '10		Monitor production.
February '10		Begin deliveries and collect COD.
March '10		Continue deliveries. Collect payments.

Sample Production

Patternmaking

One of the first steps in producing a design is to create the patterns from which your samples will be made. It is critical to find good talent at this stage of production. A great patternmaker will pinpoint problems in the design, construction process, and materials. In fact, a great patternmaker can reach celebrity status among designers. Nicholas Caito, after gaining extensive experience at Lanvin and Rochas, is praised for bringing the technical craftsmanship of Milan and Paris to America. Elle magazine calls him "New York's most in-demand patternmaker,"[1] and his fortunate clients include Peter Som, Proenza Schouler, and Hermes.

Designer Marni Joy says, "Finding a great patternmaker is one of the most important parts of the design process. I found someone early on whom I completely trusted and who did an amazing job. I left her because of cost, but I was back the following season realizing that it was worth the cost to avoid problems later on."[2]

An expert pattern is the foundation of a good product. Most importantly, it determines fit, which is one of the most common reasons that items don't sell. Signature items that help put many designers on the map, such as the Chaiken pant or the Shoshanna swimsuit, are the results of a great pattern.

Who should make the patterns? You don't have to hire a patternmaker if you can do it yourself. Many new designers learn patternmaking in design school; some even teach themselves. Making your own patterns will save substantial money and give you control. It can help you to interpret your design as well as possible and to manage alterations and turnaround time.

However, it's critical that you really have the skills to do an expert job, or you will make mistakes and waste time and money fixing the production. Factory managers have told designers that they won't work with their self-made patterns anymore because the mistakes cause time delays at the factory. Even if you are extremely deft at patterns, they are time consuming, and as your company grows, you may have to outsource this task to focus on other aspects of the business.

If you don't make patterns, I still highly advise that you acquire a basic understanding of patternmaking. The knowledge will help you better understand construction and fit, better communicate with patternmakers and other contractors, and pinpoint and understand problems. A designer can be at the mercy of patternmakers if he doesn't speak the language. The patternmaker can blame problems with the pattern on the fabric or design, and the designer won't know the difference.

Where to find a patternmaker. The best way to find a patternmaker is through personal referrals from people in the industry. However, designers are often protective of their best resources and will not always share. Ask contractors or factories if they can recommend someone. Contact the fashion schools and see if they will refer you to alumni in the field or even to current students who have strong patternmaking skills.

If you know patternmakers who work for large companies, discreetly ask them if they do freelance work or if they know anyone who does. But keep in mind that this person has a full-time job and your work will come last.

Services, such as Infomat and Fashiondex, have websites, publications, and referral services to patternmakers and other contractors. Industry papers, such as *WWD* and *California Apparel News*, sometimes list pattern services in their classified sections. Don't be limited by geography since email and the Internet make it possible to work with patternmakers from afar.

You get what you pay for. Good patternmakers are expensive, but money spent here can save considerable money later on. Most designers are willing to spend whatever is necessary for good patterns and will make their budget cutbacks elsewhere.

Generally, patternmakers charge by the piece and by the complexity and amount of detail in the garment. Others charge an hourly rate and will provide an estimate of the number of hours required once they understand the garment. The more complex the pattern or garment, the more time it takes, and the more it will cost. Pricing can vary widely among different patternmakers and services and different areas of the country. Jackets fit into one price range, from $250 to $450, while skirt patterns usually cost less, from $100 to $200. Generally, the patternmaker will require a deposit before beginning work.

Confirm that the patternmaker will make revisions if you don't like the final sample. Revisions should be included in the price if something is wrong with the pattern, but if you change the design based on the final sample, you will have to pay for the new pattern.

Communicate clearly. Before the patternmaker can begin, the designer must know exactly how the finished garment should look, including the details of shape and fit down to pocket placement. Both patternmakers and factories tell stories of designers with ideas that are impossible to make, and designers are often frustrated when shown a sample that is nothing like what they envisioned.

Sketches of the front and back of the garment, technical drawings, and detailed specification sheets are valuable tools to communicate the measurements for the garment, such as the width of the pant leg at the hem, and sewing details, including specific types of seams, spacing between pleats, size of pockets, special linings, and placement of trims.

Another option is to show the patternmaker a garment with similar attributes, in a similar fabric, to help explain what you want. One designer who works for a large fashion brand says he never bothers making patterns from scratch; he just goes to Gap and buys a similar item to use as a starting pattern.

The most important thing is to have a clear conversation with the patternmaker. While communicating, be sure to listen to this person's advice and feedback. The patternmaker can suggest improvements and help you avoid problems in the design and save money in production. Often new designers want a design in a fabric that just won't support the garment or fit correctly. A patternmaker can point this out up front before you waste time and money.

Tips and Considerations When Hiring a Patternmaker

by Sally Beers (www.pattern-design.com)

- Think about what kind of patternmaker you want. Are you creating a new, innovative line or one that is more classic?

- Do you want your patternmaker to set your standards, fit, and body specs? How serious are you about creating or maintaining your own proprietary fit?

- What services do you need the patternmaker to complete? Do you just need the first patterns, or do you want her to do production patterns, specs, cutting directions, and grading?

- Look for a patternmaker with appropriate expertise (for example, if you design coats, he should have coat experience), but don't be completely limited by his experience. You may hit it off with a bathing suit patternmaker who is versatile.

- Ask her if she prefers draping or flat patternmaking and why. A good patternmaker should be proficient in draping.

- Find a patternmaker with manual skills, rather than just computer skills, and ask how many years he's been doing it. It can take 10 to 20 years to become proficient at manual patternmaking.

- Ideally, a patternmaker should understand the entire production process to create patterns that will result in good garments that fit.

- What is your budget for a patternmaker? You should be able to find a good one for $50 to $75 per hour. I recommend a budget for patterns between $500 and $1,000 per new style. Versions of existing styles might cost less, but this is a good rule of thumb for a professional pattern that is production-ready.

- You can ask for a set price for an entire collection of patterns. For example, you can tell her you have $5,000 and need to complete 10 to 12 styles and see if she can commit to your budget.

- Ask him for a time estimate for the pattern. If you want a quick first pattern or drape, it usually takes between four and eight hours, depending on the complexity. I recommend setting aside three months

to develop a small line, especially if the patternmaker is to establish the fit and sizing for you.

- Find out whom she has worked with before and ask to see examples of her past patterns, as well as samples made from them. Try her out with one style to evaluate her work.

- Make sure he considers his clients' work proprietary. Would he share another company's slopers? Does he start from scratch when developing new client slopers? Would he sign a noncompete agreement?

The First Samples

The samples are the most critical tool for sales and require time and effort to perfect. Emerging designers spend as much as $80,000 for one season's sample collection. Each sample can easily cost $1,000. Most young designers have a bad habit of oversampling. Keep your eye on the budget and limit the number of styles in the collection.

Who should make the samples? A designer does not need to sew. Many of the biggest names in the fashion business would be lost behind a sewing machine. However, while you aren't expected make your own garments, basic sewing skills are vital to understanding construction and fit and will help you pinpoint the problem with a sample that doesn't look right. Perhaps more importantly, basic sewing skills help a designer communicate better with the factory and sample maker.

Making your own samples will save you money and allow more control over the product and production schedule. Some new designers are extremely talented with a sewing machine and produce immaculate samples. But generally, it's easy to spot samples made by a designer because they lack the quality and expert finish of a professional. Whether it's an issue of skill or just equipment, be honest with yourself. If your in-house samples aren't as good as they could be, outsource.

The same criteria you use for hiring a patternmaker applies to a sample maker. Inquire about expertise in the type of product you design, see examples of past work, and ask about turnaround time. Sample price is affected by the

number of pattern pieces; the complexity of the garment; and the extra details of lining, topstitching, buttonholes, and finishing.

The factory you have found for production may offer sample-making services. If the factory makes the first sample, it will better understand the garment and give a more accurate estimate of production lead time and cost. However, the cost of that first sample may be quite high. Sometimes, especially in New York, a factory will inflate the sample price considerably because it is concerned that after the designer receives the sample, it will be given, along with the entire production job, to a cheap factory overseas. To counter this, the factory prices the sample high and then makes up for it in a cheaper production price as an incentive for the designer to keep the work there. Many overseas factories produce samples as part of their production package and then ship them to you for approval. Some even visit New York each season during the sample-making process to create samples or review them in person with the designer.

Be a perfectionist. Terry Gillis, owner of the store TG-170 in New York, says when working with new designers, she finds the biggest problem is usually the fit.[3] A designer should do everything to ensure proper fit. Test each sample on a fit model who accurately represents the proportions of the target customer. The fit model will give movement to a garment and show whether it hangs correctly or if it pulls or sags. A model can also tell you about comfort and ease. Most likely, at least one round of alterations will be needed after trying the sample on the model, and the sample should be redone until it's right.

Some designers act as their own fit model, but with clothing, it's very difficult to get a full perspective of a garment on your own body and to pinpoint where it needs alteration. Before you finalize the collection, try the samples on a few "real" people to hear feedback and see how the samples hang on different bodies. I have seen shock on designer's faces when after creating all their samples and perfecting them on a model, they realize how different the garment looks on a "real" body.

In addition to fit, check the sewing and construction details of the item. For clothing, do a wash test of the first sample to alert you to any shrinkage, fading, and stretching that result from care and cleaning.

The first cost estimate. Throughout the entire design and development process, it's important to keep track of every cost associated with the design and development of the first samples and be aware of how the costs of production will affect the final retail price. You don't want to create a product that no one can afford to buy.

The first sample will allow you to create the first production cost estimate for the item and to verify that you can actually afford to produce and sell it at the appropriate price point. Designers roughly guess that the production cost for each item will be half the price of the sample, but as you price out different quantities with suppliers and factories, your estimate will become more accurate.

Production costs will change based on the orders you receive. The larger the orders, the less things cost because of volume discounts for materials and sewing. Small orders of each style can lead to production and material surcharges, even if the overall sales figures are impressive. Wholesale pricing should be based on the costs of goods sold using quantity estimates.

Costs of goods sold (COGs) includes all the materials and labor specifically required to produce the actual items ordered by the stores. It covers materials such as fabric, trimmings, zippers and buttons, handles, lining, fusing, thread, labels, and hangtags, as well as the labor costs for production patterns, marking, grading, cutting, sewing, and packing. Don't forget the costs of the specific hangers, ticketing, and shipping required by the retailers. Create a cost sheet to track the costs and redo the sheet for each new item (see figure 6.2).

If the actual costs of the fabrics, trims, and design details of each sample are too high to result in a realistic and profitable wholesale price, the design will need to be altered to bring the cost down. When starting out, the designers of menwear line Morgan D'Alessandro designed a great trouser with lots of funky button and D-ring embellishments. But they realized that because their production quantities were small, the cost of adding just those elements was more than $20 for each pair of pants. They had to cut back on the details to keep the pants at a reasonable retail price.

 The Costs of Production

Shoe production is extremely expensive because of the high cost of each component. Assuming you have a European factory to work with you, plan on the following costs for high-end shoe samples:

- Last (the solid form around which a shoe is molded): €75, each pair

- Heel: €825, each pair

- Prototype: €250, each style

This adds up to approximately €1,150 per pair, not including any special hardware or other features. To put a small collection of 20 styles together, using four lasts and three heels, would cost at least €7,775. And it can easily cost more. One high-end shoe designer stated that just the model development of a collection of half-pair sales samples usually costs about $20,000, and this does not include costs of new heels or lasts.

Shoe designers create two to four sample collections each year. Although the lasts can be reused, you will need to add more eventually, as buyers want new shapes each season.

The final collection. When the first samples are complete, edit the line to remove any samples that should not go to market. Some will need to be eliminated because they are too expensive, take too long to produce, or simply don't fit the collection. Once the line is finalized, make whatever duplicate samples are required for the selling process. You may need one set of samples for a New York showroom and one set to send to a West Coast sales representative.

FIGURE 6.2 Sample Cost of Goods Worksheet

Style #	Season:			
Description:				

Piece Goods	Width/Style	Cost per Yard	Yardage	Cost
Fabric 1				
Fabric 2				
Lining				
Interfacing				
Other				
Allowance				
		Sub Total Piece Goods Costs		

Notions	Style/Size	Unit Cost	# of Units	Cost
Buttons				
Zippers				
Thread				
Labels				
Trim 1				
Trim 2				
		Sub Total Notions Costs		

Labor				Cost
Production Samplemaker				
Cutting				
Grading				
Sewing				
		Sub Total Labor Costs		

Shipping				Cost
Hangers				
Bags/Shipping Boxes				
Hangtags				
Other Costs				
		Sub Total Shipping		

Total Cost of Goods Sold	
Wholesale Markup	
Wholesale Price	
Retail Markup	
Suggested Retail Price	

Fabric Name:	Sketch
Content:	
Source:	
Swatch:	

Production Options

Production sources need to be lined up and ready before you begin to take orders. In fact, many designers recommend that you research and find your production options before you even start your company. Although there are alternatives, the majority of designers choose to give their production to a factory or contractor.

Not Everyone Wants to Work with You

Like the fabric suppliers, factory owners often feel that new designers are not worth the extra work. New designers have more problems, pattern mistakes, materials that aren't appropriate for the product, incorrect cutting, and other issues that take time to organize and fix. To a factory, time is money.

Factories often require references, especially overseas. Micheal Spaulding of Gunmetal says, "You can't just walk into a factory in Italy and have them work with you. A last factory won't even give you an appointment without a recommendation from someone in the industry."[4] Holly Dunlap of Hollywould approached the Italian Trade Commission, which introduced her to the factories.[5]

Factories are concerned about your credibility and whether you can pay. They will ask about your business history and, most importantly, the projected production run. If you are brand new and don't have any orders yet, you don't need to tell them.

Minimums (Again)

Factories also require minimums because small production runs are time consuming and less profitable. When reviewing a factory, find out its production minimum and try not to waste time with factories that are not an option for you. Many factories specialize in small lots or are at least open to negotiation, especially in New York and increasingly in Italy, where more manufacturers are taking their production to Asia, forcing local factories to be more flexible and open to small companies.

Designers utilize several tricks to try to get around minimums, but in such a small industry, it's better to be straightforward and try to negotiate. If you don't meet the minimum, offer to pay more. For example, if the factory requires a 500-piece minimum at a price of $20 each, say you will pay $22 each for 250

pieces. Realize if you negotiate this minimum up front and end up after market with orders for only 200 pieces, you must decide if you can take the loss on the extra 50 items or try to sell them elsewhere. In general, extra stock simply ties up your money, and you will probably have some returns and end up with extra inventory. Be very careful never to cut more than a 3 percent overage on your orders. If you can't sell enough to meet the factory minimum, it's best not to produce the piece at all.

Also, make sure you understand the definition of minimum. Some factories may have a minimum of 200 of each style, but that may include all sizes and several color options.

When negotiating, try to convince the factory owner that working with you now will lead to a large production run in the future. Ask about the production capacity of the factory to imply that you are planning to have big volume soon.

 Design Trick

Cutting the same silhouettes in different colors and fabric combinations and incorporating different trims will save money on patterns and production and help meet minimums. Even though the garments look like different styles, to production, the cutting and sewing steps are the same, and you will be charged a lower price as if it is all the same garment. Observe collections in the stores to see the smart ways that designers save money on fabric and production. At the Rebecca Taylor store, for instance, a tuxedo pant is offered in several different colors of wool, and the same silhouette is available in satin and with varying trims.

Referrals to Factories and Contractors

Finding and reviewing factories is time consuming and can be frustrating. Ideally, you will receive recommendations from designers or others in the industry. Fabric shows are also a good source of information, and in general, you just need to ask around. For example, if you are making leggings, ask the supplier of

the stretch fabric which factory could sew them. Panjiva is a New York–based company that helps fashion brands find and evaluate factories with a database of more than 40,000 apparel suppliers around the globe. The chambers of commerce of Italy, China, Hong Kong, and India can help you find factories in those countries.

Don't disregard the importance of the garment industry's "old boys' club." The factory owners know everyone and will refer you to other contractors, suppliers, and a wide range of specialists. There are ads for contractors in trade papers, and referrals are available at the Fashion Information Center and the Garment Industry Development Corporation in New York, as well as the Garment Contractors Association in Los Angeles. Infomat and Fashiondex have resources online and in their books. While these sources will provide long lists of potential options, you will need to research and knock on doors to find the place that is right for you.

Different Factories Offer Different Services

Every day, young designers in New York are seen schlepping from place to place just to complete one garment. They carry the fabric from the cutter, to another place for marking, to another for sewing, and then wait in line for an hour or more elsewhere to have the buttons put on. Transportation from one place to another can be tedious and expensive, and the designer has to manage the flow between vendors and contractors.

Production can be simplified by choosing a "vertical" factory that offers multiple services, such as fabric selection, patternmaking, production, and shipping, at one place. Having fewer organizations involved means less opportunity for things to go wrong and processes to run late. The designer has more control, and because one factory handles many steps of the process, it is more likely to provide accurate cost and timing estimates up front.

Consolidation results in efficiencies and savings. Factories that order fabric and trim place orders for multiple brands, resulting in bulk discounts, particularly with standard fabrics, such as denim, and performance fabrics for swimwear or activewear. Designers don't have to run to the factory every time it is short a button, because the factory sourced the button and can order more.

Many overseas factories offer "packages" that include the entire process from sourcing and sampling to producing, finishing, and shipping the goods. Increasingly in New York, if you ask for a full package, the factory will comply. However, while packages make the production management job easier, some designers feel that packages limit the choice of materials and process too much, leaving less room for maintaining quality standards and process control.

Consolidation is not always available, and it doesn't always make sense. Many of the best factories only offer cut, make, and trim (CMT). They cut the fabric, sew (make) each item, and trim by pressing, tagging, hanging, and packing for shipment. The other steps of the process, such as marking and grading, need to be outsourced. In some cases, the best sewers for the fabrication might be in a sewing room that doesn't offer other services, or the designs may require a cutter or sewer with special equipment. Sometimes it's simply less expensive to cut certain quantities in a cutting room or to hire an independent grading service.

Where to Produce?

Domestic production. When starting out, it's highly advisable to produce domestically or even locally if possible. The ability to oversee each process and communicate directly with people at the factory will make it easier to keep production on schedule and meet quality standards. You can also benefit from faster delivery to market and less danger of piracy, a potential problem in overseas factories. Also, it can be easier to negotiate terms when you are dealing face-to-face. The biggest downsides are that domestic labor costs are high and you may not find a factory with the expertise you need.

While most small designers in the United States produce in New York, there are production opportunities everywhere. California is actually the largest producer of apparel in the United States, and driving your production around in Los Angeles is easier than dragging it from block to block in New York. The Evans Group, with locations in Los Angeles and San Francisco, is one vertical company that specializes in contemporary and young-designer production and has on-site patternmakers and sample makers.

There are designers in San Francisco, Dallas, Chicago, and Portland who produce in those cities and cite the advantages of working locally to produce specialized pieces, quick reorders, and small runs. Many smaller cities are working to support the local fashion industry by launching fashion weeks or creating programs that support designers. For example, Mayor Richard M. Daley announced the City of Chicago's plans for the Chicago Fashion Incubator at Macy's on State Street, an initiative that provides six emerging designers with mentoring on the business of fashion. Designers will be offered sample production and showroom space at the State Street store. The incubator will also provide workshops and seminars for the local fashion community.

Off-shore production. Designers generally choose to produce overseas for either cost or quality reasons. Italian factories are credited with producing the highest quality of designer goods, from men's suits to shoes. They understand designer clothes and have highly trained craftspeople and artisans who have learned from generations of experts and take pride in their work. As a result, buyers are often more interested in items made in Italy.

Other countries have specialties, too: beading in India, knits in Peru, sweats in Canada, and embroidery and other skills in Mexico, Turkey, Africa, and the Caribbean. However, China has taken a great share of the market from these countries. Asia is credited with the cheapest production because of low labor costs. In the last few years, China and Hong Kong have responded remarkably well to small companies. The myths that the factories in Asia are not interested in small designers and that their quality isn't as good are no longer true. There is a wide selection of factories in terms of size, quality, and expertise. There are factory owners who care about the quality and the vision for the product. The majority of emerging designers produce their knits in China because Chinese factories offer convenient packages and there are no longer as many knit producers in New York. Recently, there has been some consumer backlash against goods produced in China, which may affect sales to a select group of customers. Reports of high levels of toxins, such as formaldehyde, in clothing and fabric have created some apprehension about the Made in China label, especially in the childrenswear market.

However, there are challenges with communication, cost, timing, and quality when producing anywhere abroad.

Communication

- *Language.* Even if your contacts speak English, little misunderstandings because of language differences can cause big production problems. If you don't know the language where you produce, communicate clearly and take extra care to ensure that you understand each other. You may need to hire a production manager who is fluent in the local language or at least find an intern with the necessary language skills.

- *Training.* It's important to train the overseas factory to make sure it thoroughly understands how the product should look and fit. Don't take anything for granted. If the people who work in the factory wear saris most of the time, you can't expect them to immediately grasp the tailoring details in the patterns or the importance of grain lines.

Cost

- *Shipping.* Even with inexpensive labor, producing overseas can cost as much as producing domestically because of shipping. Sending materials to the factory and having it send product back to you is expensive, and designers also spend to send samples back and forth numerous times during the production cycle to monitor quality. For each shipment, duty and taxes must be paid.

- *Exchange rates.* Designers who produce overseas follow the exchange rates daily because of how greatly they affect their costs. Always confirm in which currency you are dealing. The recent high valuation of the euro versus the U.S. dollar has been challenging for many American designers who produce in Italy. Shoe designer Kristen Lee states that part of her reason for moving production out of Europe was because the exchange rate was pushing her wholesale pricing out of the contemporary market where her product is positioned.

- *Terms.* Minimums are generally high at overseas factories. Many of them require you to have a line of credit, and most international factories expect a 50 percent down payment with the remaining 50 percent due at customs.

Timing

- *Holiday schedules.* Most countries have more national holidays than the United States. European factories are generally closed for the entire month of August when womenswear designers are finishing Fall production as well as Spring samples. In fact, as New York Spring fashion week creeps closer

to August, Italian factories are starting to feel the pressure to cut their traditional holidays or lose some of their larger customers to Asia. China and Hong Kong have several festivals throughout the year during which businesses close for at least one week. Designers must allow for this time in their production schedule.

- *Lead times.* Overseas production can take twice the time of domestic production. Designers must pad their schedules and ship materials and patterns early to try to prevent late deliveries. Customs paperwork can cause delays, and duty needs to be paid. Many designers warn that samples from Europe can arrive too late to make critical trade show dates, and a menswear designer who was participating in his first New York runway show received only part of his collection when several boxes were delayed at customs. He was forced to send several models onto the runway wearing shirts and jackets with only underwear, but fortunately he pulled it off with good styling.

- *Culture.* The working practices and customs in each country are different, and people in other countries don't work at the same fast pace as workers in the United States or Asia. Countless designers have told me about the frustration of getting work done in Italy, where it always seems to be time to break for lunch. A designer needs to schedule extra time to avoid late deliveries.

Quality

It is more difficult to control the quality of production when you are thousands of miles away. Most large manufacturers have full-time employees who travel to or live in the production country and oversee the factory every day. New designers generally can't afford to do this and, therefore, must work with an agent or have the factory send samples at several stages of the production process for approval. This takes time, and if there are problems with the final product when it arrives, a local factory will need to fix it quickly.

How to Choose a Factory

Take the time to meet with several factories and choose one that gives you confidence. This should be done well in advance of your first sales season. A factory owner compared it to choosing a babysitter and said, "You don't just hand your baby over to anyone." This is a critical relationship. You will deal with these people often and need to trust them.

In reality, some factory owners care about the quality of their work and the success of the line, while others only care about getting the job done and getting paid. When meeting the owner or manager of each factory, try to get a sense of the person, his priorities, and whether he takes pride in his work. There are several types of questions to ask, and if there are things you don't understand, ask him to explain. Don't be intimidated.

Factory Expertise

- Each factory has areas of expertise with the corresponding equipment and knowledgeable workers. Factories that excel at knits might not be able to produce outerwear or leather goods. Factories used to working with cotton or wool may not be competent with delicate silks. If a collection includes leather jackets, knit dresses, and woven pants, the designer may need to work with three different contractors.

- Find out which production services the factory provides and whether they subcontract work out to others or do it all in-house. Many factories offer multiple services to attract more business, but subcontracted work is difficult to oversee. If you don't think the subcontractors can handle a process effectively, don't give them the job.

Delivery

- Ask if the factory regularly meets deadlines and establish the lead time for each job. Show your contact a sample or ask her to have one made one to help estimate timing as accurately as possible.

- Inquire about the turnaround time for reorders. Reorders should be finished faster than the initial run.

- Confirm what the factory means by delivery. To some, it may mean the product is just leaving the plant or is on a boat, but you need to know when it will be in your possession.

- What recourse will you have if the factory is late in delivering the goods?

Customer Service

- Find out whom you will deal with every day.

- How does the factory ensure quality at each stage of production?

- See some of the factory's finished work to analyze its quality.

- Ask the factory owner how to lower your costs and improve the production process.

Credibility

- How long has the factory been in business?

- Who are some of its clients, and how long have they been clients? Call these clients for a recommendation.

- Visit the factory and ask for a tour. Nancy Caton of Nancy Whiskey and the Sewing Factory advises, "Look for signs of good working conditions. Is the factory clean? Can you walk through it, or is the fabric stacked up to the people's shoulders? Do the people look happy?"[6]

- If you doubt that the factory is legal, ask to see its business license and watch for signs of labor abuse.

- How many employees are at the factory? Find out the factory's history of employee strikes and its policy if a strike causes production to stop.

- What happens if your goods are damaged at the factory or during transport? What kind of insurance does the factory have?

- Get a sense of how trustworthy the factory is regarding copyrights and private information. Probe the factory owner about other clients to see if the owner tells you things he shouldn't. If proprietary details about another customer are shared, the owner would likely share the same information about you.

Ask the factory to make a finished production sample after you receive the cost estimate but before you give that factory the job. This will help you judge the quality of the work and help the factory owner provide you with an accurate price. Making a sample helps the workers understand the piece, and it will give you a sense of what it is like to work with them. At this point, they want your business and will be as responsive as they can be. Some factories, mostly overseas, will create the sample for free to try and secure your business, but as explained earlier, others will charge you three times the production price out of fear that you are using them just to get a sample.

Price and payment terms. Unfortunately, the cost of production often ends up being the last concern for a young designer. In the panic of finding the right materials, contracting quality production, and trying to get product delivered on time, a designer will pay almost anything.

Before you contract with a factory, it should give you an initial cost estimate made from the sample or spec sheet. The greater the quantity of items produced, the less each item will cost. Remember that everything is negotiable, but if the price seems too good to be true, revisit any concerns about quality and delivery.

Generally you will pay the factory COD, but often with a deposit of at least one-third of the price up front. Some factories require progress payments as the job passes through different stages of production. If a factory has had bad experiences with small designers, it's not unheard of for it to demand full payment in advance.

Pay fabric and production people on time, and they will help you with discounts, better terms, flexibility on minimums, and other issues. The more work you give them, the happier and more supportive they will be in terms of price and service.

Pricing terms specify which party covers which parts of shipping. FOB includes the transportation to the shipping port but not the shipping, duty, or other costs from that point on. CIF includes shipping but not duty. As when shipping fabric, ask for LDP in which the shipping and duty is included in the quoted price.

The Agreement

The written agreement should include pricing; the number and description of articles covered by the contract; delivery date; the repercussions if delivery is late; detailed finishing, packing, and labeling instructions according to the store requirements; the shipping method (local messenger, trucking, sea, or air); the payment due date; and the method of payment.

Before you begin, confirm the number of units to be produced; which stages of production are being handled by which contractors; and that all samples, materials, and patterns will be returned to you. Be very clear about the delivery date. Larger jobs take priority at factories, and despite the agreement, it's smart to give early deadlines to be safe.

Regardless of all this contract advice, not everything is written down. As one designer said, "Italian factories won't work with contracts unless your name

is Prada, Gucci, or Ferragamo. You have to rely on the word of many people and be prepared for things to change without a moment's notice."

Factory Alternatives

In-house. Several emerging designers produce all, or at least part, of their line in-house with a small team, which generally includes a patternmaker and a few sewers. Obviously this method can be very expensive and requires a significant outlay of funds for cutting, sewing, and pressing equipment, as well as the permits, insurance, and licenses legally required to run a production facility. A designer I know with a very small in-house sewing room spends $20,000 a month to keep it running. She says it's worth the extra expense because of the control it gives her. With in-house production, the designer can oversee the entire process every day and manage the timing and quality of each garment as it's produced. There is no competition from other designers, and it's easy to react quickly for reorders and work around missing materials.

Designer Gustavo Cadile couldn't meet the minimums at the beading factories for his intricate eveningwear gowns, so he manages an in-house team of extremely talented and experienced couture sewers who handle all his beading, sample production, and special orders.

Producing in-house results in a tight team of people who learn to work together efficiently, and the designer has the opportunity to train and teach the team to become experts in signature fits and finishes. Some designers take sewers on field trips to high-end stores, such as Saks Fifth Avenue, to study the technique and finishing of different garments and set expectations.

An in-house sewing room can help protect proprietary information about design and fit. A designer told me she sends out her jackets, blouses, and dresses to a factory but will never contract out her pants. She has worked tirelessly to develop a signature fit, and with many other jobs moving through the factories, she doesn't want to risk someone stealing her pattern.

In recent years, many New York factories have shut their doors, leaving a number of highly skilled workers out of a job. These are ideal people to hire for in-house production. Keep in mind, however, that even with your own in-house

team, you won't have all the special skills required for each collection and will still have to contract out specialty work, such as beading or knitwear.

In-house production requires you to be there every day with the sewers, directing them and reviewing their work. Some designers who have an intense focus on quality are happy to spend all day measuring seams and checking finishes to ensure that each item is consistent. But not every designer wants the time-consuming responsibility of managing manufacturing processes and people.

A full-time production staff brings additional pressure. The sewers are employees and bring a serious financial obligation in terms of their salaries and benefits. You need to have the work to keep them busy, and you know that if the business fails, you won't be the only one left without a job.

Freelance sewers. If your orders are small or require special skills, individual sewers (or craftspeople) can be hired on a freelance basis to handle the production. Freelance sewers are expensive and generally take longer to produce, but they can be the best option when filling a one-time order for a store or creating specialty items that require detail or handwork. However, if you anticipate a large reorder or increased business with the store, you should get a factory involved to keep the production quality consistent on all runs and to provide quantity discounts and cost-effective measures.

Patch NYC started its business with a collection of crochet hats made completely by the mother of one of the designers and then embellished by designers John Ross and Don Carney. John says, "After one especially crazy crochet season, we realized Mom just couldn't keep up. We brought in two of Don's aunts and one of Mom's friends to help that season. Suddenly, there were all these variations in the hats since each person crochets slightly differently. We stopped wholesaling the crochet hats and only added knits back into our collection seasons later when we found a factory that would produce quality hats and scarves."[7]

Nathalie "Alabama" Chanin, the designer of Project Alabama, returned to her hometown of Florence, Alabama, to find "quilting circles" that could supply the handwork needed to produce her T-shirts. She supports the hometown economy by subcontracting to more than 100 women to do the stitching.[8]

Production Management

Once you have taken the collection through the sales process and confirmed the orders, you will know which items will be produced, in what quantities, and with what required delivery dates. Now it's time to start production.

When designers were asked, "If you could hire just one employee, what would it be?" almost every designer surveyed answered "a production manager." The production process is extremely critical and time consuming. Between constant problems and a tight schedule, it requires someone to manage each stage of the process, from dealing with raw material deliveries to final shipping and quality control. Whether you are fortunate enough to have a production manager or if, like most start-up designers, you are attentively filling the role yourself, careful production management is critical to ensuring quality construction, consistent fit, on-time delivery, and loyal customers.

Quality Control

The buck stops with you. You cannot accept bad work or compromise on quality. Quality control is critical at all stages of production right through to labeling and shipping. The buyers and the end customers have rules and expectations and if you don't meet their standards, the customers will return the product, stores will charge it back to you, and neither will give you another chance.

The store doesn't care if the factory messed up. It's your responsibility. Designer Nicole Miller tells of her experience when all the beads popped off an entire shipment of sweaters for Saks Fifth Avenue. She had to eat the loss for the shipment because the store could not accept it and the factory was already paid with a letter of credit and could not be held liable.[9]

Stay on Schedule

Delivery is key, and if you are late, orders can be canceled and returned to you. Do everything possible to be on time, or the stores might not work with you again. During production, try to anticipate delays, and if you know that a shipment will be late, call the retailer immediately to ask for an extension and permission to ship. Find out if the store will accept a partial order on time and the rest later. If it won't accept that, you at least have some time to find another store that will.

Technology

A significant amount of software and technology are available to help apparel and accessories companies become more efficient from the beginning of the design and planning process through sourcing production, shipping, and sales. There are systems that can collect data, plan better delivery cycles, manage costs and inventory, assist with patternmaking and fit, comply with electronic data interchange (EDI) and other department store requirements, track samples and PR, and more.

However, most technology investments are extremely expensive and should not be a priority for small companies, which need to preserve capital until they build up enough volume to warrant making these investments. You should first concentrate on growing your sales and volume and shipping on time and then slowly add infrastructure to your business.

COO of Loeffler Randall Amanda Thomas's biggest advice to a design entrepreneur is to get good computer education in Excel and your other software, as you will spend much time on the computer organizing, planning, scheduling, and analyzing.

In fact, most early-stage designers rely on Excel to handle a majority of their needs. For costing, you can design a spreadsheet to track all of your expenses and calculate the total cost, wholesale price, and profit margin for each collection. Excel is also good for creating and managing production schedules, working backwards from your delivery dates through each stage of production and raw materials sourcing. Excel can also generate business reports, such as sales by city and state, sales by size and color, this season's profit versus previous seasons', and more to analyze your best and worst markets and styles and help you plan for next season. For accounting, most early-stage designers rely on QuickBooks. But if your business scales up significantly, you may need more sophisticated financial software.

Once you start to research other technology, the place to start is with an Internet-based software system that will work with your existing Microsoft or other operating system and allow you to avoid making any significant hardware investments.

Internet-based systems are ideal for helping you communicate more efficiently with factories and suppliers. For example, sending a multipage paper fax to India

with the unreliable phone lines and frequent disconnections can lead to delays in production, mistakes in communication, and time wasted following up and resending information. With a Web-based system, you create a central repository for all of your schedules, inventory, and production requirements and can communicate in real time with mills, factories, customers, sales, and warehousing. A Web-based system enables all parties to access and work off the same accurate and up-to-date information using a secure user ID and password. Some Internet-based solutions make it easy to share visuals with your suppliers and vendors, illustrating communications regarding materials, samples, and production.

In general, the key efficiencies a designer should seek are applications that integrate order entry, production planning, and financial operations, saving significant time on administrative activities. For example, enterprise resource planning (ERP) and merchandising software, such as LogOns small business solutions, help track information across all sizes and styles to help with the sales cycle, production planning and management, inventory management, and financial accounting, including invoicing, costing, accounts receivable, and accounts payable. Also, some Web-based programs help with sales order processing, customer relationship management (CRM), and even e-commerce issues such as online shopping carts.

A good software will create reports on what has been shipped and hasn't, what supplies have been delivered when and where, returns, factor reports, accounting and tax reports, customer management and communications, contact and mailing lists, commissions to salespeople or showrooms, retail discounts, markup and profit margins, duty tracking, invoice and packing slip creation, as well as inventory management issues, such as styles by color, size, and style number; season; price; fabric content; delivery date; inventory allocation to orders; the percentage of stock that sold at full price versus on mark-down; comparing forecasts to actual sales; and building new forecasts based on past trends.

Supply chain management (SCM) technology is generally the most sophisticated option available to plan the flow of goods and information, starting with raw materials sourcing through production and shipping to final delivery and reorder. It can organize and automate communication and scheduling throughout the design and production chain, and it helps you analyze the efficiency of the entire operation versus just each part. For example, China may be the cheapest place to produce, but if it takes

an extra week to get the goods from China versus producing in Los Angeles, it may be worth the extra cost of production to get the goods earlier and onto the floor selling at full price. A truly efficient supply chain will shorten lead times, ensure on-time delivery, raise productivity, reduce costs, and minimize inventory by helping the designer produce what has been sold rather than selling what has been produced.

Design software is another key area of interest for early-stage companies. It lets designers create their collections and store all styles and materials in the application's memory to make easy updates and modifications in color, design, or fabric. These programs can help you create specs and draw flats; some even include fit applications and three-dimensional models in a broad range of colors and materials. They can also help you review collections, reduce the number of actual samples required, and communicate in visual detail with the factory.

Specific technology resources and vendors are included in the Resource section at the back of this book.

Ordering Production Materials

Wait until you have responses from buyers before ordering production materials. Although large companies make sales predictions and order their fabric and trims in advance, small companies should "cut to order," meaning only producing exactly what is necessary to ship. The mills do not accept returns, and if fabric is ordered in advance and the style doesn't sell, the designer will be left with it. Some new designers overstock in hopes of reorders, but they learn quickly that this just wastes money. However, if some of your fabric is from overseas and has a long lead time, you may need to order the production yardage before sales are finalized to stay on schedule. In this case, wait as long as you can and work closely with the salespeople to get accurate quantity projections.

Clearly order the correct fabric using a swatch. Confirm the delivery lead time, cost, and shipping information. Know how much yardage it takes to produce each piece and don't buy too much. A very small amount of excess can cover damaged or unusable goods, but too much stock will go unused and eat up your profit margin.

Track the Production Materials

Create a system or chart to keep track of every material needed for production and where it is in the ordering process. The chart should include everything required for the item from fabric, lining, thread, and interfacing to buttons and zippers.

Do everything you can to ensure all materials arrive at the factory on time and in the right quantities to avoid scheduling problems at the factory. Most factories won't start a job until all the components are there. They don't want to risk setting all their machines with your green thread just to find out that the zippers aren't arriving for three more days. If the fabric or other materials will be late, tell the factory manager immediately so he can plan and make arrangements to fit your job in later.

Production Pattern and Samples

Once you are ready for production, the factory will create the production pattern. This pattern is made from the sample but includes modifications made during sales to perfect the fit, the design details, and the sewing guidelines and to eliminate fabric and trim waste. A slight change in the seam allowance can save significant cost in production.

If the factory didn't make a sample earlier in the process, have it create one now. Meet to inspect the production sample and discuss changes, quality concerns, scheduling, and specific costs. Factory managers are busy, but you want to utilize their time and expertise. Ask them for their concerns about the samples and the overall job. The production samples that you agree on set the standard to monitor quality during production. Communicate that all units should be produced from the specifications and processes accepted on this sample and will be rejected otherwise.

Cutting Tickets

Cutting tickets are actual orders for production that specify the details for the entire job. These are used to check the order and as a basis for any disputes. The cutting ticket should include as much information as possible. Write it all down and keep proof of the communication. Include the style number, the quantity of each style to be cut, the size range, the delivery date, a technical drawing, a fabric swatch, a list of all fabrics and trims, pattern pieces, and sewing and fin-

ishing instructions. Be specific regarding measurements and where to sew, how to lay the fabric, and whether it should be cut in a specific direction.

Grading for Size

For garments to sell, the sizing must be correct and consistent from season to season. Unfortunately, there are no standard measurements for size. The basic guidelines are based on a 60-year-old study by the U.S. Department of Commerce, and not surprisingly, manufacturers have started using their own systems. In fact, sizing became marketing driven when manufacturers realized that a woman who is a size 10 is much happier if she fits into a garment with a size 8 label. However, sizing does need to relate to general consumer expectations, or the clothing will be left in the sales bins. The most important thing is to be consistent from season to season. Basic sizing guidelines can be found on websites such as *www.fashiondex.com*.

Grading is the process of adjusting the production pattern up and down to meet the sizes that were ordered. Grading is often offered by the factory or contractor, and there are grading services that specialize in this work. Grading is charged per pattern piece and affected by the complexity of the pattern. Although it is usually too costly for new designers, some recommend testing the grading and fit by making samples of a full size range before continuing production to avoid problems on delivery.

Marking

Marking determines the best layout for cutting pattern pieces from the fabric. A good marker will save time, eliminate fabric waste, and help you determine exactly how much fabric you need. Depending on the number of garments produced, a quarter inch of fabric saved by a good marker can eventually save yards of production fabric. The marker ensures that the pattern pieces are properly laid out with the grain of the fabric and accommodate any patterns in the fabric, such as lining up stripes. A new marker is created for each size in the range.

Cut and Sew

Once the marker is set and the fabric has been carefully checked, it can be cut. Usually the fabric is spread on tables and cut in large stacks. Make sure pieces

from the same dye lots are cut together, or else the pieces within one garment may not match. Once cut, the pieces are bundled together with the thread, trims, and other items ready to be sewn.

Don't Forget Labels

The company label, the size label, and the fabric content and care labels required by Federal Trade Commission regulations have to be sewn into the garments. Care labels must include complete instructions for regular care of the garment, including information about bleaching, ironing, and drying, and warnings if the garment cannot be cleaned without harm. Labels must state the country where the garment was made, if made outside of the United States. Complete information about labeling requirements can be found at www.ftc.gov in a document entitled "Threading Your Way through the Labeling Requirements under the Textile and Wool Acts." If you sell to other countries, be sure of their labeling requirements; for example, Canada requires bilingual content and "made in" labels.

Factory Management

It takes time and experience to learn all that you need to know to manage production. Many factory owners and industry experts advise designers who want to have their own line to spend a few months in an internship or job at a factory. While students prefer to intern in the design room or even the production area of a big company, a few gritty months in a factory will provide a wealth of useful experience and knowledge. One factory owner says, "If you don't know anything, how can you tell anyone what to do? You need to know how to manage people, pinpoint problems, and identify mistakes."

Amanda Thomas of Loeffler Randall loves spending time in the factory. She says that people in the factory love to teach and will take you around and show and explain processes to you. This is so helpful to production, and it is key in an organization to have someone who thinks like a manufacturer. A designer should learn this and be interested in this. She says, "If you want to make things, you should learn how they are made."[10]

It shows in the construction and quality of a garment when the designer has experience with the engineering and production process. Designer Bruno

Grizzo says it was on his first job, working in the factory of made-to-order designer Frank Tignino, that he received an invaluable education on how to make clothes. He still works out of Tignino's spacious Garment District atelier, benefiting from a family-like relationship with his manufacturer.[11]

When you work with a factory, be specific and communicate clearly and often. Don't be afraid to ask questions, but don't be difficult or annoying. You need the factory's patience in case materials are late or cutting tickets change during production because of new or revised orders. Know what you need before you call or show up, and if you have a dispute or misunderstanding, sit down and work it out calmly.

It may be necessary to train the sewers on each garment. In most factories, each worker focuses on just one part of the garment, sewing just the side pant seam or sleeve inset before the garment is passed on to the next sewer. They don't always have a sense of the entire garment and final product. Realize that even if you personally trained the team leader on your job, if a rush order comes in from a bigger brand, the lead sewer could get pulled off your job, leaving the less-trained workers to handle the remaining production. Ana Beatriz produces her high-end womenswear line, Lerario Beatriz, in Brazil. She has a talented, full-time production manager located there, but production is still constantly stressful. Each garment and process has to be carefully watched for quality to avoid retail returns, such as when she had dresses returned due to a tiny spot left by a pin. She chose to work with a very small factory in Brazil where she could specially train a small group of five to seven workers specifically on her fabrics and techniques. She also has all of her intricate embroidery handled through a non-profit organization that helps abused women make a living in embroidery.[12]

Relationships are everything, and designers, such as Duckie Brown, work with factory owners who have become important mentors. Some designers have received financial support from their factory, and rarely, a factory has produced the designer's sample collection for the runway at cost.

Increasingly, factories are looking to partner with smaller labels and even invest in their businesses. Many Chinese companies are seeking opportunities to continue their growth and increase their market shares, and they seek to partner, produce, and help fund new labels. As larger manufacturers move production to Asia, Italian and other European factories are becoming more flexible,

not just working with small labels but seeking to invest in them for increased efficiency, profit, and future loyalty. Manufacturers in places such as India often seek designers to create their own lower-priced lines, and they will partner to do your production in exchange for your design skills.

As much as you might feel desperate to find a factory to do your work, finding the right one is essential, and if you don't like its work or you aren't comfortable with the operation, find another factory.

Quality Control

Be there. If at all possible, you need to be there. Call and visit the factory often during all steps of the production process. Over the phone, factories may be misleading about the job. Big companies pay big bucks to have their production finished quickly, and the young designers get pushed aside. If you are at the factory, you can ensure that your job isn't continually bumped.

A designer should catch mistakes as they are happening, before the product is complete. Workers are paid by the piece. Their incentive is not to be careful but to be fast. As they speed up, they may take shortcuts, and the quality will suffer. If you show up regularly at the factory, they will take more care with your garments and work more slowly. At a minimum, check on the work during the beginning, middle, and end of the production run.

Return phone calls immediately. The factory should call you when things go wrong or if something doesn't look right. If your factory calls you for each concern, consider yourself lucky, because others will only call once for every ten mistakes. Call back immediately, and if the factory needs you to come in, get there as soon as possible. Sometimes designers have to go to the factory four times a day to deal with problems. Factory owners say that 95 percent of small designers don't call back right away, and because time is money to the factory, they won't sit around waiting. The factory will move on to something else and won't bother to call next time.

Check quality carefully. When you inspect production, compare everything against the standard set by your production sample. Measure the seams, test that the buttons and labels are secure, and check that the stitching is straight. Look for color consistency and for stains from the machine oil or glue. Inspect the pressing and packaging. Inspect a number of items again before you pay at the end of production and refuse to pay if they're not up to standard. If the factory can't get the quality right, change factories.

Overseas. If you choose to produce overseas, you need an agent or production manager whom you trust to babysit production for you. Even if you have an agent or manager there, you may need to go yourself as well. Designers have moved from Los Angeles to New York specifically to lessen the flight time to Europe where they do their production. Without proper oversight, you can't ensure quality. In fact, you won't even know if the factory is outsourcing the production to someplace else.

Designer Diego Binetti produces some of his womenswear line in China, and his business partner, Ada Lee, who is fluent in Chinese, travels to China for a month or more to oversee production each season. She is there to instruct the factory, explain the fit and stitching detail, and manage the quality every step of the way. If the factory in China makes mistakes that aren't caught before shipping, Diego has to use a factory in New York to fix everything. Being at the factory also led Ada to discover that the factory was using their pattern to make cheaper garments in different materials to sell as their own. This occasional shady practice can be stopped if someone is there to represent the designer.[13]

Producing in Italy has its own challenges, and designers say it's very hard to manage production and get things done on time. Flying in for 24 hours to check on everything is not enough. Ideally, you need someone who is 100 percent on your side to be there all the time. Menswear designer Douglas Mandel of Kamkyl says the most frustrating thing for him about producing in Italy is being constantly pushed back by bigger manufacturers, resulting in his jobs being late.[14] Shoe designer Kristen Lee agrees: "You are pushed to the end for delivery and production from the tanneries, sole makers, last makers, heel suppliers, component suppliers, and dye-dip houses. Just one delay in the many components can cause a whole delivery to be late."[15] She is now producing in Brazil where she found a production agent whom she trusts. She has to oversee her production more now in terms of quality and has to be more spe-

cific with instruction. She visits Brazil once a season and then ships samples back and forth for review. She also has the new challenge of having less options for sourcing materials and must ship leather and hardware from Spain, Italy, and elsewhere.

Shoe production is complex and challenging, which is why so many of the big brands license their shoe lines rather than produce them themselves. Shoe designers are experts on Italy because they spend significant time there. Most designers visit several times a year, even if they have a production agent located there. Also, attending the Linea Pelle leather show is key for meeting with the tanners, heel makers, and fit specialists. Holly Dunlap, designer of Hollywould shoes, actually moved to Florence, and Michael Spaulding of Gunmetal shoes goes every month. He says, "In Italy, a little charm goes a long way. Drink their wine and tell them when it's the best prosciutto you've ever tasted. Then tell them you are not leaving until they finish your job."[16]

Designer Alicia Bell manufactured some pieces overseas to save significantly on her production costs, but when she received her shipment, along with the beautiful beaded pieces, there were endless problems—stains and dirt on the garments, pen marks where the buttons were sewn on, buttons falling off...even a size 6 shirt with a size 12 sleeve on it! She had to spend many long days fixing the problem garments herself at her U.S. factory. Fortunately, she had an iron-clad contract and didn't have to pay for the faulty production. Her attention to quality control and detail saved the collection.

There are ways to build relationships and find overseas factories to trust. Wendy Mullin of Built by Wendy recently moved some production to Shanghai. She knows the owners of the Shanghai factory from when they had a factory in New York. They call her their "American daughter," and she knows her production is in great hands.[17]

If you don't have someone to monitor production at the factory, have the factory send samples from multiple stages of the production run for your approval. Shipping will become a significant expense because of the constant back and forth, but it's critical to guarantee good quality. Many Asian factories have very efficient and quick sample approval systems in place, and some visit New York each season to meet with their U.S. clients, review fabric and materials options, and even test first samples.

Packing and Shipping

At most small companies, the designers and their staff personally pack and ship the goods. On the bright side, it's an ideal time to be in touch with each product and check that quality standards have been met. The designer can control the packing process and make sure that directions from the stores are carefully followed.

Retailers, and in particular department stores, have specific packing and shipping instructions that must be followed, or the store will refuse the goods or issue charge back fees.

Read the routing guide from the store thoroughly and follow the directions. Packing details cover whether the garments should be on hangers or packed flat in bags, wrapped in plastic, or tagged in a specific place with specific information. Shipping instructions indicate the shipping method that should be used, the documentation and packing slips required, and the format for labeling the boxes. Don't forget to order packing materials in advance. While some of these requirements seem overly demanding, realize that the stores receive thousands of items each day. To get your goods onto the selling floor quickly, the box labels, packing slips, packing bags, and hangtags must provide all the information to help the stores quickly process the boxes and items. They should be able to tell the style name and number, the size, the color, and even the neckline style or sleeve-length without unpacking or unfolding each item.

Take your time and pull each order, one at a time. Confirm whether the shipment is insured by the shipper or the retailer. Once shipped, track the deliveries. When shipping small amounts overseas, FedEx, DHL, or UPS can act as a customs broker. Once you start shipping in volume, it's preferable to use a freight forwarder or fulfillment service, which can help with paperwork and international shipping regulations, book the shipping, arrange for insurance, and save money through consolidation.

 Fulfillment Centers

At some point, you will want to work with a fulfillment center rather than handle all the tagging, shipping, and packaging of product in your own studio. As your

volume grows, shipping becomes too time consuming and complicated and takes up too much space. When selling to department stores, it can be critical to work with a fulfillment center to meet all the vendor compliance requirements correctly and avoid chargebacks and returns. Shoe label Loeffler Randall, which produces shoes in Italy, bags in Korea, and apparel in New York, now works with a fulfillment center. Their COO, Amanda Thomas, names growing pains in shipping as their biggest current challenge. With just a 15- to 20-day window, they need to coordinate items coming from all over the world to be packaged together in mixed orders for multiple accounts.

Fulfillment centers offer a range of services and capabilities, and you can negotiate a package based on your business needs. They will charge you for storage, for shipping, and then according to your selections from a menu of other services. A fulfillment center may offer warehousing and inventory management, garment on hanger (GOH) shipping, pick order or batch order processing (assembling mixed orders of items that arrive from different manufacturers for shipping to multiple customers), processing returns, customs clearance, hangtag and price ticket application, credit checks, invoicing, and a range of barcode and EDI-compliant services.

Electronic data interchange (EDI) is the electronic exchange of information between two computers. Most department stores require vendors to be EDI-compliant and to use barcode technology on their shipments. Department stores receive thousands of items each week and need to organize and process them quickly to get the goods onto the selling floor. EDI and barcode technology, used to label boxes and individual hangtags on the items, enable this process. However, it is generally too expensive for a newer designer to invest in this technology, so you should ask for an exemption from a department store for at least the first few seasons. However, if a fulfillment center has the EDI and barcode software, you will be able to comply earlier without making the investment yourself. As a result, the stores will get your goods onto the floor more quickly, allowing them more time to sell at full price, and you will avoid the expensive charge backs that result from packing and shipping errors.

Many fulfillment companies have a minimum, so you need to make sure you have the orders to meet the requirements. Make sure your fulfillment company has insurance and that it is EDI-compliant and can meet the requirements of your department store clients. Ask what discounts it has with the major shipping companies, such as UPS and Fed-Ex, how fast it can turn around orders and ship, and if it offers same day shipping.

7

Marketing and Branding Materials

The fashion business is as much about marketing as it is about design. Image is everything. It differentiates the label and establishes an emotional connection with the customer. The Versace customer seeks to emulate an ornate and glamorous lifestyle, while the Calvin Klein customer desires minimalism and a clean aesthetic. Successful designers market their identity and lifestyle as much as their product. It extends to all areas of life, enabling Ralph Lauren to sell paint and Christian Lacroix to sell espresso cups.

Brands aren't formed overnight but grow organically over time as people hear about them or interact with them in different ways. Everything must be designed. Each visual interaction with a brand shapes the consumer's impression, and designers need to send the same message continually in their logos and labels, marketing materials, invitations, hangtags, website design, and packaging. Think of the iconic power of the Tiffany blue box.

Consistency is key. Focus on one simple idea that umbrellas over everything you do. The product itself, and the point of view that you develop, are the root of the brand, but every surrounding decision and detail, such as the stores you sell in and how the merchandise is presented, are part of crafting the right image. Renowned advertising copywriter and agency founder David Ogilvy defined a brand as "the intangible sum of a product's attributes: its name, packaging, and price, its history, its reputation, and the way it's advertised." (www.ogilvy.com) If your brand image is strong enough, it can be communicated even without showing the product, as with the 1989

DKNY advertising campaign that for one year focused on scenes of New York City without showing any DKNY designs.[1]

Be Your Brand

Designers themselves must represent the brand. What you wear, where you eat, and where you go out is an extension of your brand. Ralph Lauren is photographed on horses and sailboats, reflecting his all-American outdoor brand. Valentino is seen at celebrity parties, strolling in Gstaad, and lounging on his luxurious yachts, reflecting European jet-set glamour. Even Martin Margiela, who refuses to be photographed for the press, fits perfectly with the somber, deconstructivist tone of his design. If possible, a designer should wear his own designs or at least represent the design aesthetic. The Betsey Johnson label would not make sense if Betsey herself wore Armani. Men who design womenswear obviously can't wear their own line, but they should still fit the image. Zac Posen's debonair style complements that of the women he dresses, and Marc Jacobs's menswear line represents the male counterpoint of his female muse.

Logos

The first impression of your brand is most often your company name and logo. For most designers, their logo is simply their name, but the font, size, color, and shape used to display it creates an image for the company and collection. Ralph Lauren's polo player, Chanel's double Cs, Target's bull's-eye, and the LV of Louis Vuitton each represent a specific attitude and lifestyle. If your label is minimal, your logo should be simple and clean, whereas if your collection is fun and girly, your logo should be more embellished and feminine.

Press and Sales Kits

Press and sales kits provide a first and lasting impression of a new label. They introduce the line to the buyers and press, announce that the designer is ready to sell, and continually reinforce the brand. At a minimum, the kit should start with a clean and simple two-pocket folder and include a lookbook or photos of

your collection, line sheets for buyers, a biography, a collection summary, and copies of past press. The materials must be intriguing, professional, and at least look as though you made an effort. An unprofessional press kit can damage your image and ruin your chance of sales or press coverage. As senior vice president of the fashion office and public relations at Bergdorf Goodman, Robert Burke received a variety of press kits and said "the vast majority are really bad."[2] Too often, I've seen designers show up to open calls with crumpled sketches and line sheets shoved loosely into a manila folder.

If you are a recent fashion school graduate, it's important to understand the difference between your student portfolio and what you show as a designer with your own line. A student book is great for getting a job as a designer, but it's not appropriate to show to buyers and press. Photos and illustrations can offer an intriguing hint at inspiration but should not look like your school inspiration boards. Also, whether you are new to this or not, if you can't sketch well, don't show sketches. Amateur drawings will make you look amateur. If you must illustrate a line in development, use a croquis, which is a figure outline used for drawing clothes on a body.

Be creative and edit carefully. Buyers and editors are visual people who receive hundreds of packages each month. Think about what will make your materials stand out just enough for others to want to pick them up. Designers often get too elaborate and sabotage themselves with over-the-top presentations. It doesn't need to be wrapped in taffeta or have glitter pouring out of it. Simple is best. You don't need to spend a lot of money on fancy paper, bindings, or customized packaging. In fact, keep the costs down and find inexpensive ways to be creative and make your package stand out. A brightly colored envelope can grab attention.

The buyers and editors really just want to see several well-photographed outfits on a model, with a simple note explaining your history and point of view. Don't show everything you've ever done. Stick to your strengths and only include the strong, carefully edited looks that make up your current collection.

Lookbook

The lookbook will work harder for you than anything else. It is your most important sales tool and often the sole reason for landing an appointment or receiving a call from a buyer or editor. The lookbook should consist of strong, clear photos of all the items in the collection. Lookbooks are not cheap to create, and you need to watch your costs carefully because they can quickly climb into the tens of thousands. Fortunately, there are ways to reduce costs, and when first starting out, you should be able to spend as little as $2,000 on your book each season. Start by trying to find photographers, stylists, and hair and makeup artists who are new to the business. They are likely to work in exchange for prints and a photo credit, which could lead to considerable savings. But choose with care, because a good lookbook needs the photographer, models, styling, and set all to work together holistically.

Photographer. Photographing fashion product is a specialized skill. Ideally, you will use an experienced photographer who can shoot clear, impactful images. The lookbook should include a mix of full-product shots and close-ups that show detail. If you work with an amateur photographer or one who lacks fashion experience, several things can go wrong. For example, the photos might come back blurred, or they may be shot too far away from the product or at the wrong angle. The cost for a photographer varies greatly and can be extremely high. Shop around, meet with several, and review their books to get a sense of the quality and style of their work. Word of mouth is the best way to find a good photographer. Also, modeling agencies can help you find more than just models; call and tell them that you are a new designer and are looking for photographers and stylists who want to test.

These photos give two perspectives on an outfit. One gives a sense of the overall look and the other focuses on an important detail.

These photos give two perspectives on one outfit providing an understanding of the overall look while highlighting the details.

A lookbook from the Tom Scott collection includes photos of full looks along with close-ups to show detail.

Four exquisite close-ups show details of the Doo.Ri collection. Printed courtesy of Doo.Ri.

Models. Clothes should be photographed on a live model. While some designers have created strong lookbooks using mannequins or other methods of garment display, I don't recommend it. A live model gives dimension to each piece and emphasizes detail and fit. Casting the right model, who fits the personality of the line, will communicate the right mood and energy without distracting from the clothes. If you don't have personal connections to an appropriate model, you will need to call an agency. Know in advance the type of model you want for your shoot—whether dark and sultry, blond and all-American, Brazilian, or Russian in look. Be up front with the booker if you don't have a budget. Many new mod-

els will work in exchange for prints for their book. You simply need to make the booker and model understand that you are a professional with a serious business and that you are working with a decent photographer. Realize that without a budget, you have less choice in the model you get. Don't call IMG Models and ask if Gisele will work for trade. While you don't need a live model to shoot accessories, jewelry does look better when photographed on a three-dimensional form.

Set and background. The background for your photographs should be clean and professional and not overwhelm or distract from the clothes. A good choice is a simple white wall. Many designers who have runway shows create their lookbook from the show photos, which generally feature a white backdrop. Of course, you can create a background that lends mood and ambience. A romantic, Victorian-inspired collection could be photographed in front of antique wallpaper or with the model on an antique settee. But be careful to not overwhelm the clothing with the set. A beautiful shoot can still miss the point. Shadows from props and furniture or a model's pose can bury the product. Lookbooks that alternate artistically styled photos with pages of clear, straight product shots work well. The viewer is enticed by the story but still able to see the line clearly. Please don't use an amateur set such as a dark apartment hallway or your parent's suburban driveway unless that is specifically the inspiration for the collection.

Printed courtesy of Helena Frederikson Photographer: Redrick deLeon

This outdoor backdrop reflects the inspiration of the line in a subtle manner.

Photography by Andrea Thompson - Art Direction and Clothing Design by Egami.

This backdrop sets an intriguing tone without overwhelming the clothes.

Courtesy of Tashkent, Photo: Greg Morris/ Insight Visual www.iy-photo.com

This background in this photo compliments the shoe fabric and style.

Styling. You want to style each look intriguingly, using shoes, accessories, hair, and makeup to reveal your inspiration. Be careful: elaborate styling can overshadow the purpose of the shoot and be too creative. As a designer, you may want to drive the overall vision for the shoot, but it can be beneficial to work with a stylist who can give creative input as well as help find your location, accessories, and other needs. Accessories and shoes can be your own, vintage, borrowed from a showroom, or, in the manner of many stylists, purchased and then returned to the store. Hair and makeup should also be carefully conceived to complement the clothing. Wild hair looks silly with a sophisticated suit collection, and a smoky eye doesn't work well with beachwear. An additional concern is that some buyers are better than others at separating the clothing from the styling. If you have cotton prairie skirts rocked out with heavy leather jackets and biker boots, the buyer whose customer loves prairie skirts may not buy because she can't get past the rocker image.

Stretch Pearl Cluster Bracelet
Rhinestone & Crystal Drop Earrings
Pearl Cluster Earrings
(Pearl Cuff · Perry Ellis · Spring '05)

Party Cluster Earrings
Tassel Fringe Earrings
Swedon Treasure Necklace
Orchid Pollen Drop Earrings
Swan Wing Earrings

SUBVERSIVE JEWELRY · SUBVERSIVE JEWELRY

The styling for this lookbook balances clear photos of the jewelry while projecting a strong identity for the line.

A well-styled product shot that positions the bag in the life of a chic customer.

past collection

The models' pose and styling in these photos project dignity and strength while clearly showing the clothes.

Presentation. Photos, which should be in color, can be presented as a lookbook in numerous ways—bound together as a 4" × 6" spiral notebook, blown up and put loosely in a pocket folder, printed with several images on each page, or printed all on one foldout poster or accordion-style foldout. Another favorite format is a stack of neat postcard photos with one look per card, kept together in an envelope. The viewer can flip through the postcards as a group, and the designer can mail the cards out separately as reminders of the line throughout the season. Keep in mind that printing and binding costs add up quickly, and the format affects the mailing cost for each one.

Some buyers prefer to see the collection in a digital format via email, CD, or website. If you send images by email, make sure they are high quality but not so big that the recipient's firewall blocks them or they clog the recipient's email in-box. To be safe, resize each image to 4" × 6" or smaller. If the recipient is just reviewing the images, you can send them at 72 dots per inch (dpi), but if the images will be used for print, send them at 350 dpi. If you send a CD or DVD of the full collection, include a few photo printouts in case editors have trouble running the CD or find it too much hassle.

A lookbook should include your company name, the season of the collection, and your contact information in case it is separated from your other materials. It's also a good idea to include a style number for each item or even a full description of each look on the back of each page, on the bottom of the print, or on a single page in the back of the book.

Photos by Dan Lecca. Printed courtesy of Milly.

This spiral bound lookbook makes the most of strong runway photos.

Photos courtesy of Loungewear Betty. Photographer Marco Pedde.

Printed courtesy of Linea Nervenkitt.

BRISTOL	ESME	DEAN	SOBEL
sterling silver white topaz	turquoise 24k gold vermeil	blue topaz briolette aquamarine briolette 14k chain 23k gold vermeil	sterling silver deconstructed chainmail faceted smokey quartz

This lookbook shows the product clearly next to descriptive information.

This lookbook/mailer features several clear shots on one page.

Printed courtesy of Lewis Cho, Elizabeth Young (photographer), Denise See (layout)

This lookbook shows several full looks with detailed shots in a two page spread.

Line Sheets

Line sheets show each item in the collection with the information needed by buyers. They include a flat drawing or clear, simple photograph that shows the shape and details of each item. This is not a place for artistic sketches. The line sheet is arranged with several items on one page and includes the style number, name, description, wholesale price, colors and sizes available, fabric content, the minimum order, and the delivery and cut-off dates. They may also include fabric swatches. Your company name and contact information should be on every single page of your line sheet.

Hope McGrath of Asha says, "It's important to have separate line sheets for press and buyers. The buyers should receive wholesale information, but editors need retail pricing for their audience."[3]

Be protective of your line sheets and don't just hand them out to anyone. They show the specific detail of your items and are a good guide for knockoffs if they fall in the wrong hands.

This line sheet incorporates clear runway shots with detailed product and delivery information.

This linesheet focuses on product pricing and descriptions with simple flat drawings.

This line sheet includes clear photos of the product in place of line drawings.

The artistic illustrations on this linesheet clearly show the design details.

Biography and Collection Summary

Buyers want a brief paragraph or two about the designer and a brief description of the line and collection. Keep it all short and to the point and don't forget to spell-check.

The bio should include the designer's origin, education, and relevant work experience, along with anything special and intriguing. Everyone wants to know the story behind the clothes. Designer Miguel Adrover grew up on an almond farm in Majorca, and this distinctive background helped him attract attention. Designers use childhood experiences, such as visiting their father's chemistry lab, playing dress-up in their mother's Lily Pulitzer, or spending years in teenage rebellion, to put their line in context. Some designers who don't have an interesting background make one up.

When describing your line, it's important to have a story to explain why you are different and provide some framework for the collection. Laird Borelli, senior fashion editor of Style.com suggests, "If John Galliano says his collection is influenced by 'Russian princesses on vacation in Deauville,' it creates excitement and intrigue. But don't be too sugary or make up irrelevant stories. If you were influenced by circles and squares, or the color red at 5:00 PM, simply explain that in one or two sentences."[4]

Include information on where the collection sells. Many publications feel an obligation to showcase only products their readers can buy now and may not cover you if you don't sell. Mention your website if you have one and list celebrities who have worn or carried your designs and any industry awards or recognition you have received.

Other Marketing Materials

Clear Copies of Press Coverage

Professional color copies of press are much more appealing than black-and-white copies; therefore, it's worth spending the extra cash to get the most impressive images. Don't include every press item you have ever received and take out anything that is not relevant to your current work. If your item is included on a

magazine page with many other products, circle or highlight your item to make it easier for the buyer or editor to find.

Postcards and Promotional Mailers

Lookbooks are expensive to produce and mail, so it's smart to have another low-cost promotional item to send to buyers and editors as an introduction, reminder, or announcement of each new season. The best choice is a postcard or simple mailer, which includes a single photograph, collage, or sketch that is eye-catching and representative of your work. Make sure the card includes your name, contact information, and website if you have one. You can send reminder email images to buyers and press—it is definitely much cheaper—but keep in mind that people are hesitant to open email attachments and therefore may not see your images.

A postcard provides clear shots of several different designs and their color options.

A postcard makes a bold statement and creates intrigue for the line. Printed courtesy of Lost Art.

Printed courtesy of Lisa Levine. Photography by James Westman.

A postcard that shows the jewelry on a model, lending personality to the line.

Printed courtesy of Hollywould.

A postcard that clearly highlights several items from the collection.

Website

A designer today needs to have a website. It is an extremely convenient way for buyers and press to find and review your work. Collections, press coverage, and information about you and the line can be posted on the site, saving the considerable expense of mailing full lookbooks and press kits to everyone. Email announcements can easily send people to see your latest work with the click of a button and help them find you again without shuffling through piles and files of press kits. Some designers worry about posting their latest collection in case others copy it before it reaches the stores. This is a valid concern, and if you decide to post collections before they are on the runway or in stores, consider creating a password-protected area accessible only by buyers and editors.

A website can be simple, but it should reflect the brand and include clear, high-quality photographs. It must be easy to navigate and up-to-date. A website that hasn't been updated reflects badly on the business. It makes the designer appear disorganized and may lead people to believe that the designer is no longer in business. If you are behind, post a home page with your contact information and a note that the site is in the process of being updated. There are several examples of emerging designer websites in the Resources section of this book. One excellent site belongs to Rodarte at www.rodarte.net. They show the collec-

tion in multiple ways through a range of clear product shots and artistic, romantic images that reflect the brand. There are detail shots, photos from fittings and the runway, and models in the garments in front of a basic white wall.

Managing a website is quite time consuming. If website maintenance is not in your skill set, you may need to get outside help. Agencies that specialize in Web design and management are too expensive for a small company's budget, but you can find excellent freelance designers and programmers to help create your site. Ask friends and colleagues for recommendations and research other independent designers online to see who created their sites. Many talented Web and graphic designers are not creatively stimulated by their day jobs and would be excited to work on a fashion designer's site as a side project. Even if you don't want a full website or don't have time to manage one, I highly suggest having a simple home page with your logo, contact information, and one or two images of your work just to have an online identity and to ensure that anyone searching for you on the Internet can find you.

Samples

Proper, well-made samples are critical for your sales and press appointments. The buyer assumes that these items are an exact example of what she will receive if an order is placed. The quality of stitching, fabrication, and construction will set expectations. Buyers stress the importance of first impressions when previewing a new collection. A store will never take a chance on a new collection that doesn't look professional.

Before each appointment, check that your samples are clean and undamaged. Clothing should be pressed and carried in a sturdy garment bag on good hangers. Accessories and jewelry should be packed in neat bags, boxes, or trays. Hangtags should include your company name and address, style number, size range, color options, fiber content, wholesale price, and where the item was made.

If you can afford it, cut the samples in each of the available color options. Although you can show the items in one color with swatches of color options, several designers told me that the buyers have trouble envisioning the options and are more likely to buy if they see the actual item in each color.

As discussed in chapter 6, duplicate sets of samples may be necessary, depending on who is handling your press and sales. At some point, a designer may need to produce one set for the New York sales showroom, one for the Los Angeles showroom, and one for the public relations firm.

8

···

Sales

Regardless of design talent, the designers who focus on selling are the ones who stay in business. Sales are what enable a company to expand and make money, and without them, the effort put into designing the collection and producing the samples is irrelevant. However, selling a collection as a new designer is more complicated than you think. While it is exciting to have a store interested in buying your designs, smart selling requires a careful strategy for working with the right stores, negotiating the terms, and pricing the goods correctly.

A designer generally has two different sets of customers, the retail store and the final consumer. You have to focus on both. The goal is not just to get the merchandise into the stores. Jeffrey Tweedy, former executive vice president of Sean Jean said, "When we do a strategy, we really think about how we get it in the shopping bag and out the door."[1] When you sell to a store, you partner to achieve a common goal. You both believe the customers will want what you design and will pay the price to buy it.

The Financial Realities of Selling

Wholesaling to retail stores is the best sales route for new designers. The stores are known by consumers and have the resources and presence to build a national or even international clientele quickly for an unknown designer. Danny Bensi, formerly of Cloak, says, "This whole entire thing is about the store. The store is what matters and we are at the mercy of the buyers."[2] Fortunately, it has

become increasingly important for stores to carry new designers. But realize that the demands of retailers can be strangling. Stores do not like risk, and they put pressure on designers in numerous ways to share costs and guarantee profit. A designer must understand the store policies and make her own retail terms and conditions known on sales agreements and forms. Some agreements are never written down, and as designer Alicia Bell says, "Many things in fashion are done on a handshake and a prayer."[3] Realize that stores make exceptions all the time. You should negotiate everything. In the end, you must weigh the pros and cons of each store demand and decide if you can afford to do business with that store.

Charge Backs

Charge backs are fees charged to the designer for not meeting specific requirements of the store. Do what you can to keep these charges to a minimum. They add up quickly; can eliminate your margin; and can damage your relationships with the stores, factors, and your showroom. Most department stores have very strict policies for packaging, labeling, and shipping product. They may require clothing to come packed on specific hangers (such as double-strand wire or solid plastic), while other items need to be poly-bagged. Product may need to be preticketed for the sales floor, and both the packing slip and the shipping label must include specific information. The store may specify which company to use for shipping and may even require a certain type of box. Department stores provide a "Routing Guide"—an extensive document that outlines all of the store's requirements—and if you don't follow it precisely, you will be charged. The charges are expensive—ranging from $0.10 per item for not attaching price tags and $5 per carton for no packing slip to $60 for boxes that exceed the weight requirement and $250 for sending a box to the wrong address. Charge backs may also be issued if items arrive damaged or need to be repaired at the store. Many retailers keep copies of their routing guide and requirements on their websites. For example, to see a copy of the Saks Fifth Avenue documents, you can look under vendor relations at *www.saksincorporated.com*.

The best way to avoid charge backs is to read the routing guide carefully, and if there are requirements you can't meet, to tell the store up front. When

you receive a charge back form, inquire immediately if a charge is unjustified. Don't be intimidated; you *can* dispute it.

EDI (Electronic Data Interchange)

Most department stores require their vendors to be EDI-compliant. EDI is a paperless electronic transmission system that allows the store to communicate quickly and automatically with the vendor, shipper, and warehouse at a detailed level. With EDI, each box and merchandise item is identified by a barcode, which can be scanned at any time and communicate information to all parties involved. For example, boxes can be scanned when they leave the warehouse or when they arrive at the store, and the shipper, retail storeroom, and buyer all know automatically exactly which merchandise has arrived. This saves significant time and cost spent having staff open boxes and confirm and communicate delivery by email or phone. Unfortunately, for a designer to become EDI-compliant is expensive and complex. Department stores will grant exemption to most new brands for several seasons, understanding that the company is too small to justify such an investment. Any small company selling to a department store should request at least a two-season exemption from being compliant with EDI or other software requirements to see first if the relationship will be worth the effort. Once you decide to become EDI compliant, the first step should be to work with a fulfillment house that has the software and ability to integrate EDI into your labeling and shipping.

Markdown Money and Guaranteed Sell-Through

Guaranteed sell-through requires the designer to agree that a certain percentage of goods will sell at full price. If that percentage doesn't sell, the store can charge the designer "markdown money" or a "markdown allowance" to cover the loss when the goods are put on sale. For example, if you sign a sell-through agreement of 70 percent and 72 percent of the goods sell at full price, you won't have to pay markdown money. But if only 60 percent of the goods sell at full price,

the store can require you to pay money to cover the markdown for the 10 percent that was guaranteed, as well as for the remaining 30 percent.

The arrangement indemnifies the store, taking the risk out of the buy and allowing the store to overbuy. Big manufacturers are able to support these policies because they have high volume and still make a profit, even with the markdowns. But for small companies, the allowances eat up profit quickly. Many designers and showrooms do successfully refuse markdown allowances and guarantees by explaining that the company is too small to support the policy financially. Showroom owner Greg Mills advises designers to say no to markdown allowances or at least negotiate.[4] Tell them you will agree to the sell-through guarantee if they make a commitment to buy for the next two years. Perhaps offer to give them mark-down money as a credit toward their next season's order. But realize if you say no, the store may buy less and you will be less important to them. The best thing is to try to sell only what you believe the store can sell at full price.

Discounts

Most department stores expect to receive a discount off the wholesale price. Their reasoning is that they generally buy in greater quantities and will sell more product in total. The discount can range from 3 percent to 15 percent and dangerously eat up your profit. Weigh the pros and cons of each discount and decide how much you think the store can sell for you and whether being there will lead to bigger buys and other accounts. For example, a store like Barneys New York can be important to new designers, even if they don't sell well. The store acts like a showroom because buyers from other stores go there to search for new names. If they see your label there, it can result in new business. If you really want to be in a store, determine whether you can afford to give the discount. Most new designers can't avoid discounts, but try to negotiate. The better your relationship with the buyer and the better the goods sell at the store, the more negotiating power you have.

Cancellations and Returns

Stores will return merchandise for a multitude of reasons, including overshipment, unauthorized substitutions, bad fit, early or late delivery, low sell-through, or defect. One designer received a large department store order for a blouse, but

before delivery, the buyer saw a knock-off version of the blouse in a low-end store window and canceled the order. While some reasons for returns or cancellations are justified, some are not. The tragedy of September 11, 2001, resulted in many stores refusing shipments without cause or returning them for absurd reasons, such as in the case of one designer who had T-shirts returned because of their skyscraper motif.

If merchandise is returned, first try to fix or replace the unacceptable product and get it back to the store immediately. If you can't replace the items, ask the store to accept a credit for next season, rather than just refunding its money. If the merchandise is too old, don't accept it. One department store tried to return styles to a designer that it had held for eight months, and the designer rightly refused the return.

Another designer had a dress returned to the store by a customer who had worn it once. Afterwards, the designer found yellow sweat marks under the armpits. The store returned the entire shipment of dresses to the designer, even though only one dress was affected and the stains were probably caused by the customer's deodorant. If something like this happens, try to push the responsibility back on the store or take one garment back to do an inspection before accepting the entire return.

To avoid returns, always call the store before you ship. Many stores require designers to make a "delivery appointment" with the receiving department; failure to keep these appointments results in a charge back. Try to negotiate if a store wants to cancel. A designer had a store call midproduction to cancel an order, and the designer simply refused based on the fabric's being purchased, cut, and already on the machines. The negotiation resulted in a tedious shipment plan, sending small batches every few weeks, but at least the merchandise made it into the store.

Pricing

Pricing must be determined before you have appointments. The price of each item must be carefully balanced between its fair market value and the needs of your business. Each item must look its price, accurately reflecting its value and quality, and pricing must stay consistent from season to season. Price defines your profit margin—the difference between costs and sales. If you price the collection too high, it will not sell; if it's too low, you lose your margin, and this will eventually drive you out of business.

Photo by Dan & Corina Lecca

Unicorn sweater from Fall 2004 collection.

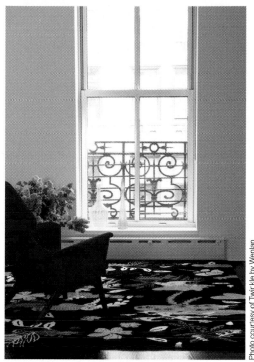

Photo courtesy of Twinkle by Wenlan

Formosa rug for Twinkle Living.

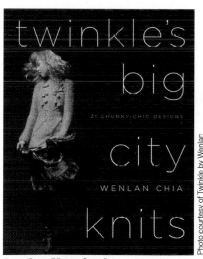

Photo courtesy of Twinkle by Wenlan

Big City Knits book.

Photo courtesy of Twinkle by Wenlan

Unicorn necklace by Twinkle Jewels.

twinkle by wenlan

Twinkle by Wenlan extends her brand and imagery across multiple product lines.

Spring 2008 collection.

Photo by Dan & Corina Lecca

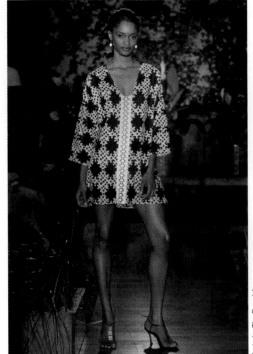

The Cabana 2007 collection.

Photo by Tim Darwish

Beach towel.

Courtesy of Milly

Invitations to Milly events.

Courtesy of Milly

Milly

Milly's flair for textile design distinguishes all her products and communications

Blazer with piping

Photo by Alex Muccilli

Double breasted cardigan.

Photo by Alex Muccilli

Yoko Devereaux store.

Courtesy of Yoko Devereaux.

A collaboration between Yoko Devereaux and artist Charles Lutz. These hand treated suitcases were created exclusively for the 10th anniversary issue of Surface magazine and featured in the Terminal 5 art exhibition.

Yoko Devereaux

Yoko Devereaux's artistic and casual edge unites his designs and collaborations

A runway shot from the Keanan Duffty
womens collection.

From the Keanan Duffty menswear collection.

Bearbrick - a collaboration
with Jon Savage - noted UK
rock journalist and author
of 'England's Dreaming'

From the Keanan Duffty menswear collection.

*British musician turned designer, Keanan Duffty, draws
inspiration from British punk for his range of products*

Inspiration board for Coney Island collection.

Coney Island is the inspiration for the Beckerman Spring 2008 collection and lookbook.

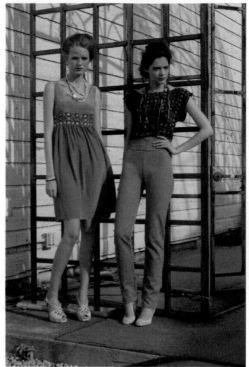

Inspiration for Helena Fredriksson Spring 2008 collection

KRISTEN LEE

NEW YORK • LOS ANGELES

Inspiration for Kristen Lee Spring 2008 collection

© Stephen Green-Armytage, from his book "Extraordinary Chickens" (Harry N Abrams)

Photo: Dylan Griffin

Inspiration behind a Yarborough jewelry design

Courtesy of Bruno Grizzo

Photo: ioulex

Inspiration for the Bruno Grizzo collection

Photos courtesy of Bliss Lau

Photos courtesy of Bliss Lau

Inspiration behind a Bliss Lau signature bag

Photo by Anne Hamilton

Courtesy of Tom Scott. Photo - Stephen Rose

Inspiration for a Tom Scott Fall/Winter 2007 look

Understand the price range for your market. Before you establish price, compare the items in your line with similar collections to establish a range that makes sense in the marketplace. Even established designers send employees to the stores regularly to research the price of competitive items and use that as a guide for their own product. If a designer is starting to produce leather coats, she will search for a leather coat that is similar in quality and image and plan to price in the same general range.

Many new designers are positioning their product in the contemporary market alongside brands such as Rebecca Taylor and Catherine Malandrino. This positioning requires high quality at a lower price point, which you must be able to sustain from season to season.

Be ready to explain your price point to the buyer and how the qualities of the fabric, production, and construction define the cost. Never underprice your product to get into certain stores. Stores buy you to fit a certain price point, and you can't adjust that later. The loss you take from underpricing will only accumulate as your orders grow.

Covering your costs. One of the biggest mistakes new designers make is not charging enough to cover their costs, much less provide a profit. The price must cover the cost of goods sold, as well as all other indirect expenses.

Cost of goods sold (COGS) includes all expenses related to producing the items ordered by the stores. This covers the obvious expenses tracked throughout production, such as buttons, zippers, marking, grading, fabric, construction, and shipping.

Indirect costs include design and development costs and sales, as well as general and administrative costs. Design and development costs include all the expenses of the sample collection, such as fabrics and first patterns, as well as research and development expenses, such as trips to fabric shows. Remember to account for your own labor if you make the patterns or samples; otherwise, the pricing won't cover your costs when you start to outsource this work.

Sales, general, and administrative costs include the costs of running the business, selling, and promoting the line. These include overhead, including rent, bookkeeping, salaries, and telephone; sales expenses, such as lookbooks and trade shows; advertising; and public relations. Markdown allowances, dis-

counts, returns, and canceled orders are sales expenses, and if they apply to you, your pricing must cover them.

Cost of goods sold is attributed to each specific item, but design and development costs and sales, general, and administrative costs need to be divided up and allocated across the entire collection. The process takes time, and designers become Excel wizards as they work to allocate costs correctly.

Calculating wholesale price is not an exact science and can become complex. If you work with a sales representative, ask the rep to help you. Several pricing methodologies exist, but one of the best approaches is to apply the same markup margin the retailer uses to the cost of goods sold. The markup will cover all indirect costs and provide the profit margin.

Retail pricing strategies may vary by store, but generally, retail markup equals double the wholesale price plus 20 to 80 percent, referred to as 2.2 or 2.8. Apparel is at the low end of the scale; jewelry and shoes are at the high end. Markup can be as high as 3.0 for product made in Europe because of the extra cost of duty and freight. To price product with the same markup margin as the retailer (or 2.2 in this example) the math works like this:

COGS = $50

Wholesale price = $110 ($50 × 2.2)

Retail price = $242 ($110 × 2.2)

At this stage, return to your research and determine whether the resulting retail price makes sense in the marketplace. If it seems too high, it means the wholesale price and COGS are too high. To save your margin, you must find a way to simplify the item design, use less expensive materials, or gain production efficiencies with larger runs to bring down the COGS. When manufacturing in Italy became too expensive, shoe designer Kristen Lee moved her production to Brazil to keep her pricing in line with the contemporary shoe market. Examine the resulting margin to determine if it is sufficient to cover your rent, salaries, and other fixed costs. If not, again you may need to alter the COGS.

Generally, the goal is for pricing to leave roughly 15 percent net profit margin after all direct and indirect costs. In the end, it's not about the volume of product you sell; it's all about the margin. The only way to increase your margin is to increase your price or lower your costs. As you are in the business longer,

you will build in efficiencies, and some costs will go down. For example, you will accumulate patterns that can be used again or adjusted just by switching out sleeves or collars. You will meet the minimums for cheaper production and discounts in fabric and materials. The margin will increase as the business grows.

Where to Sell

Wholesale

Department stores. Designers want to be in department stores because of the prestige, exposure, and sales volume they can provide. One buyer from a big chain of department stores can land your merchandise in 20 locations across the country, dramatically growing the business and providing economies of scale for sourcing and production. The department stores have established customers and regular traffic and benefit from extensive promotional budgets, catalog, and online sales reach. They can also put newer designers in the company of established, highly desirable brands. However, department stores put significant stress on designers to contribute to their margins and to cover their costs. Many are owned by large public companies pressured to make money for their shareholders. Their decisions are based on daily sales and don't allow time for a new designer's business to develop.

There is a saying that at department stores "the clothes are on wheels." The store wants to wheel the clothes in completely prepped for the sales floor and, if they don't sell, wheel them back out without any loss or responsibility. Big brands, such as Ralph Lauren and Tommy Hilfiger, essentially rent real estate from the department stores. They spend thousands of their own dollars to build and maintain branded areas in the stores and hire the people who staff them. It can be difficult for a small brand to compete in this arena.

Boutique and specialty stores. New designers should start by selling to small boutiques, and many choose to continue working primarily with small stores once they are well established. Small boutiques are more flexible regarding delivery, and they share in the risk. They don't demand markdown money or issue significant charge backs, and if they return items that didn't sell, they are more

likely to accept credit for next season rather than demand a refund. Working with small boutiques allows you to keep more control in the beginning, to try out new things, and to make sure you have your production thoroughly in order before you enter the department store business.

Rich Rosenthal, CEO of Alvin Valley, says, "It's risky to produce over 15 percent of your sales for department stores. Chain retailers will deduct 30 to 40 percent of your invoice for freight and trade discounts, vendor compliance charge backs, and markdown allowances, as allowed. It's wiser to build sales with specialty stores which pay in full and spread your risk."[5]

A product that doesn't sell well in a big department store may do well in a small boutique. Department stores tend to overbuy, and your label must compete with hundreds of others on a crowded floor with bulging racks and too few sales-people. In a small store, the owner is generally the buyer, knows the customer well, and buys specifically for them. The sales staff in the store often includes the owner or is made up of people whom the owner personally hired and trained.

Working with smaller stores does have its challenges. Each store needs to be tracked and serviced separately, regardless of how big or small its order. Each believes it is your most important account, and because it places small orders, you may need several stores to buy an item to meet its production minimums. Most importantly, small stores are less known and can be financially unstable. They may go out of business or simply not pay. You have to be meticulous about checking their credit before accepting an order. As menswear designer Andy Salzer states, "Servicing small boutiques and special 'cool' stores is harder than servicing the big—they order three of something, or don't pay for six months."[6] Some of the more influential and trendsetting boutiques are even starting to only buy on consignment or demand discounts because they know the designers really want to sell there. These key boutiques can be instrumental in building a new brand and desirable product image before launching with the department stores, but they won't necessarily contribute to your profitability.

The New York selling market is extremely competitive, and many design-ers who are based there don't have a single account in New York. Alternatively, across the United States, there are significant areas of wealth with customers who want high-end fashion. Large luxury brands, such as Hermes, are opening

boutiques in smaller cities, including Charlotte, North Carolina, and Naples, Florida. The exclusive boutiques in small cities represent a huge opportunity for new labels to build loyalty with a high-end, full-price luxury shopper who wants to discover something unique to call her own.

National chain stores and boutiques. Many of the smaller exclusive boutiques, such as Scoop, Intermix, and Calypso, are opening multiple locations, increasing their influence and the size of their buy. As a result, many are beginning to make the same demands as department stores. Other established national chains, such as Urban Outfitters and Anthropologie, have become significant customers for new designer product and will partner to sell the product either under the designer's own label or as private-label merchandise for the store. Any of these accounts can launch a new label in multiple markets, but they also increase the risk of doing too much business with a single customer. While it is efficient to grow the amount of product with each account, regardless of the type of store, designers should not rely too heavily on one customer for the majority of their sales. If a store drops you or cancels an order, it can put you out of business. You need to spread the risk over multiple customers.

Export. Exporting opens up many possible sales opportunities and spreads the risk that comes from selling in only one country, where economic or currency issues might result in a bad season. It's best to focus first on selling and delivering successfully in one overseas market. Then it will become easier to expand to other countries, and buyers, showrooms, and distributors may even approach you. For many young designers, their first overseas accounts are in Japan, where fortunately the stores are very honorable about paying on time. Japan offers a large market of consumers excited about new fashion and with money to spend. Many women in Japan live at home, work for a salary, and still receive spending money from their families. They love to shop and spend hours poring over fashion magazines. Designers such as Anna Sui and Jill Stuart are received like rock stars in Tokyo. Outside of Japan, there are also lucrative markets in Europe, other parts of Asia, and South America. Due to the recent devaluation of the dollar, many small U.S. labels are focused on launching their brands in Europe. This is especially true in the contemporary market, which is just starting to open

up in Europe. Designers have an opportunity to expand their distribution and develop new PR opportunities as a new label in a new market.

In general, the rules for dealing with foreign stores are the same as in the United States, but there are additional challenges. It is more difficult to collect late payment from a store on the other side of the world than from one across town. If you are far away, people may try to take advantage of you. The stores may only offer consignment or difficult terms. Factoring, COD terms, and letters of credit will help protect you. But if you aren't working with a showroom, you may want to ask for payment up front and only sell to stores that agree. Fortunately, markdown money and charge backs are less prevalent overseas, but there are differences in labeling requirements, sizing, payment terms, markups, sales commissions, and contracts. Shipping and insurance costs are high, plus there is duty and the expense of handling overseas returns and customer service. All of the costs depend on foreign exchange rates and add up when the dollar is weak. A designer usually needs separate price lists for different countries to cover the variance in costs and the shipping terms. Lead times are longer for shipping, customs paperwork can cause delays, and you can't be late in overseas markets, either! Delivery times may differ dramatically in a foreign market, putting additional strain on your production. Europe, for example, generally wants a pre-Fall delivery in June when stores in the United States expect a Summer delivery.

The place where you produce can affect your export abilities. If a designer who produces in New York wants to sell to Selfridges in London, the taxes to import American-made product into England can result in a retail price too high to sell realistically. But an American designer who produces in Italy can sell to Selfridges under the European Union (EU) agreements that promote free trade between EU countries, keeping the price down and allowing Selfridges to buy.

To land overseas accounts, you can contact specific stores directly. Some large foreign department stores have offices in New York, and buyers from overseas regularly visit. Other methods include participating in foreign trade shows, hiring a showroom in the foreign market, or approaching the New York buying offices that represent large foreign retailers.

Alternatively, a distributor can represent you in another country. Distributors buy goods directly from the designer at a significant discount. They handle credit checks, delivery, and collecting from each store. Many designers advise

that to really grow in Japan, you must have a distributor agreement. Designer Keanan Duffty says, "Distribution agreements are the only way to go overseas. It's too much hassle to collect payment, deal with customs, and negotiate who pays shipping and landing duty with dozens of small foreign stores."[7] A distribution deal can also provide pricing leverage with fabric suppliers and factories. But like everything else, with a distributor there are risks. You must thoroughly check the distributor's credit and have a lawyer review the agreement, because there can be big differences in law and business methods from country to country. Research the distributor's other clients and pay attention to how it promotes them. Distributors can harm your image by oversaturating the market, selling to the wrong stores, and discounting your product.

Online stores. The Internet is an increasingly important selling market for fashion labels, as more customers are buying their apparel and accessories online. The biggest attraction of online stores is their power to extend your market reach. A traditional store is generally limited to the customers in the local geographic area, but online stores are national or even international in reach and can bring thousands of new customers to your product. Online stores capture information, and the buyer can tell you where your product sells best, exactly what each customer is purchasing, and specifically why an item was returned. More designers are working to build their presence on the websites of department stores, such as *www.saksfifthavenue.com*, to grow their volume and extend their brand reach beyond the limited floor space they are allocated in the brick-and-mortar store.

There are a wide variety of online stores, and each appeals to a specific customer. Some specialize in expensive, high-end labels; some in edgy new labels; and others in overstock and marked-down items. As with a traditional store, you need to make sure the site is right for your product and will draw the appropriate customers. Find out what it will do to promote and support you. The websites www.shopbop. com, www.revolveclothing.com, and www.activeendeavors.com send out regular emails featuring new merchandise. Many sites highlight specific designers and even send out samples to magazines to garner press for the designers and the site.

As with traditional stores, you can't deliver late; websites need to be timely, too. They want the merchandise before or at least at the same time as regular stores. When they reorder, they need the items immediately because the customer has

probably already placed the order. Most websites ask for an online exclusive, meaning you cannot sell on other websites except perhaps your own. In return, ask the site what it will do to support your business. Realize that while some online companies, such as Shopbop.com, buy merchandise like a traditional store, many work on consignment basis, leaving you with leftover merchandise if the items don't sell.

Selling online offers the ability to connect with customers directly. In some cases, the designer handles shipping to the customer. In others, the online store ships items in the designer's packaging. Charming or professional packaging can represent your brand, include information on your line, and even advertise your own website.

Direct to the Consumer

There are several avenues to bypass the retailer and sell directly to the consumer.

Your own website. Establishing a strong retail business on your own website is difficult, but several designers, especially in the accessories category, have done well with this approach. It probably won't make you rich, but it can help with cash flow and provide higher margins by paying you the retail, rather than the wholesale price. If you sell the same items on your website and in retail stores, the pricing on your site must be the same as the suggested price for stores. Also, don't post your collection on your site before it hits the stores. The stores want to have the items first, and posting too soon also increases the risk of being knocked off before the product arrives at retailers.

Driving customer traffic to a website is challenging. The Web address should be as close as possible to the name of your line, and you should include it on all promotional materials, including the hangtags on your product. Register with search engines such as Google and Yahoo! and invest in key word advertising. Trade website links with sites that draw a similar customer and put some effort into getting press. Designers often conduct monthly giveaways that attract people to the site, then encourage them to register their email addresses, providing a mailing list for future promotions. Holly Dunlap of Hollywould awards a "customer of the month" with a gift certificate, and her website blog attracts regular visits to the site while deepening her relationship with the customer.

Designers use their websites to test product and conduct market research. Many designers encourage on-site communication with customers. They ask for feedback and photos of customers wearing their clothes. As a result, they can see where in the country there is demand and use that to entice stores in those areas to buy the collection.

The customer service related to selling on your site can be very time consuming. Each customer must be dealt with individually in regards to sizing, shipping, and payment problems. Online customers expect a great return policy, and fit is key so you must be consistent and explain your sizing in detail on the site.

Good photos accompanied by precise and thorough information regarding measurements and materials will help avoid returns and customer complaints. Items such as T-shirts and accessories are easier for customers to purchase without trying them on, but items such as tailored pants, in which the fit is critical, may result in more returns. As with selling to other online stores, you need to stock product and absorb the loss if it doesn't sell. The site will require good e-tailing software, and even if you are computer savvy, you will probably need someone to help set up and monitor an e-commerce site.

If your product is popular, you may be able to find a partner to manage your Web sales and customer service. Ria Brown used to sell her famous Mella flip-flops direct to customers on her website and handle all the back-end operations herself. Then she made an agreement with Shopbop.com to be the exclusive online partner for her website. They do a seasonal buy of merchandise for their site, and then she links from her site to theirs for all sales. She receives a commission on every sale that comes from her website to *www.shopbop.com*.[8]

Your own store. Your own store offers a valuable opportunity to display and control your image, as well as provide a steady revenue stream and higher margins, throughout the season. Wendy Mullin of Built by Wendy says, "Production is very expensive and leaves little margin at wholesale, but I can make it up at retail in my own store."[9]

Designer Tory Burch introduced her line through her own store in New York rather than launching through the traditional wholesale route. She felt that this would ensure consistency in the image and brand of the company and she could control more details regarding the store environment and the shoppers' experience.[10]

In your own store, you can test product; get direct customer feedback; and immediately see which sizes, colors, and styles sell best. A designer can operate a wholesale business from the store, using it as a showroom for buyers and editors and as a place to sell overstock and merchandise returned from other stores.

Ria Brown, who is a partner at womenswear label Mayle, believes that the direct-to-consumer retail connection is key to staying in touch with the customer. The volume is smaller, but the margins are twice as big and take less effort and expertise to manage. She says it's easy to find a good person to work in your store, while it's much harder to find a person who can manage all of your compliance issues for production for wholesale to a department store. In addition, retail customers are loyal, and often you find that a few regular customers account for a majority percentage of your business.[11]

However, a store is expensive. Rent, equipment, décor, credit card fees, and staff add up, and you have to have product in the store and bring in new items on a regular basis to keep it fresh. A fabric supplier said that if a small designer opens her own store, he considers her a credit risk and may not sell to her because of the financial demands of the store. A business advisor at the Service Corps of Retired Executives (SCORE) knows a designer who had a very strong wholesale business and decided to open a store. He became distracted by the process of designing the space and exceeded his budget, using expensive materials and fixtures and making changes that caused construction delays. The store opened one year late, he missed deliveries to his wholesale accounts, and he ended up $800,000 in debt.

Running a store is a full-time job. Someone must be there to keep it open during regular retail hours. If editors or customers come by during business hours and the store is closed, it looks unprofessional. Retailers work long hours, weekends, and holidays, and when you are busy servicing customers, it is hard to find time to get to the factory to oversee production or to meet with fabric suppliers. Designer Doo-ri Chung recommends you never open a store without a partner to share in the responsibility and help with the sales. In the end, she thought, "What am I doing wasting my time as a shop girl?"[12] and she closed her store to focus on the wholesale business.

If you have a store, you need to keep it busy and continually attract new people. A promotional plan can include mailings, collection previews, cocktail

parties, and other in-store events and incentives to draw customers. Collect contact information from people who visit and inform them about events, sales, and the arrival of new merchandise. Invite the press and entice them to cover the store opening and to list events and sales. Be creative and align with artists, restaurants, and neighborhood shopping events to attract new customers and generate buzz.

Building Strong Customer Relationships

By focusing on her end customer, Wendy Mullin of Built by Wendy has developed a strong, loyal audience despite her decision to cut back on wholesale accounts. Through her own store and website, she creates a direct relationship with her customer. Her business used to be 80 percent wholesale, but it came with the stress of dealing with difficult stores that didn't pay and didn't know how to buy or merchandise the collection well. When Wendy's patternmaker died of a stress-related heart attack, she decided life was too short and cut back to sell only to stores that really believed in the clothes and had good credit or paid a deposit. As a result, the number of stores to service is smaller, and the customers are flexible, loyal, and willing to work with her.

Wendy promotes her retail store and website by sponsoring small events and advertising to her customers in niche places, such as literary, music, and art magazines. The fashion magazine world is crowded and competitive, and it's really not the place to reach her customers. Ads in alternative publications are inexpensive, they reach her customers at their place of interest, and they stand out because of the lack of other clothing advertisers. Built by Wendy has sponsored Lady Fest, which supports contemporary female artists, and she even bought an ad in a high school fanzine and sponsored a charity fundraising event for $300 when a customer emailed to request her support. The result is a personal customer connection that she further develops by involving customers directly with the brand. They walk in her runway shows and send their photos to be posted on the website, and she deals directly with her best customers in the store and on the Web. She even travels to bring sample sales to her customers in their town. In Chicago, she sold $20,000 in goods in two days. She says, "It's about my relationship with my customer. At the end of the day, the stores and press will not be loyal, but the customers will."[13]

Flea Markets

Flea markets and selling arenas such as the Young Designer Market in New York's Nolita area offer a place to test product, make a little cash, get rid of samples, and sell to the public without making a commitment to a full-time store location. They also offer an opportunity to connect with other new designers. Dana Foley and Anna Corinna met when they each had booths at the 26th Street flea market in New York. They partnered to open their successful Lower East Side boutique and wholesale business Foley + Corinna. Although they made a successful transition, there is some danger that designers who sell at these markets won't be taken as seriously by buyers from high-end stores.

A renewed interest in crafting and handmade wares has resulted in several events and websites for small craftspeople and designers to sell their wares directly to consumers in needle crafts. Etsy (www.etsy.com) is an online co-op of thousands of artists, designers, and crafters selling their custom-designed, one-of-a-kind products. These sites and events allow designers the advantage of making to order and avoiding wholesale issues with stores, but of course servicing each customer individually is time consuming and it's difficult to build enough volume to sustain a business.

Shopping Events

An increasing number of shopping events is created each year to bring dozens of clothing and accessories designers into one space to sell directly to consumers for a limited period of time—generally from one night up to four days. Gen Art, Shecky's, Lucky magazine, and numerous others host regular events several times per year in cities nationwide. There are also many one-time charity-related or holiday season events. By participating, the designer can sell and interact directly with the consumer, get firsthand feedback, and potentially unload old merchandise. The events draw shoppers by offering a diverse and unique selection of merchandise that isn't normally available, as well as an opportunity to interact with the designers. Cocktails, beauty treatments, gift bags, DJs, and other entertainment are regular features at shopping events. Each event targets a specific audience, some with expensive, high-end merchandise and others with inexpensive, mass vendors. Designers are charged a fee to participate—some as

high as $1,500, others as low as $500. A few events require just a small $75 to $100 setup fee plus a percentage of each designer's sales.

If you decide to participate in a shopping event, find the one with the right mix of designers and appropriate target market for your image and product. Some types of product do better at these events than others, and you should ask the organizers which type of vendors have the most success. Ask them how they promote the event to ensure enough of the proper traffic, and do what you can to spread the word of your participation.

Television

Millions of dollars of merchandise are sold each year on television networks such as QVC and the Home Shopping Network. The sheer volume of shoppers they attract is staggering. While this is not the image many designers want for their brand, the image of some of these outlets has improved, and high-end brands, such as Prescriptives, have started selling here. A few emerging designers, including Liz Collins and Alice Roi, have sold limited-edition product on QVC. Chloe Dao, winner of season two of Project Runway, launched a line of affordable separates called Simply Chloe Dao on QVC. Dao designs the clothes and is paid a percentage of the sale of total pieces sold, while an outside production company takes on the risk of sourcing and manufacturing.[14]

Incubators

Certain stores, which call themselves incubators, have nontraditional arrangements with new designers to provide an opportunity to retail. Some of the arrangements also provide a showroom space for wholesale and press appointments, studio space, and business training.

Rather than buy the collection, these stores charge designers a monthly fee to have their product in the store, and some places take a percentage of sales as well. While the concept of a true incubator has a lot of potential, especially if it includes production capabilities, unfortunately many places that identify themselves by that term seem to come and go. A few have even shut their doors without paying commissions owed to the designers. If a designer isn't selling anywhere else, it can be beneficial to place the collection in one of these stores

to meet the retail requirement often required by press and to be able to tell other stores that you sell. But incubator stores can be expensive, especially if your product isn't selling well. Many are located off the beaten path and may have trouble attracting steady traffic. Incubators can make a line appear amateurish, and if the mix of aesthetics and the quality of the other designers in the store isn't consistent, it might not be positive for your image.

Custom Clientele

Some designers operate a portion, or even all, of their business for individual clients. The risk is low because there is no investment in materials or production until there is an order and the designer can require a deposit to pay for the materials. Designer Gary Graham said that when he was starting out, private clients gave him confidence, feedback, and free PR when they wore his clothing out and mixed it with well-known labels.[15]

It takes many individual customers to build enough volume to sustain your custom business. As Jordan Betten, designer of custom leather brand Lost Art, points out, press is extremely important because he doesn't have a presence in stores to tell people about his work. He sends out weekly emails and has held trunk shows in Los Angeles and Japan to build clientele.[16]

Individual customers are time consuming because you have to service each one. Ideally, you want to try to grow the amount that each client orders, rather than just the total number of customers, and avoid making custom pieces, which require even more time and provide small margins.

Selling to the Stores

Research

When asked where they want to sell, new designers predictably list the same few high-end, high-profile stores, such as Barneys New York, Colette, Neiman Marcus, or Fred Segal. But after seeing their product, one often wonders if they have ever even set foot in these stores. I can't stress enough how important it is to research carefully and learn about the stores before you reach out to them. Henri Bendel and Maxfield are dream stores for new labels, but it would be rare

to find a product that fits both. Not every store is right for your line. Designers must target places that cater to their customers and have the proper image and product mix for their designs.

If you aspire to sell to a specific store, go there and study it. Look at the layout of each floor and each section. Review the merchandise, visual display, and price points. Observe the customers. Before you contact a buyer, you need to know exactly which floor your product should be on and what designers you should be next to in terms of aesthetic, price point, and customer target. Note whether the store has lines similar to yours or if you would fill a gap.

Talk to the salespeople in the store and ask them what sells well, what doesn't, and which items fly off the floor as soon as they arrive. Find out if any items are on a wait list. Notice the merchandise on the sales racks because those things won't be reordered. Ask them about your competition and the lines you admire. When consultant Robert Burke, was senior vice president of the fashion office and public relations of Bergdorf Goodman, he observed, "When Zac Posen comes in to the store, he is there on the floor asking about Dolce and Gabbana's delivery dates, how many deliveries they have, how they price and flow the goods into the store."[17] Store research will help you significantly at your sales appointments. The buyer will see that you have done your homework and are serious about working with him.

Whom to Contact

Many of the large department stores have fashion directors. Their job is to find the next new thing for the store, and they spend considerable time in the market researching new sources and talking to editors. If the store has a fashion director, approach that person first. You should also call the store or ask the salesperson for the name of the specific buyer who buys for the section in which you should sell. For boutiques and stores nationwide, you can purchase lists of stores and buyer contacts from places such as Infomat or Fashiondex, but these are mass lists that require further research to pinpoint the appropriate places and contacts. If you aren't familiar with a store, don't just blindly sell to them. One high-end jewelry designer visited one of her new "boutique" accounts in Texas and was shocked to find her merchandise on display in a hair salon.

When to Contact

Get your collections ready early. Many buying decisions are made before market week. Womenswear designers should try to meet the buyers a few weeks before New York Fashion Week, in early to mid-August for Spring, and early to mid-January for Fall. The menswear market takes place in mid-July and mid-January, but buyers ideally want to start seeing samples in late June or December.

Once market week comes, buyers are besieged by dozens of brands all vying for their attention at the same time. If you are a designer in Los Angeles, where market week is later, you need to have your collection ready much earlier to be ready when the New York market begins. The money for new sources is limited, and if you wait, you may miss out. Michael Fink, senior fashion director of Saks Fifth Avenue, explains, "You want buyers to see your product before the money is spent."[18] If you simply don't have the collection ready before market week, you might be better off waiting until it passes and the buyers are less busy and are spending any reserve money. Realize that in this case, you will have less time to produce and more challenge in meeting the required delivery dates.

Sales and Delivery Dates

Collection	Sales Dates	Delivery Dates
Spring Womenswear	Mid-August through October	Late January and February
Spring Menswear	Late June and July	January
Fall Womenswear	Late January through March	August and September
Fall Menswear	January through February	August
Holiday (Women's)	May/June	October
Resort (Women's)	June/July	November

Accessories and shoes are planned to go with ready-to-wear and may be bought later as the icing on the cake. But most high-end shoe and accessory designers start

to sell earlier, in sync with ready-to–wear, as follows: Pre-Fall in early December, Fall in late January/early February, Resort in June, and Spring in August.

There are opportunities to sell throughout the year. New product is shown constantly, and items such as T-shirts are bought year-round.

Landing an Appointment

Before calling a buyer, first send a simple image or lookbook in the mail or by email with a short paragraph about you and the line. The package should provide a quick and easy taste of your collection and background, giving the buyer a point of reference when you call.

Follow up with a brief, concise phone call. Be professional as you introduce yourself and remind the buyer of the mailing. Give a one- or two-sentence description of your line and where it sells and ask for an appointment. Pique interest with any pertinent information, such as your successful sell-through at other stores (you can exaggerate a little, but don't overdo it), press coverage, or celebrity clients. Don't ramble on or your good impression will fizzle quickly. For a designer, it can be nerve-racking to pick up the phone and place these calls. However, it will get easier over time, and eventually you will develop relationships at the stores. Keep in mind that buyers get hundreds of calls each week. If they are short or seem unreceptive on the phone, it's not personal.

It's not always easy to get the buyer on the phone. Leave a brief, polite message with your name, contact number, and reference to your mailing. Don't call more than once per week. Getting on a buyer's nerves will not result in an order. But Terri Gillis, owner of TG-170, a store in New York, says, "Do follow up as sometimes I need to be reminded. Call until you get me or until I say, 'We'll call you if we are interested.'"[19]

When you can't get in front of the buyer, be creative and think about what you can do to obligate her to contact you. Find out if there is something in particular that she loves that relates to your collection or something personal that would appeal to her you can put in a note, message or package. You want her to think that you worked hard and really made an effort to specifically get her attention and, therefore, she has to give you five minutes.

Cold Calling
By Rachel Shechtman

I love to cold call. I really do. You're probably thinking, "Who in the world likes cold calling?" I do. In fact, I don't just like it, I actually love it!

I love the challenge and rush of calling a complete stranger, such as the CEO of a billion-dollar retailer, and within a month of the call signing a strategic partnership. I love communicating what excites me and translating it into value and meaning for the stranger I am calling. I can't tell you where it came from or why, but I have been a cold-calling addict for ten years and hope my tips are helpful to you. These are my rules for loving and succeeding at cold calling.

What are the key points you should include in a cold call?

Every great cold call follows a simple strategy: Attract, Make Relevant, and Attack!

Attract: Within the first **10 seconds** of the cold call: Who are you and why are you calling? (And you'd better make it interesting!)

Make Relevant: Within the first **30 seconds** of the cold call: Why would talking to you be meaningful for him or her?

Attack: You have about **4 to 6 minutes** to connect and be clear. Determine follow-up and say your goodbyes.

What will grab the attention of buyers or editors?

Being personal and having a sense of humor is the easiest way to grab someone's attention. When they answer the phone, take a moment before you sell or pitch. If you are calling a handbag buyer, when they answer the phone you can say, "I hear you are the Queen/King of handbags, and I just want a minute of your time to tell you what I do and send you a lookbook." Use unique and descriptive attributes that you can use when you follow up.

Do you leave a message?

First try calling the person you are trying to reach at various days and times of day and do not leave a message. I believe you should try calling at least four to six times, and if you still do not get a live person, then leave a voicemail. Here are my voicemail rules:

- Call after 7:00 P.M. (or before 8 A.M. if you're an early bird). Why? Assistants typically answer the phones from 8:30 to 6:00, depending on the boss. If you call after-hours or before, you can typically access a phone directory and go directly into the voicemail of the person you are trying to reach, bypassing the assistant.

- Your voicemail must consist of the following elements, communicated clearly and slowly:

- Who are you?

- Why are you calling?

- Why should he/she call back?

- "I hope all is well in California [or wherever this person is located] and look forward to speaking soon!"

- Leave an anticipated follow-up date / time, along with an excuse for future contact.

- No voicemail should be longer than 1 minute.

Example

Hi Sally, It's Anna Richards from XYZ designs. Since this is one of many voicemails you have, I will keep it brief. I am following up on the _____ [press kit/lookbook] I sent you. I admire your style and would value your feedback. My new collection would be great for your _____ [magazine/stores]. If you would like to reach me, you can call me at _____ [phone number]; otherwise, I will give you a call back next Tuesday to touch base about _____ [what you want from them]. Hope all is well in _____ [wherever they are located], and have a great day.

What if you don't hear back? How often can you follow up?

Follow-up is important, but stalking is not recommended! If after a week you don't hear back, you can call again. If after a second call, you still do not get a response, you can send a package related to what you are calling about. Put the materials in a differently colored envelope and make it distinctive, so if you don't hear back, you can follow up and say, "Hi, it's the person who sent the orange envelope."

What about email versus the phone for cold calling?

Email can be effective, but it depends on what you are trying to pitch. If you have a PDF or digital lookbook, then emailing it can be effective, and you can call to follow up if you don't hear back. Again, be clear, brief, and to the point in your email. Make sure the person reading will understand the value of reading to the end. Answer the questions that they are asking themselves: "What is in it for me?" "Why should I read this?"

Is there a best day of week or time of day?

The rule is very, very simple. Yet there are many of you who break this rule day in and day out. Here it is: No calls on Monday, no calls on Friday. But, but, but…what if? No way, no how, no calling on Monday and Fridays.

As you know for yourself, Monday is the day that we get back to work and need to catch up and reacclimatize ourselves to the pace of work. We just had a relaxing weekend and are not happy to be back at a desk or in an office…or at least most of us. Mondays are about adjustment, catching up, and getting back into the groove. We are not in absorption mode, and therefore any calls or encounters to encourage and promote new opportunities will be less effective if not entirely ineffective.

Unlike Monday, Friday is about smiles…talking about plans for the weekend, trying to leave early, a two-hour lunch and so on. So you are thinking, everyone is in a good mood and happy, so let's call and capitalize on their good mood, right? Wrong! Or it's more like wishful thinking. Friday is about wrapping things up and getting onto the weekend.

Therefore, any new opportunity presented will appear as an obstacle, delay, or nuisance in terms of this goal.

So Tuesday to Thursday is your window, and please avoid the following times:

- 9:00 A.M.: People just got to work and are getting settled.

- 11:30 A.M.–2:30 P.M.: People are thinking of food, eating it, or tired after just consuming it.

- 5:30–6:30 P.M.: People are getting ready to leave.

What if I'm really shy—how do I get myself to pick up the phone?

No one said you have to make the call. If you know that you will not be able to get across what you need to get across because it is simply not part of your personality, there is nothing wrong with that. Reach out to someone who knows you and

your collection well enough to make the pitch and act as your PR or sales associate. It is not uncommon for designers to find it challenging to "sell themselves," and often there can be more freedom when someone else is making the pitch. They can say things that you might not feel comfortable saying about yourself.

What percentage of cold calls should I expect to actually work? At what point do I get discouraged?

You should expect to get a response at least 50 percent of the time. But if you call multiple times and don't hear back, stop calling! At some point, you need to move on. Stalking does not get you anywhere faster and may turn off the person you are calling. There are numerous reasons why someone doesn't return a call, and only one is that they are not interested. It could be timing, mood, wrong contact information, or numerous other things beyond your control. Harping on an unreturned call only perpetuates the inefficient use of your energy, so look forward and move on to the next! If it is meant to be, you will cross paths with the contact one way or another.

Should I qualify my cold call leads at all? How should I prioritize whom I call?

It depends on your business objective. If you want editorial exposure, then reach out to press and bloggers before stores. Do the reverse if you are interested in retail distribution. Never start your cold calls with your first choice. Instead, warm up and make sure you feel comfortable by the time you're calling your top choices.

Now what? How do I start?

You're probably saying, "Now what? How do I start?" Some of you will embrace these tips and embark on your cold-calling mission tomorrow. Some of you still feel uneasy. And then there are those of you who are intrigued by these ideas but may not have someone to call.

If you approach cold calling with the sole objective of getting a meeting with an important CEO or a personal audience with Oprah, then chances are your attempt may not yield your desired results. However, if you embrace and acknowledge that the call is about making a connection and, most importantly, telling your story…it just might happen!

Rachel Shechtman is founder of Cube Ventures, a retail consulting firm based in New York City (www.cubeventures.com) and director of strategic partnerships at the Council of Fashion Designers of America. Rachel is writing a book on cold calling, expected to be out next year.

The Appointment

Once you get in the door, be concise and to the point; buyers have limited time. Present your collection in a professional, friendly manner and let your store research pay off. Share your successes and to what other stores you sell. Make it easy for the buyer. Explain how the product fills a void in the market and how it can be displayed and fit in to the store. Julie Gilhart, vice president and fashion director of Barneys New York, says, "Do what it takes to be super-organized. It is better to do less well. Be precise and creative in presenting the collection. Have well-thought-out pricing and be ready to state a delivery date that can be done. Be earnest and honest.[21]"

Buyers and sales reps both agree it's not just about the design—it's the whole package.

What Do They Look For?

Stores are always interested in new. The buyers look to fill a gap and avoid repetition of the lines they already carry. They see too many things that look alike and crave something unique that stands on its own but makes sense to their customer. Many buyers say that despite the increasing number of new designers, product is often too basic or trying too hard, and many designers aren't really designing but just copying others.

The product and price must make sense for the store. Designer and showroom owner Ana Beatriz states that price point is one of the most critical factors determining whether or not you get the sale. Increasingly, the buyers are playing it safe and won't buy if a product is slightly higher priced, even if the materials and construction are worth it.[22]

Your collection must have "hanger appeal" to attract customers to the rack and help it sell. Buyers also look at the value and quality of the production and how well the silhouettes, colors, and fabrics fit in with current trends. Some stores are more trend driven than others. P45 in Chicago focuses on promoting individual style; therefore, owner Tricia Tunstall does not go to market looking for trends. If sequins are hot, she may buy a few sequined items from her best designers, but in general, she feels that trends too often cause customers to burn out on a good thing.

Consistency is key. Buyers want to look at the product and immediately understand your viewpoint, even if they don't like it. Buyer Terri Gillis of the store TG-170 wants young designers to be true to themselves and stand for something. Being too driven by trends will dilute your identity, and it becomes difficult for buyers to know what to expect from you. She cites Tracy Feith, Paul & Joe, and Rebecca Taylor as all having clear identities and a sense of consistency from season to season.

The buyer must believe that you are ready as a business. The store's credibility is on the line, and buyers need to be confident in your production ability and quality control. Michael Fink of Saks Fifth Avenue says in the first season, his biggest concerns are if the product will be delivered on time and whether it will fit. Business stamina is important as well. Buyers don't want to pick up a line, promote it, and start building your customer base just to have you burn out financially, flake on your deliveries, and leave them hanging. You are a risk, and as we've already established, stores don't like risk.

Buyers say that press coverage might make them reconsider a designer or item if they are on the fence, but it won't sway them on an item they don't like. Julie Gilhart of Barneys New York says, "My biggest concern is that they can actually do what they need to do to make their things commercially successful. This means delivering on time and producing good-quality merchandise. In the end, no matter how much hype or press you have, these two things are essential for long-term success."

Press tied to the store can help increase or secure the order. For example, if you are going to be in *Lucky* magazine, a store might purchase your product to be listed in *Lucky* as the place to buy the item.

Buyers Are a Great Resource

Buyers' feedback is important whether or not they buy (and whether or not you agree with them!). They know what sells and what succeeds. Listen to their comments as they review the line and note what they do or don't like. The appointment is a rare opportunity for free, qualified advice that can help enormously with development of the line and with the next sales appointment. However, Ron Frasch, chief merchant at Saks Fifth Avenue, advises, "Don't listen to the buyers too much. Retailers tend to look too much into the rearview mirror at what worked

well in the past versus having the vision to look forward."[23] A designer needs to weigh the feedback of buyers against her vision and make sure she stays true to the focus and direction of the line. As designer Kristen Lee says, "You get direction in every direction over the years and have to really filter the buyer feedback."[24]

When a buyer sees a new designer, he may pick up the designer right away but more often will wait a season or two. Accessories are easier to pick up quickly because they require less space, but generally before a buyer commits to any line, he will watch to see if the business is stable and the line is creatively consistent from season to season. Don't be afraid to ask the buyer directly, "What do I have to do to sit on the floor at your store?"

After the appointment, thank the buyer for the time and consider the individual's reaction. If the store doesn't place an order, remember that rejection is not personal. Send a thank-you note and promptly provide any requested information or materials. Landing one good store can make the difference. Many designers have said that once they sold to a store such as Fred Segal or Henri Bendel, the rest of the stores came.

The Order

Only take orders you can produce and deliver on time.

An enthusiastic buyer who loves your product and wants to place a large order is every designer's dream. But you need to be realistic and up front about what you can and can't do. Generally, first orders are small, and chain or department stores will test a new vendor in one or two locations. But designer Rebecca Taylor warned not to take on too many department store doors or locations too soon. She shipped about 26 doors at Saks Fifth Avenue in her first season and says, "They came back with some charge backs and it practically put us out of business right then and there."[25] She recommends only doing six doors at the most at the major department stores. Too many locations with one store demands more up-front financing and creates more risk of shipping problems, charge backs, and returns.

While designers dream of getting their labels into luxury department store Bergdorf Goodman, Wen Zhou, CEO of 3.1 Phillip Lim, held them at bay for

more than a year before taking a small initial order to avoid overwhelming the company's overseas manufacturers or flood that market with too many clothes.[26]

Know your production schedule, and if the buyer requests a delivery date you can't guarantee, don't take the order. Try to negotiate the date or tell the buyer you don't want to jeopardize her business and therefore need to wait until she can provide more advance notice. While some designers have successfully taken on crazy deadlines just to land an important account, there is significant risk. If the store is important and you miss the delivery or have a quality issue because of the rush, it won't order from you again.

Delivery Dates

As your business grows, offering more deliveries will spread out the production payments and cash flow. The buyers like to keep fresh product flowing into the store, and additional deliveries each season, as well as holiday and resort deliveries, provide more opportunity to sell and stay in contact with the buyers. You don't have to create an entire collection for each delivery, just a new group or a few items. While you may start with one or two deliveries each season, eventually you will grow to have ten or more per year. A typical annual schedule could include three Spring deliveries, three Fall deliveries, one Holiday delivery, and one Resort delivery. Many designers add a Summer collection specifically to keep money coming in between Spring and Fall, which can be a long time without any cash inflow.

Generally, the designer sets the delivery dates, but the store sets the terms, which affect the dates. For example, for Spring, the designer may set a date, such as January 30, or specify a window, such as January 15 to January 30, to allow some flexibility. The store may specify a start date, which is when it will begin to accept the goods, or it may ask that the goods be delivered "as ready." There is always a cancel or complete date, which is the final deadline for delivery, and if product arrives after this day, the store can refuse it with no obligation. Stores with very fashion-forward customers may request early delivery to get fresh product on the floor before their competitors. For example, while most Spring menswear deliveries are in January, these stores may want delivery as soon as December 15. A designer should strive to offer earlier delivery to increase

the likelihood of the goods selling at full price on the floor, but you should only promise what you can truly deliver according to your production abilities.

Generally, designers break up their deliveries for a season by category. For example, the first Fall delivery would be T-shirts, lightweight pants, and jackets. The second would be heavier fabrics and fall colors, and the third would be winter jackets. A product that has a long season or is affected by weather may have other deliveries. For example, T-shirts may have Summer deliveries in May, June, and July.

Small Orders Can Be Unprofitable

Know how many of each item you need to sell to justify producing it. A certain quantity of a style might be necessary to meet the minimum arranged with the factory, and it may not be worth paying the high sample price for fabric to make a small number of a particular dress. Once you have all of your orders, you may need to call the buyers to drop a style. Communicate this as soon as possible. Although the buyer won't be happy, he understands minimums and expects this to happen occasionally. Try to get the buyer to replace the dropped item with another style in your line, rather than just canceling the order. Tell the buyer about other pieces that have been best sellers or point out similar styles. It's worth communicating the quantity you need to sell to produce the dropped style. If the buyer really wants it, he might adjust the order to meet the minimum.

Production limitations can sometimes be used to your advantage. Menswear label Duckie Brown often has only enough fabric to make a limited number of each jacket style, and its sales representative tells the buyer this up front. The limited quality makes the jacket more exclusive and creates demand. Sometimes it's OK to be sold out.

The Selection

A great collection can look terrible on the rack if the selection is wrong, and a buyer can make you look good or bad depending on what is chosen. For example, several designers caution against letting a store order too many of one style. A large rack with all the same style can look like a sale rack, and customers will assume it is all there because no one wanted it.

It's important to keep some control. Make suggestions on the right styles, sizes, and color combinations for the buyer's market. While some buyers have a

great sense for the collection and know what works for their store and customer, others need to be coached and pushed toward what will sell. Have options ready for the store. For example, if a dress is at a high price point because it's made from expensive silk jersey, offer the dress in cotton as a lower-priced option.

Assist buyers with the selection and then step back to avoid pressuring them when writing the order.

When buyers review a line, they look at both collections and items. Key items are often where they see themselves doing the most volume. Some designers are reluctant to sell items to a buyer who isn't interested in the whole collection, but showroom owner Denise Williamson says, "Designers should be flexible on that. The buyer knows what the store wants and if he sees the potential within the blouses, and that's what he really wants to promote in the store, I think it's great. It's a stepping stone. Perhaps next season he will come and say those blouses did so well, the pants look great too, let's add those on."[27]

Designers should be conservative with the stores when starting out, but as they get to know their customer and the buyers, they may be more willing to take more risk. For example, if a buyer from a chain of department stores doesn't order a particular item but you know the store in San Francisco really wants that style based on conversations with the sales staff, a designer could ship that particular item to just that store and guarantee it personally. If it doesn't sell, the designer will have to take the product back, but she knows the customer wants it and is willing to take the risk.

Special Requests

Buyers often ask designers to alter items or even create a special item to round out a collection or fit a trend. They may want a skirt to be shortened or request special colors or fabrics. If Roberto Cavalli is showing crochet-over print dresses, a store may want you to make a version to round out your line and attract trend-focused customers. It's important to adapt to wholesale customers and help them meet the shoppers' demands.

However, when making special items for stores, there are no guarantees. If it doesn't sell, the designer is stuck with something unwanted in the first place. Designers shouldn't agree to special requests unless it makes sense for their line. If a buyer requests crochet and crochet is not what you do, no one will win.

Buyer influence can push a designer too far into the mainstream, diluting what makes him special. Designer Alice Roi says stores regularly ask for items to be added to collection. She will agree, but "if they want something pink, it has to be my pink and done in my way."[28]

Some designers make extra money by creating private-label merchandise for a store. They might offer one of their popular items in different colors or slightly different styles and at a lower price because the order quantities are large.

Exclusives

Stores compete to find the next new star and differentiate themselves from their competition. They don't want to sell the same items as their competitors, especially if they are in close proximity to each other, and they will ask the designer for the exclusive on a line. An exclusive means you can only sell the line to that store according to the terms of agreement. Exclusive is loosely defined and changes according to each retailer. Some specify a geographic area. For example, in New York, an Uptown exclusive may mean you can only sell to Henri Bendel Uptown but you can still sell to Kirna Zabete Downtown. A Los Angeles store may require the exclusive for a five-mile radius. Some exclusives specify one particular competitive store and others require a period of time, such as six weeks, before the line can go to other stores.

Exclusivity is not always a bad thing. You don't want to overdistribute your product. If it's in every store, it won't seem special, and the sales results won't be good anywhere. Be strategic about exclusives and choose the right alliances to meet your goals. Womenswear designer and Project Runway contestant Alison Kelly designed an exclusive collection for Shopbop.com and says, "It was a very good move for me, as it would be my first wholesale order and I felt I could handle only one retailer that season."[29]

Loyalty is important to the buyer. When Tricia at P45 in Chicago picks up a new designer, she wants the exclusive in the city at least for one year in exchange for helping to launch the designer. When deciding between exclusives, pick the store that supports you the most.

Showroom owner Denise Williamson says that from her point of view, "You should never promise an exclusive until you see the actual order. If the

order amounts to $3,000, it's probably not beneficial to your business to only be at that one store. If it's a $15,000 order and the store is willing to get behind you with promotions, an in-store event, or by putting merchandise in the windows, it probably is worth it."[30]

If a buyer really wants the exclusive, you could require a bigger buy in exchange. Exclusives work within the season; next season is open for renegotiation. If you really don't want to agree to a collection exclusive with one store, you can offer exclusive items to be sold only at that store. Even if you have exclusives, you should stay in contact with other stores in the area in case anything changes. Designer Alicia Bell had an exclusive with a store in Texas, and another nearby store wanted the goods. The original store closed down, and she was able to ship the goods to the other store, avoiding returns and delays and ending up with a bigger order.

Controlled Distribution

Ana Beatriz, designer for Lerario Beatriz and owner of showroom Fiftytwo, says her biggest business challenge is growing at the right pace. While you need to grow your number of accounts and volume, you must also maintain image control.

Increasingly, as the market for new labels becomes more competitive, many designers are committing to a small, controlled distribution strategy. This approach emphasizes building retail accounts slowly and selectively with a focus on quality control and image. When a designer is just starting out, it is tempting to go for the money and sacrifice store quality. However, keeping a tight control over your image by carefully choosing the stores where you sell and slowly increasing your accounts each season can be key to creating a strong desire for your product and help you to stay "new" longer. Buyers want to have a sense of discovery and feel that they found something new and cutting-edge. While designers can't win the price battle against the H&Ms and cheap trend-driven brands, they can create something special that feels exclusive and highly coveted by both the retailer and the end customers.

Order Form

The purchase order should include the store delivery address, billing address, the style number and description of each item ordered (including fabric, sizes, and colors), the quantity of each, the price of each, and the correct delivery due date. The order form should be numbered and include your company information and terms (see figure 8.1).

All the pertinent information should be in writing. Review the terms and make sure they work for you. Confirm who is paying the cost of shipping and insurance. Double-check the packing and shipping requirements to make sure that you understand them and, again, tell the store up front if you can't comply. Don't process the order until you are satisfied with the terms.

Pricing terms specify which party covers which parts of shipping. FOB (free on board) is preferable, because it means you cover transportation to the shipping point and, from that point on, the costs are covered by the store. Many stores require the designer to cover the cost of shipping to the store's warehouse, and then the store will cover shipping from the warehouse to each individual location. For overseas delivery, LDP (landed duty paid) means that shipping and duty are included in the quoted price and paid by you, not the retailer.

Have a date to stop taking orders for the season. Once you close the selling season, confirm all orders and organize them on a master schedule for production and delivery.

FIGURE 8.1 Sample Order Form

Designer Name		Customer P.O. _____
Designer Address		
Designer phone and fax		Department No. _____
BILL TO _____		SHIP TO _____
ADDRESS _____		ADDRESS _____
CITY _____		CITY _____
STATE _____ ZIP _____		STATE _____ ZIP _____
PHONE _____		PHONE _____
FAX _____		FAX _____
BUYER NAME _____		ORDER DATE _____
TERMS 6/30		START DATE As Ready
SHIP VIA UPS		COMPLETE DATE 6/30
SALESPERSON _____		IN STORE DATE _____

SPECIAL INSTRUCTION:

			A	29	30	31	32	33	34	35			
			B	2	4	6	8	10	12	14			
			C	XS		S		M		L			
Style	**Color**	**Description**	D								**Total Units**	**Unit Price**	**Total**
2417	Navy	Wrap Tee			1		2		2		6	20 00	120 00
2789	Beige	Pocket Skirt				2	2	2	2		8	39 00	312 00
THIS ORDER SUBJECT TO TERMS AND CONDITIONS AS NOTED ON OTHER SIDE OF THIS FORM												**TOTAL**	432 00

BUYERS SIGNATURE _____

TERMS AND CONDITIONS

1. This order is an offer upon the terms below that cannot be withdrawn by Buyer prior to cancellation date. It shall be a binding contract upon acceptance by Seller. Seller shall indicate acceptance by shipment of goods to Buyer. Buyer understands that certain styles and/or sizes and/or colors may be unavailable. Buyer will accept all available styles, sizes, and colors.

2. This order is not cancelable prior to completion date and shall be subject to the terms and conditions.

3. No returns accepted without Seller's written permission.

4. Seller will not issue credit for any allowances, deductions, or materials returned unless Buyer obtains the Seller's written consent of same within 14 days of receipt of goods.

5. Any merchandise returned to Seller which is not found to have been non-confirming in breach of the herein warranty shall be returned to Buyer.

6. Buyer shall be responsible for all shipping costs incurred in returning the allegedly non-conforming merchandise to Seller and the merchandise must be shipped pre-paid.

7. Deliveries against this order are subject to credit approval by the Seller's credit department and/or its factor at time of shipment. Seller or its factor may, at any time and from time to time, in its sole discretion, limit or cancel credit of the buyer as to time and amount, and as a consequence, may require anticipation or demand payment in cash for delivery of any untitled portion of this order.

8. Terms are F.O.B shipping point and title passes to Buyer upon delivery to buyer or the carrier.

9. Prices on this order are based on present contracts for finished garments, yarns, fabric, and supplies, and on present labor cost. Should prices for any items be increased, the prices on this order will be subject to increase.

10. All orders are taken subject to delays or non-delivery caused by any reason beyond our control.

11. All claims must be made within five days of receipt of goods.

12. Past due charges at the rate of 1½% times the prime rate will be accessed on invoices not paid when due.

13. No waiver, amendment, or modification of this agreement by Seller shall be effective unless in writing and signed by Seller. No failure or delay by Seller in exercising any right, power, or remedy shall operate as a waiver of the right, power, or remedy. No waiver of any term, condition, or default of this agreement by Seller shall be construed as a waiver of any other term/condition or default.

14. To be Shipped By means Day By which goods are shipped from our warehouse.

15. C.O.D POLICY

 a. A 25% to 50% deposit is required at the time each purchase order is written.

 b. All shipments must be paid by cash or certified check.

 c. All or any part of the order that is not accepted is subject to a non-refund or your deposit. If a shipment is refused there will $50.00 handling fee deducted from your deposit.

 d. Your deposit amount will be applied towards your outstanding balance once the last shipment of the corresponding purchase order.

 e. Due to processing, The Shipper will be allowed to ship 15 days after completion date.

 f. Your store will be contracted before any shipment is made. If you do not respond to our initial call (with an approval) within 7 days, your order will be considered cancelled and your deposit will not be refunded.

Consignment

Sometimes, rather than place an order, a buyer will offer consignment at the store. The buyer won't buy the product but will put it in the store and pay you, minus a commission, for anything the customers buy. Consignment has pros and cons that largely depend on how much you value the store. It can get you in the door at a place you really want to be, and it's a great way for you and the store to test your product. Michelle Smith from Milly agreed to sell her first season at Bergdorf Goodman on consignment to get in the door. The collection sold well, and the next season the store bought.

Consignment in one store could also entice other potential accounts and pacify magazine editors who want to refer their readers to a place to purchase your product. It may also be your only option if you approach buyers midseason or after their budgets are spent.

However, some designers call consignment the C-word and resent the lack of commitment from the store. Consignment definitely works to the retailer's advantage: the designer is taking all the risk by producing stock for the store, which will be returned if it doesn't sell. David Ludwig, owner of DL27 showroom, says he would only recommend consignment if you already have the merchandise and need to move it out of your warehouse.[31]

Trunk Shows

If a buyer isn't ready to make a commitment but really likes the product, she might offer to hold a trunk show. This allows the designer to bring product into the store to sell for a day or two. It's a great opportunity, but realize it's a test and you must do everything you can to get the good results that will encourage the buyer to place an order with you. Try to schedule the date during a busy weekend and send out an email or mailer to encourage as many people as possible to come into the store on that day.

Eveningwear, hats, and other expensive or special item departments will sometimes host a special order trunk show for a designer. This provides a great opportunity for the designer to presell a few special-order items while being paid up front.

Immediates

Retailers increasingly want to buy "immediates"—items from the current season that can be delivered quickly to the store. Buyers are becoming accustomed to the fast turnaround offered by large manufacturers. Whereas buying six months in advance has more risk, immediates allow the store to respond quickly to a new hot trend or the demand created when a celebrity wears a particular item or label. The ability to sell immediates may help a new designer get into an elusive store or seize the opportunity created when another designer cancels a delivery or item and the buyer needs a quick replacement. At trade shows, many designers offer immediate delivery on specific items. While it may be tempting to over-cut best sellers to use for immediate deliveries during the season, there is always a chance that the store won't reorder and you will be stuck with the overstock.

Immediate can mean "tomorrow" if you already have the items, but otherwise it depends on how quickly you can produce. Anywhere from two to five weeks is considered immediate. Despite the incremental sales and increased cash flow provided by these orders, a designer has to be honest about what can be handled. Immediates increase the pressure to produce and deliver quickly, and they demand organization. If you take immediate orders for Fall, you will be producing that product as well as producing holiday and selling Spring at the same time. It can be confusing, and designers have been known to mix up items from different orders because of the crazy shipping schedule.

Getting Paid

Designers John Ross and Don Carney of Patch NYC said, "There are so many challenges working with stores and, unfortunately, the biggest challenge has been getting paid."[32] Unfortunately, getting paid by the stores is not as easy as it should be. After several calls to a well-known, reputable store, one designer who has been in business for 10 years had to show up personally with an intimidating friend to collect $20,000 in late payments. Another designer lost $45,000 to a well-known chain store that kept the goods and never paid. The story is too common, and while there are few guarantees, you can take measures to help get your money.

Check Credit

It is critical to check the credit of stores before you work with them. Set up an account with Dun and Bradstreet, and for an annual fee, you can call to get credit ratings on each new store. Have the store fill out a credit application and provide references. Call other designers who sell at the store to ask if it pays on time. Alternatively, you can rely on a factor. Wenlan Chia from Twinkle says, "Factoring is like buying insurance on the store orders."[33] She deals with numerous unknown stores, and her factor handles credit checks and guarantees payment on the stores it approves. She knows that she will get paid whether the store pays or not. (See "Factoring" by Tim Moore in chapter 3 for more information.)

Payment Terms

Some stores won't pass a credit check or be approved by your factor, but this doesn't mean you shouldn't sell to them. You simply eliminate the risk with appropriate payment terms. The terms greatly affect your cash flow, and the goal is to get your money as soon as possible. Negotiating power lies in how badly the store wants the product. Everything is negotiable, and stores make exceptions all the time. They may pay 50 percent up front when a combination of press, buzz, and customer demand creates urgency for the product. The sample order form in figure 8.1 includes an example of payment terms.

COD. When working with a new store, you don't have to extend credit. COD is your best option until you have sold to it for a few seasons and have established trust. When a store pays COD, it either provides a check on delivery or arranges with its bank to transfer funds into your account immediately upon delivery. Some designers require the store to pay COD with a certified check or money order at delivery because they have had a bad experience letting a new store pay COD with a business check that then bounced. If this happens, it can be a hassle to call and chase after the store owner to get your money or, in the case of one designer, go there and personally escort the owner to the bank.

As you build trust, you can adjust your COD terms in good faith for the store. COD 30 means you agree to hold the check received upon delivery for 30 days

before you deposit it. Unfortunately, some stores already postdate their COD checks by 30 or 60 days without prior agreement, and there is really little you can do.

Credit card. Accepting credit card payment from small stores is a great arrangement for both parties. The designer is paid immediately, and the store can pay off the balance over time. Ideally, you want full payment on the card up front, but the store may only agree to half up front and half on delivery or full payment on delivery. To accept credit cards, a designer needs to set up an account with Visa, Mastercard, and/or American Express, which will charge between 1 and 4 percent of the credit card sales. This expense needs to be built into your pricing.

Deposit. While not easy to obtain, a deposit provides much-needed cash to use for production. For new stores, you can ask for a deposit with the balance due COD until their credit is proven. Alternatively, if they pay a deposit, you might allow them 30 days from delivery to pay off the balance or even give them a discount on the total cost of the order. Many small stores justifiably refuse to pay a deposit because of being burned by paying up front for product that is delivered late or does not meet quality expectations.

Letter of credit. A store can also pay you with a letter of credit from a bank. It essentially vouches for the store's creditworthiness and guarantees the bank will pay you. With a letter of credit, you can be confident you'll receive payment, but most stores refuse to provide them because they are expensive to obtain.

Net terms. Generally, you should offer the big, well-known stores terms such as net 30 and require COD from small stores. Net 30 gives the store 30 days from the date of the invoice to pay you for the goods. Some stores even require net 60 or net 90 terms. The delayed payment can severely strain your cash flow. With any terms, be sure to invoice immediately when you ship to avoid further delays in payment. It is common to offer stores a discount if they pay sooner. For example, 8/10 terms offer the store an 8 percent discount if it pays within 10 days of the invoice date.

The payment terms on your sales forms should include a late fee of at least 5 percent for past due payments.

Past Due Accounts

Collection is tedious, frustrating work and takes up valuable time. Generally, your showroom won't help collect because the amount of effort isn't worth the small commission it would receive. While a designer desperately wants to collect $5,000, a $500 commission is not as motivating for the showroom. Most young designers cannot afford a retainer fee for a lawyer, and lawyers won't find the small percentage they would receive as enough payment either.

The problem is in your hands. Legal-looking letters can go a long way in getting payment or other restitution. One designer writes letters and copies a fake law firm on the bottom, but it might be better to ask a friend in the legal world if you can use the name of his law firm.

They key is to try to prevent the problem by being firm with your terms when the buyer places the order. Again, offer a discount conditional on receiving payment on time. Designers have had to bully or even threaten stores, and while sometimes this approach is effective, at other times, the simple reality is that the money isn't there and being mean won't make it come any faster.

Customer Service and Supporting Sales

The relationship with the store really kicks in once you have the confirmed order. You need to service each account and help the stores sell the product. Designer Liz Collins says, "The goal is to get the clothes into the stores and into the customers' closets. Not just get the clothes into the stores and then onto the sales racks, and then over to Century 21 [a New York designer outlet]."[34]

Delivery Is First and Foremost

"Nothing will kill a collection quicker for a retailer than for it to come in late," says Robert Burke, consultant and former senior vice president of the Fashion Office of Bergdorf Goodman.[35] A collection is expected to sell best during the first few weeks on the floor. The buyer needs to have the merchandise there, proving the right choice has been made. If the merchandise arrives late, the store can cancel the order, send it all back, and issue significant charge backs.

Avoid late deliveries at all costs, but if for some reason the product is going to be late, let the store know as soon as possible to give it a chance to make allowances or, if it cancels, give you enough time to try to resell the goods elsewhere. Many stores will try to work with you, but others won't. Michael Fink of Saks Fifth Avenue says, "If you're late, it's a big deal. We reserved dollars, floor space, and you let us down."[36] A store may put a late shipment on the floor and try to sell it, but if the merchandise doesn't sell, the store won't take responsibility and the situation will make it very hard to justify doing business with you again. If the buyer wants to cancel, offer a discount as an enticement to take the goods. If you can't sell them at any other store, you may even want to offer them on consignment.

You Are Only as Good as Your Sell-Through

For the larger stores and their buyers, it's all about the margins. They don't make decisions based on the drape, design, or detail of your fabric. Marty Staff, president and CEO of the Joseph Abboud Group, said, "A buyer is never rewarded for having a great T-shirt or sweater. The only thing they are rewarded for is the numbers."[37]

Retailers measure your success by sell-through—the percentage of items they buy that sell at full retail price. For example, if they buy 100 pairs of pants and sell 5 pairs in the first week, the sell-through for that store thus far is 5 percent. Department and large chain stores issue sell-through reports to the designer each week and judge the line, and whether or not they will order it again, based on these reports. Each store is different, but as a guideline, 75 to 80 percent sell-through is fantastic, 60 to 65 percent in the designer area will probably give you a reorder, and 30 percent is really bad—buyers will definitely not reorder from you. Sell-through expectation changes by classification. Up to 90 percent may be expected in a highly competitive category such as denim, T-shirts, jewelry, and accessories.

Good sell-through gives you power. Designers testify that buyers will negotiate discounts and be lenient with charge backs and allowances if the sell-through is good. A designer told me about a store that said it would never buy from him again because of delivery problems, but because of his strong sell-through, he is selling there still. Good sell-through can be used to entice new accounts and larger buys for next season.

Your Job Is Only Half Done

Monitor the sell-through reports from the bigger stores and call the buyer at small boutiques regularly to check on sales. You can't rely on the store to move the goods. Stores provide an opportunity, but designers need to take things into their own hands to make sure the product sells. There several things you should do.

Confirm delivery. Always confirm with the buyer that the merchandise was received and verify when it hits the floor. One designer shipped her goods and called the buyer a few times to check on sales. After a couple of weeks, the designer was shocked that not a single item had sold. She went to the store herself to check on the goods and couldn't find them on the floor. After an intense search, the store located her collection still in its box in a storage room. It had never been put on the floor.

Go to the store. The above example is one reason to visit the store once your merchandise arrives. Of course, you may be limited to visiting only the stores in your area, but many designers and sales reps travel to their accounts to check on the merchandise and find out what is selling.

It's important to see where the merchandise is placed at the store and how it is displayed. Check to see that your product is positioned with other appropriate designers in the store. A New York–based designer was fortunate enough to sell her collection to Jeffrey New York, but when I asked her how it looked, she said she didn't go see it for fear of being disappointed. That is exactly why you should go. Nothing will sell if your merchandise is smashed onto an overcrowded rack or hidden in a corner in the back. If the display or location is bad, you can fix it by informing the buyer or telling the staff on the floor.

When designer Shoshanna Gruss was starting her line, Shoshanna, I saw her multiple times at Bloomingdale's, checking to see what was selling and making sure her product was neat and displayed properly. I'm sure her dedication and ownership affected her sell-through and helped grow her business to where it is today.

Help the salespeople sell. The sales staff on the selling floor can be your greatest asset. They interact with the customer every day and have the ability to increase your sell-through.

Ideally, you want an opportunity to train the salespeople on selling your collection. Sales seminars are a common practice at both big and small stores. Simply ask the buyer to arrange a time for you. If you don't have a formal opportunity to train, at least stop by the store on your own and introduce yourself to the sales staff in your section. Salespeople love to meet the designer. It creates a personal connection and gives meaning to the line. Tell them about the collection, the materials, the inspiration, and where and how it is made. Show them ways the items can be combined and worn. If the sales staff has met you and understands the product, the next time a customer wants a black skirt, the salesperson will be more likely to suggest your black skirt.

Designers often work with the buyer to arrange incentives and rewards for the salespeople. A free handbag could be given to the person that sells the most that month. Maybe a pair of earrings could be the prize for the first person to sell one of the new necklaces in the line.

Learn from the sales floor. Salespeople have valuable information for your business. Ask them to describe the customer who buys your product. Inquire whether many customers buy one thing or just a few customers buy several. Find out which items get the best reaction, which get the worst, and why. Salespeople hear the customers' comments as they see your line and try things on. They can tell you about fit problems, issues with the fabric, or complaints about the price. Designers are removed from their retail customer; salespeople provide the link to real feedback.

If you can, get behind the counter for a day or two at a store and sell your own product. There is no better way to have firsthand contact with your customers and to understand what the salespeople need. Menswear designer Thom Brown worked weekends at Bergdorf Goodman selling his own line directly to customers. No one knew the product better than he, and I'm sure he received valuable feedback from all the customers shopping for suits.

In-store appearances. Many designers complain that the stores are not loyal and are more focused on building their own brand than yours. Too often, a customer who buys merchandise from a new label can tell you where the item was purchased but cannot name the brand. The best way to make the store more loyal

is to go directly to the customer and create demand there. If the customers request your product, the retailer will want to buy it and build a relationship with you.

Customers love to meet the designer. It provides a special connection or experience to enhance their purchases. A customer can show her friends a new handbag and tell them she met the designer and learned about the inspiration and materials in the bag. Personal connection results in customer loyalty. Make them feel special, and they will come back for more.

At a trunk show, the designer shows the collection, often on models, to a group of the store's best customers who then can place orders for the items. A personal appearance is a chance to meet customers, talk with them about the collection, and help them shop.

Personal appearances do result in sales. Oscar de la Renta once sold $2.4 million in clothes at a single trunk show at Bergdorf Goodman.[38] Designer Zac Posen is constantly on the road, appearing in stores to meet his customers and support his line. A designer should seek out opportunities to meet customers in the stores. When Michelle Smith of Milly traveled to Chicago for a Gen Art runway show, she scheduled a personal appearance for the next day in one of the Chicago stores that sells her collection. Designer Diego Binetti set up his hotel room as a showroom for appointments in Miami. Anytime you travel, try to arrange a trunk show or an appointment at a local store. The buyers appreciate the support and the reason to invite their best customers into the store.

Store advertising and promotion. When a designer's merchandise is featured in a store catalog or advertisement, nine out of ten times, the designer paid for it. The designer shares the cost of the page with the retailer to support the goods in the store.

Advertising is very expensive, and for a new designer, catalog co-op can be cost-prohibitive. But if you have any budget for advertising, partnering with the store is the best strategy. Store catalogs and ads are targeted, often to the customers who spend the most money, and will drive them to the right place.

Stores hold other promotions that you may choose to support. Special discount days may require you to cover the discount at the store, and customer incen-

tives might require a gift with purchase. Weigh the cost for each opportunity carefully to decide if it really results in more sales or just eats up your margin.

Reacting to Sell-Through

If your merchandise is selling out, you need to know to offer a reorder and quickly produce more of the bestselling items while they are hot. If merchandise isn't selling, you need to take action to help it out. Schedule an in-store appearance, create an incentive for the sales staff, or swap out some of the merchandise.

Swap outs. If specific items are not selling at the store, send the store other items that do sell well to replace them. You want the store to have product it can move to increase your sell-through. For your own image, you want to keep your goods off the markdown rack. If swap outs don't work and nothing is selling, consider having the store return the merchandise before it is marked down so you can sell it elsewhere. Less merchandise in the store will make your sell-through look better.

Realize that each market is different. One store will tell you the clothes are running big, and another will tell you the same clothes are running small. Different markets respond to different product, and designers can often swap items between stores. If a particular store is really struggling with your line, send a few of the bestselling items to see if they get a response. If that doesn't help, the store is not right for your product.

Don't get beaten up. As much as you need to take sales responsibility into your own hands, sometimes it's appropriate to be firm in dealing with the stores and push some responsibility back on to them. For example, if your line is selling great at some stores, ask the buyer why it isn't selling at his. Tell him about your great sell-through elsewhere and ask him politely what he could be doing to improve sales.

How Buyers Decide to Buy Again

The efficient way to grow your business and brand is to not just grow the number of accounts but to grow the amount of product in each store and keep consistent orders from season to season. For a designer collection that is selling well, a 10 percent increase is typical for the next season.

The key to getting a store to return each season is having good sell-though and keeping your goods off the markdown rack. However, other factors are influential as well. It's important for the product to mix well into the store and to provoke good customer response. The stores also consider whether the designer did a good job in getting press to support the line in the store. If you have product in a magazine, the best way to reward a good account or entice a reorder is to give that store the press credit as the place where shoppers can find your line.

The designer's customer service is another important factor. Tricia Tunstall, owner of P45, says designers Rebecca Taylor and Michelle Mason provide great service to her store. They arrange for swap outs, call to check on the sales, and make suggestions for the order. If a designer isn't willing to build the relationship and provide customer service, a buyer may choose not to work with her. There are plenty of designers out there without having to deal with ones who aren't pleasant. Customer service is very time consuming, and for some designers it's too personal to handle by themselves. If this is the case, hire someone with strong phone skills to make the calls for you.

Getting Rid of Leftover Merchandise or Overstock

Each season you need to sell off leftover or returned product before it becomes dated and results in a financial loss. Some options are to offer it to stores on consignment or try to sell it at sample sales, such as Billion Dollar Babes, or at young designer markets or shopping events. Another option is to sell the product to off-price retailers, such as Clothingline (www.clothingline.com), Find Outlet, and Century 21, who buy it at a significant discount. Online, Gilt Groupe (www.gilt.com) holds one-day, designer-specific shopping events to sell high-end product at discounted prices to its invitation-only membership. Some designers host their own sample sales, and in a few cases, they use leftover fabric and materials to create stock just for these sales, in the same manner that big manufacturers produce product specifically for outlet malls.

Who Should Sell the Line?

There are a few options for selling your collection. A designer can sell it personally, hire a sales rep or showroom to represent the line, or hire someone to handle sales in-house. Each approach can work. The designer must simply decide which will be the most effective at landing the desired accounts.

However, when starting out, sales experience is extremely valuable. Most salespeople and buyers recommend that a new designer pound the pavement and get firsthand experience selling his own line for at least the first season. Showrooms generally prefer you to come to them with a few accounts to prove the legitimacy of your business, and the selling experience will help you better manage and negotiate with an outside salesperson or showroom.

Selling Yourself

In theory, no one can sell your product as well as you. You envisioned it, chose the materials, and had it produced. Buyers love to meet the designer. It helps them understand the brand and the inspiration behind the line. But many designers simply don't want to sell or feel they don't possess the right personality or skills. It can be very difficult to pick up the phone and pitch yourself, but you should try. It gets easier with each call, and you may discover a talent for it.

By meeting directly with stores or selling at a trade show, a designer learns the sales process, develops a rapport with buyers, and develops an understanding of customer needs. The buyer feedback will reveal the retail limitations of your collection and help you to be more successful at future meetings.

The most important and most difficult part of selling your own line is not taking it personally. Realize the buyers know what they want and need at a particular time for a certain customer; it doesn't mean your product isn't good. Listen to their feedback and learn from their criticism. The buyer who doesn't seem interested today might place the biggest order next season.

Showrooms and Sales Representation

Selling is not for everyone. It is time consuming, and designers may have trouble fully concentrating on sales when they need to design, source, produce, and manage a small business.[38]

A showroom offers a fixed location for several lines. Buyers come to the showroom to review multiple collections and to place their orders. For eveningwear designer Gustavo Cadile, this aspect of a showroom is key. He says, "Not only do you benefit from the showroom's connections and reputation to make sales, but it is really important to be with other designers." If a buyer came to his studio and only liked a few styles, she probably wouldn't bother to make an order, but if she goes to a showroom, she may like five of Gustavo's styles and five of someone else's, making an order worthwhile.[39]

An independent sales representative takes one or several collections to the buyers. He may or may not have a showroom location and may travel widely representing a line entirely or only in a specific territory.

Buyers often prefer to work with showrooms or sales reps because they are efficient, know the language of sales, and get right to the point, wasting less time than a typical designer. A buyer may be more likely to give straight feedback on your collection to a rep than to the designer, who might take the feedback or rejection personally.

Salespeople have skills and experience to negotiate terms, discounts, charge backs, and markdowns and to say no to difficult demands from the stores. Andy Salzer of Yoko Devereaux was thrilled when he joined a showroom and it immediately switched all his accounts from terms to COD or required a deposit. The stores are often more responsible about paying bills on time when you're with a showroom and the showroom has a payment history with the stores via other clients. Showrooms know who is trustworthy and will check credit for you. Many even have a "blacklist" of stores they won't sell to because of past payment problems or cancellations. Steven Alan of the Steven Alan stores and showroom says, "We generally don't have trouble getting the stores to pay. As a multi-line showroom, we rep several designers and the stores know that if they don't pay, we won't sell to them anymore. For a designer who reps themselves, especially if they are not factored, there is a chance that they may get burned."[40]

A salesperson can be very helpful in development of the line. Designer Gary Graham says, "If you work with a salesperson who really gets your work, it can be exciting. They want to make money and can merchandise the line to sell it better. They can tell you they need a pant or a tank top, and you trust them."[41]

Andy Salzer agrees and says that at his showroom, the salespeople are not only connected to the buyers but also to the floor managers in the stores. They are in the stores weekly checking on the stock and presentation, and they help with product development and strategically planning the deliveries.

While that adds up to a lot of advantages, it's not all rosy. Designers warn that you don't really know what is going on at the showroom and whether it is truly representing the line well or servicing your existing customers. Things can go wrong, and there are many horror stories. A showroom started by a woman with strong industry experience and manufacturing knowledge had impressive lines and was selling to good stores. All of a sudden, she stopped returning calls to her designer clients, and the designers stopped receiving payment from the stores. One of the designers came to New York to check in and realized the owner had convinced the stores to write the checks to her, closed her showroom, and taken off with the designer's money and samples. Another showroom sent a designer's samples to a big chain store that copied them all and sent back the copies rather than the originals. Yet another mixed up the seasons and put the designer's current samples that should have been in the showroom in her sample sale. Half of the pieces were sold before the designer discovered the error.

Finding the right representation for you. Showrooms can be set up easily with little investment, and they are just as easy to close. Lawyer Steven Hahn warns that a contract isn't worth the paper it's written on if you don't trust the person. You need to find reputable people whom you trust and who can accurately represent you.

The best way to find a good sales rep is to ask experienced people in the industry. The buyers you sell to and other designers can recommend reliable people. Some designers walk the trade shows to meet the reps there. They approach them and observe how the rep presents the lines. Before you commit, meet with many potential reps and showrooms—and meet with them several times. Call a few of their clients for references and try to talk to designers who have left. In the end, consider the issues below and go with your gut.

- Business credibility. Find out how many years the showroom or rep has been in business and research her industry reputation. A reputable showroom will help you appear more legitimate and act as a prescreen for the retailer. A

buyer will know you have reached a level of acceptability by being selected for that showroom.

- Connections. Find out which stores the showrooms or rep sells to each season and where he has the strongest relationships. Ideally, he should be working with your target stores. Michelle Smith from Milly says, "Being with a sales showroom from day one really helped to propel the line quickly into the stores. The showroom already had the contacts and relationships, whereas on my own, I would have had to start from scratch."[42] Test the rep's knowledge by mentioning a few stores to see if he knows the buyers.

- Lines represented. Before you meet with a showroom, find a list of its clients and think about whether you want your product displayed with these labels. The other lines should complement yours and appeal to a similar target market, price point, and quality level to attract the right buyers. Some designers recommend avoiding a showroom with directly competitive lines, but David Ludwig of the DL27 showroom says, "Hanging with a comparable brand is no problem. If the buyer likes the aesthetic and is looking for that type of product, they will buy both."[43]

- Keep in mind that the stores have a different set of buyers for bags, shoes, and ready-to-wear. For a shoe designer, your aesthetic may fit perfectly into one of the most highly regarded and heavily trafficked showrooms. But if you are the only shoe line there, no matter how many top ready-to-wear buyers visit, they will not buy your shoes. It may be best to handle your sales in-house.

- Number of lines. Big showrooms have more lines and more salespeople and are well known and attract more traffic, but a designer there may receive less attention. If you aren't one of the hot lines being pushed or attracting a lot of press, you could be left out. At a small showroom, the salespeople are able to give more attention to each line and work one-on-one with the designers. However, they are less well known and have fewer clients to attract the buyers.

- Sales and service approach. Try to get a sense of the personality and approach of the salespeople. Their approach and the way they service customers is key to the success of your line. Aggressiveness is important to land appointments and close sales, but if the rep is too pushy or rude, buyers may avoid her. Find out if the rep will involve you in the sales process. Buyers still want to meet the designer, and ideally you should have occasional meet-and-greets at your showroom. A good sales rep will handle customer service, follow up with the stores regarding deliveries, and handle sales training. Reps can also help you

with more than sales by advising you on pricing strategy, product development, and merchandising; helping to create a strong lookbook; or getting your line into a trade show.

- Territory. Ask whether the showroom has reps or another location in other cities and whether they travel, participate in trade shows, or cover foreign markets. It's good to find a showroom with worldwide contacts but beware of road reps that insist on covering a huge, unrealistic territory. Although most buyers travel on buying trips to New York or to the trade shows, they love the convenience and one-on-one attention that comes with seeing lines in their own store. Many designers have a showroom in New York and one in Los Angeles or Europe. They may have a New York showroom and a rep that travels their line to other markets. Start with a New York representative before you branch out to Chicago, Los Angeles, Dallas, or elsewhere.

- Length of agreement. Occasionally, a showroom will offer to test your line for a season, but most require a commitment of two to three years. It takes time to build a new designer's business and get the name out to the buyers. If the rep spends a season working to build your name, he wants to be able to reap the rewards in the seasons to follow.

Getting in. It may take some time and effort to get into a reputable showroom. Generally, a showroom will consider you if there are no conflicts, the line has a strong identity, and the quality is good. Send the showroom a press kit and then call to ask for an appointment to make a presentation. At the presentation, the reps will review the collection to see how it fits in with their other clients and think about their buyers and whether your line fits their needs and tastes.

Showroom owner Denise Williamson looks at the whole presentation—the materials, the collection, the designers themselves, and their drive and willingness to work with the stores and the showroom. It's not just about the clothes; she is investing in the person. She has to believe you can deliver on time and will produce good quality. The showroom's reputation is on the line if the designer messes up.[44]

Steven Alan and Lynn Rosetti of the Steven Alan showroom and stores ask designers about their experience, whom they have worked for, and their relationships with their factories. As Lynn says, "We usually won't pick them up until they have shipped at least one store, but if the background is right we might

make an exception. We might try them in the store for a season to see if they deliver on time and have good quality."[45]

Press coverage can help sway a showroom, and in truth, it doesn't hurt if the designer is well connected or cute. If you are new, the showroom may want to wait to pick up your line until it has a customer following and a few retail accounts. At other times, a showroom may simply be full and can't take you unless you fill a gap for them.

Payment and terms. Showrooms and sales reps both charge a commission on sales. Showrooms charge from 10 to 15 percent, with 12 percent being the most common. The percentage may go down as the sales volume increases. For example, for $1 million in sales or less, the commission may be 12 percent, but at $1 million to $2 million in sales, it goes down to 11 percent. Showrooms and sales reps receive their commission upon payment from the store, not when the store places the order. This prevents them from being paid on orders that are canceled or returned. Road reps are typically paid a 10 percent commission, but many require an advance on their commission to help cover their costs until the stores pay. You will need to pay their fees for trade shows and possibly cover other expenses, such as those for travel and telephone.

Realize that a 10 or 12 percent commission may sound insignificant, but as one designer said, "What I wouldn't do to have that 12 percent back now." If you sell $300,000 in a season, 12 percent is $36,000—a lot of money for a small company.

U.S. showrooms often charge a monthly "rack fee" in addition to commission. The fee can range from $500 to more than $1,000 per month. If you are fortunate, it will be structured as a "draw," which is taken out of the commission when the stores pay. It is possible to negotiate different combinations of commission and monthly fee, but be sure to estimate the total end cost. A designer may negotiate to pay a higher commission to save money on the fee, but if it's a successful season with high sales, the designer might have been better off paying the higher monthly fee. Before you sign, read your contract carefully and negotiate the clauses that don't work in your favor.

It is standard practice to relinquish all of your existing accounts to your sales showroom. This avoids confusion about who is handling which stores and makes it clear for the buyers. But again, everything is negotiable, especially if the showroom really wants your product. A hot menswear label negotiated with one of the best showrooms to pay only half the monthly rack fee and to pay it only for the two key selling months. It also negotiated to keep its existing accounts and only pay commission on new stores.

Several showrooms offer public relations services, which can result in a higher monthly fee or commission. Combining sales and PR in one place can save you money compared to hiring an additional rep for PR, but if you don't need the PR service, you should negotiate a discount.

Manage the relationship. Don't leave a showroom to handle sales and simply trust it will be OK. Despite the commission incentive, salespeople can be overwhelmed by the number of lines they represent or may focus too heavily on another line that is getting a lot of press and is considered an easy sell. Check in constantly to ask what is selling, who has been in the showroom, and what meetings are coming up each week.

Listen to your salesperson's feedback on what the buyers want and their comments on the collection. This can offer valuable input and suggestions, but if the advice doesn't really make sense for your line, or is given to you with bad sales results, take it with a grain of salt.

If you decide to leave a showroom for any reason, be professional and try to depart on good terms. Fashion is an extremely small industry. People talk, and you may end up working with them again in the future.

In-House Sales Representative

Once you have the financial resources and are more known in the market, you may consider hiring someone to handle your sales in-house. While it's expensive to take on a full-time employee to represent your line, bringing sales inside puts control back in the designer's hands and allows one person to understand the collection fully and be involved in merchandising and developing the line and the sales materials. It is also easier to control your positioning in the mar-

ket. As Amanda Thomas of Loeffler Randall explains, if you have a $500 cashmere sweater and another label in the showroom has a $300 cashmere sweater, it's much harder to emphasize the differences in quality, design, or construction, as too often the buyer will just go on price point.[46] Customer service can be difficult to handle through a showroom. If something changes during production of the collection, the designer needs to communicate that to the buyer, something the showroom is sometimes reluctant or can't be bothered to do. An in-house salesperson can also travel to the stores to check on the merchandise, conduct sales education and training, and develop relationships with the buyers and salespeople. Hiring an experienced salesperson allows the designer to benefit from that person's past experience, contacts, and professional reputation with the buyers.[47]

Trade Shows

Trade shows create a group-selling environment by bringing dozens of designers into a single location to meet hundreds of buyers. There are dozens of shows in the United States, Europe, and Asia that each attract buyers from all over the world. Trade shows offer a great opportunity to make contact with retailers, especially if you are not with a showroom. The designers benefit from the draw of the other designers and can show their line to numerous buyers they wouldn't otherwise meet due to time and travel constraints. In addition to buyers, editors attend the shows, and there are opportunities to make contacts with importers from other countries and distribution companies that could rep your line.

The biggest downside of tradeshows is the expense. The smallest booths start at $4,000 and can be as much as $8,000, depending on the show. It costs money to create your display, ship it and the collection, create promotional materials, and hire staff. As one accessories designer put it, a trade show easily costs $10,000 by the time you pay for the space, the lighting, extra samples, and staff. The buyers generally show up with a budget in mind, looking for specific things. They are often reluctant to place an order with a new line and instead put you on their mental list for next season. You need to go back for a second

season, resulting in a $20,000 expense for the year. This can equal a significant percentage of your annual sales.

Choosing a Show

There are shows for womenswear and accessories throughout the world, such as Designers and Agents in New York, Los Angeles, and Tokyo and Coterie in New York; menswear shows, such as Capsule in New York and Pitti Uomo in Florence, Italy; and accessories-only shows, such as Accessories Circuit and Sole Commerce. Each show is different, and while the large, well-known shows may bring in thousands of buyers, your product may do best at a small specialty show that attracts buyers from small, exclusive boutiques. To review a show, first call or email the show organizer and request an exhibitor kit. This should contain a list of past exhibitors and past attendees, which will indicate whether the show is focused on your market and will attract the appropriate buyers for your line. Talk to other designers, past exhibitors, and even buyers about their experiences with the show and ask for their recommendations. Try to visit the show before you sign up. Walk around and see the booths to get a sense of the quality of the traffic and whether the exhibitors are actually writing orders. One person's experience will differ from another's. A bad show for one designer could be a great show for you, based on who walks in the door.

Getting In

Once you pick the right show, you need to be accepted. This process varies in difficulty depending on the show. Coterie, for example, is a well-established show with little room for new exhibitors. Each show will carefully review each new applicant to decide if it will even let you buy a space. The show organizers want the same things as the buyers: a focused, concise line with a clear identity, quality of construction, the ability to fill orders and deliver the goods, a price point that reflects the product, a reflection of current market trends, and a direction that fits in with other vendors or fills a gap at the show.

Being with a showroom can help if you can't get into a show as an individual. Showrooms buy large booths to display all of their lines. Even if you aren't with a showroom yet, you can try to find one that has space at the show

and product comparable to yours. Ask if the showroom would let you pay a fee and commission to come in as part of its space at the show. It's a long shot, but it happens. If it has room for another line, it may help you out in the hopes of getting more business at the show.

Before you pay for the trade show, talk about your location at the show. Small, lesser known companies aren't given the best spots on the floor, and you should make sure you aren't stuck in a bad location at the back of the show or in a corner that won't get much traffic.

Making the Most of the Show
by Barbara Kramer, coproducer of Designers and Agents

Prior to attending a trade show, the designer should do as much outreach as possible. For very little money, a designer can create a postcard that will represent his brand and send it out to their wish list of customers. A second option along these lines is to create an e-vite and forward it to all of the customers on his list. The designer would have to collect all the e-mail addresses beforehand, which entails some legwork. We then suggest that the designer place a phone call directly to the buyer or buying assistant and inquire if she received his communication and extend a further invitation to visit them at the show.

At the trade show, presenting a lookbook to first-time customers is a smart branding idea, as the buyer is first formulating her impression of this new brand and putting your personal spin on what she views is always to the designer's advantage.

How you design and create the backdrop for your booth goes a long way in telling the story of your brand. A new company can look like an established brand simply by being professional in its presentation. The look of the booth might become a corporate design that is always presented with a color or graphic change influenced by the current season it is selling. Perhaps a designer might change the look concurrent with the new theme for that season. Whatever the approach, having a clear and uncluttered space is important, because above all it is the product that must be given priority.

Proper show etiquette is very important. Make sure that your booth is organized and ready for work. After you finish working with a customer, return your merchandise back to its original spot so you are ready to greet the next client. It is important

to present a welcoming space to everyone through a smile and comfortable body language. Never eat anything that requires two hands while stationed in your booth. Leave reading materials such as books or magazines at home. If you are having a slow patch, take out your notebook and write something down. Never approach customers in another vendor's booth and avoid tagging them in the aisles. Buyers really hate to feel cornered or pressured by the seller. The more inner confidence you present the better your experience will be.

It is always the objective for a designer to procure an appointment with a buyer at the show. If a buyer has an ongoing business with a brand or designer, he is more likely to make an appointment in advance with that person than with someone who is unknown. Usually buyers initially walk the show and make notes on which stands they plan to return to for either a closer look or actually to sit down and write an order.

It is always a good idea to collect business cards from all of the visitors to a booth. I recommend making a note on the back of each card during the show so the designer doesn't end up with a pile of cards and no idea what they represent. It is also a good idea to email buyers after the show, thanking them for their visit and asking if they require further information. For buyers who have taken notes in a designer's booth, it is a good idea for the designer to make a follow-up phone call the next week and check on the possible order. We call it "dialing for dollars"! Follow-up is 50 percent of the work.

Caution

At trade shows you will meet buyers from many stores that are unknown to you. You should require COD or credit card payment or run a credit check before you accept orders from these stores. Don't accept large orders from a new store. It's better to start small with an option to reorder. Ask questions about the store and which other designers it sells to make sure it's the right place for your line. Andy Salzer of Yoko Devereax asks for photos of the stores to be sure the image is right for his line.

Don't hesitate to talk to people. Greet everyone and immediately ask where they are from. Mass manufacturers have people who walk the trade shows to look for ideas to copy. Also, beware of "consultants" and buyers from mass chain stores

who can be as likely to knock off your product as to place an order. Your booth should be welcoming, but don't have everything out in the open, and don't just give your line sheet to everyone before finding out where that person is from.

Overseas shows can open up entirely new markets for your business, but these trade shows bring greater cost and more risk and you want to make sure you are ready. If you do exhibit overseas, it's a good idea to have someone with you who speaks the local language.

Trade Show Alternatives

The high price and exclusivity of trade shows has sparked many designers to develop their own innovative ways to sell during market week. Designer Mimi Turner parks an RV across the street from Coterie and Designers and Agents for a few days each. She sets up her collection, along with those of a few other designers, in the RV as a mobile showroom. By sharing the costs, each designer spends much less than buying a booth at either show. They hand out flyers to the buyers entering and exiting the shows and invite them to see their collections. Mimi made sure to have her parking permits and insurance for the RV all in order, preventing the shows from shutting her down. Granted, some buyers were skeptical of the "unofficial" venue and wouldn't enter the "trailer." But others were intrigued by the innovative, renegade approach.

In another approach, approximately 15 designers shared a gallery space during market week in New York and invited buyers to come see them. They pooled their contacts, attracting buyers to see unknown lines and drawing on the excitement of finding something exclusive and unique.

A designer can also rent a hotel room or other space near the trade show venues during market week. For example, several designers with high-end collections set up in hotel suites in Paris during market week to meet with buyers. Just realize that the trade shows are time consuming and exhausting for the buyers. Many of them barely can get through everything at the shows, leaving little energy to hit other small groups or individual designers even a block away.

What is the single most effective thing you do that affects your sales?

"Having a showroom."—Gustavo Cadile, eveningwear

"Garner press. As a new brand trying to compete in the high-end luxury channel, the press that I get for the brand, both via magazine editorial and celebrities wearing my shoes, is critical."—Ruthie Davis, shoes

"I think the most effective thing for sales is having good product, good prices that make sense to the consumer, and knowing what advantages and qualities your product brings to the market."—Brian Wood, menswear

"Service to my clients and quality. If you work with them, they come back for more candy, especially if it sells."—Diego Binetti, womenswear

"A focused product and vision that remains consistent season after season. Brands that continually shift with the trends never become known for any one thing and thus can become obsolete with the next coming trend. By staying true to your vision, you are able to develop a loyal clientele who depends on your product to fill a particular niche season after season regardless of the outside environment."—Romain Kapadia, menswear

"The number one thing which effects sales is PR."—Ana Beatriz, Lerario Beatriz, womenswear

"Trade shows and photo line sheets."—Nina Valenti, nature vs future, womenswear

"Our showroom is amazing. Once we signed with them, things drastically changed and we try to listen to their feedback."—Annie Lewis and Helen Cho, Lewis Cho, womenswear

"Marketing and PR. Any brand will stay anonymous for years if the item is not seen in magazines, on television, and on the right arms of the 'it' celebs. I market my brand across the board from travel to business to everyday celebrity papers. It is great to get a bag in InStyle, but sales skyrocket when articles are written about the company."—Jessica Alpert-Goldman, World According to Jess, accessories

"*Doing a lookbook, effective line sheets, and keeping our website up-to-date.*"—Chloe, Samantha and Caillianne Beckerman, womenswear

"*Product. I believe PR can really help drive the sales, but at the end of day it's the product that has to hold its ground.*"—Grace Sun, womenswear

"*I would say fit. If the styling and fabric are good, the fit is the biggest factor at the retail end.*"—Jada Simons, Marie Marie, womenswear

"*Lifting up the phone. All my major accounts came to me because I am not afraid to cold call (persistently and audaciously) or call on people in my network. I cold called a major retailer and got a chance to meet the buyer, because I happened to call when she was looking to expand that line of the business. I cold called my school friend buyer at Target, sent him stuff about my company, which he forwarded on and on. I followed up and got to fly out and meet with the buyer a week later in Minneapolis. I cold emailed Donny Deutsch and two days later received a call back from the producers asking me to be part of the show. I cold called the founder of Vera Bradley hand bags, Discovery Toys, and the ex-VP of merchandising for Victoria's Secret (now member of the board for Limited) by calling everyone in the state of Ohio with that last name. All of these people are now my mentors and I am very fortunate to have them. For each of these "successes" I have dozens of dead ends, which is OK. In lifting up the phone, you have very little cost (besides fear, bitten nails, etc.), you get good at it pretty quickly, and the rewards are potentially very handsome!*"—Jane Ivanov, Eve Alexander, maternity lingerie

"*Selling our collection on our own. No one besides the designers knows all the intricacies of the garment and collection. We find buyers are more receptive because they feel special to know and work with the designers directly. We feel there is more honesty working directly with the buyers.*"—Jerry Tam, Form New York, womenswear

"*At wholesale—it's having a showroom. At retail, its trunk shows. They are my ultimate marketing expense. Coming to the stores and meeting the staff gets them excited about my product, which in turn always leads to better sales off the floor. Plus, it gets the store's customers excited and curious about who I am and my product.*"—Lara Miller, womenswear

"*Trade shows such as Designers and Agents have really helped with the growth in sales. I live in Miami which doesn't have much of a fashion industry like New York,*

so participating in a large scale buying period is essential."—Karelle Levy, Krelwear, womenswear

"I always attempt to visit the stores who carry my line."—Nicole Romano, womenswear, accessories

"I work with a showroom that understands my company and fully supports my vision for it."—Corinne Grassini, Society for Rational Dress, womenswear

"Talking to my customers. I always love hearing what my customers have to say, what they love, and what they can do without. Listening to them helps me understand their desires and what inspires them."—Christine Alcalay, womenswear

9

Press and Public Relations

Press is a driving force in fashion with the power to skyrocket a designer into the spotlight and drive demand at the stores. Press coverage is vital to helping a new name compete without the megamillion advertising budget of Gucci or Calvin Klein. The opportunities that press coverage can kindle are boundless. In addition to swaying buyer decisions and building brand awareness, press coverage can attract potential investors. Jeffrey Tweedy, former executive vice president of Sean John, said, "What got our eye into creating a joint venture with Zac Posen was the attention that he got, magazine after magazine after magazine."[1]

Good News/Bad News

The press is more interested in new designers now than ever. Television, magazines, and newspapers pay unprecedented attention to unknown names as they compete to find and declare the new stars. But the press can blow someone up too quickly, putting unrealistic pressure on a new designer who simply doesn't have the resources and support to live up to it. Success in the fashion business takes time, and even shows like *Project Runway* can't bring profitability to a designer. The show has been criticized for not producing a real success, as the designers who win seem to drift back into obscurity and face the same challenges as before. There is no *American Idol* in fashion.

Dealing with the media is a game, and you have to be thick-skinned and realize there is no loyalty. "The press in America love to build up people

and then start shooting pellets at them," designer Zac Posen warned a room full of hopeful designers.[2]

Warning!

Press is a tool—the means to an end—not an end goal in itself. It's easy to be seduced and distracted by the press and the attention it brings, but instant celebrity is not instant success and it won't keep you in business. As lawyer Charles Klein says, "The fashion cemetery is littered with the remains of fashion press darlings who focused excessively on press and not enough on the bottom line."

Many of the new "star" designers whose collections and lives are regularly triumphed in the press don't have the sales to back up the hype. Isaac Mizrahi went out of business in the late 1990s despite having a loyal following of editors and significant coverage in the newspapers and magazines. As author Teri Agins says in her book *The End of Fashion*, "What was missing from this happy ending was the only review that counted in the real world: sales in stores."[3] As another fashion magazine editor put it, "Do you want to tell your friends you were in *Nylon* or pay your rent?"

If you consistently have an 80 percent sell-through each season in a department store, or you produce pants that give women a consistently flattering fit, it's very difficult for the store or the customer to replace you. But to the press, you are entirely replaceable. Their job is to deliver fresh news every season. The writer has a story to tell and doesn't care if your clothes sell or not.

Sales Versus PR

New designers with limited time and resources should weight their focus heavily toward sales rather than PR. Designers often tell me that press coverage really doesn't affect their business, and many designers are quietly focusing on sales and getting rich. They spend their money creating a gorgeous lookbook and don't waste money on shows or chasing press. Although many people may not have heard their names, they have built a loyal clientele that provides them with great sell-through at

retail. An accessories designer told me, "My customers are smart, educated women who trust the store and the salespeople. They just don't read the magazines."

There is no denying that the press can open the door to sales. The influence of magazines on the retail business is enormous, and coverage in a magazine or WWD can land that first appointment with an important store or convince a hesitant buyer. Tricia Tunstall, owner of P45 in Chicago, says that while the press doesn't sway her to buy something that isn't already of interest, it does help if she is on the fence.[4] The coverage means that someone else sees the potential in the designer, and if shoppers are looking for the designer because of the press, her store will get more sales.

Buyers talk to editors to get their opinions and find out who is being covered. Shopping-oriented magazines that specify stores where products are available, such as Lucky, can move a lot of product, and if a buyer hears that you are going to be featured in one of these, he might pick you up just to benefit from the rush.

The PR Strategy

Sending out a mass press release or generic press kit to dozens of writers is generally not effective. Editors get hundreds of releases each week. They are busy people with long hours, tough deadlines, and specific missions. Chasing press is very time consuming, and you need a firm strategy. It's not worth spending hours answering questions and sending photos for a website that doesn't garner much traffic or isn't quite the right focus for you.

Do Your Homework

Just like researching stores, a designer should thoroughly research the publications and tailor her approach to be effective. *Elle*, *Esquire*, *Teen Vogue*, and *V* each have a different audience and target their aesthetic, opinion, and range of featured product to that readership. Spend time looking through the magazines and newspapers where you want your line featured. Determine whether your collection is truly relevant to each. Learn the section titles, the types of stories they include, and who writes them. For each target publication, determine in which specific section or column your story would best fit.

Each magazine approaches fashion differently. A celebrity angle helps considerably with *InStyle* but less so with *Lucky*, which is more concerned with where you sell. *Style.com* doesn't cover bridal or maternity, and you shouldn't contact it if you design for these categories.

Read each magazine to understand its "voice." *Nylon* speaks in a gritty, underground voice compared to *Teen Vogue*. *Esquire* is far more formal than *Black Book*. If you approach a publication using its tone, there is a greater chance of being covered. In addition, it's worth taking time to customize the press release or collection summary to the writer's individual style. It will help the writer visualize the piece in the column and save time and effort when writing it.

Magazines have editorial calendars, which are primarily used by the advertising department to send to potential advertisers. These outline the topics that will be covered in the magazine each month for the next year. If a story on beach escapes is planned for the January issue, target your pitch to that topic, and it will greatly increase your chance of coverage.

Don't aim solely for the obvious fashion magazines. Designers dream of being in *Vogue*, but plenty of other publications help build buzz and create demand. Travel, fitness, and lifestyle magazines all have fashion issues. Business magazines write about new companies and trends in fashion, and their coverage can validate your company to suppliers, lenders, retailers, and even potential investors. Websites are becoming more influential, and coverage on a magazine-affiliated site such as *www.elle.com*, *www.nylonmag.com*, or *www.style.com* can be easier to land than in the printed publication. Other independent websites or email newsletters, such as *www.hintmag.com*, *www.dailycandy.com*, *www.genartpulse.com*, or *www.refinery29.com*, have cutting-edge, influential readers and lead not only to consumers but to the large magazine editors who scour these sources for their own coverage.

What Editors Want

The writer's job is to provide interesting news and cover the trends. Think about how your story is relevant and state up front what makes you special. Sally Singer, fashion news/features director of *Vogue*, said, "The conglomerates have the ability to direct the trends, and if you are an independent with your own

point of view and it doesn't fit the trends, no matter how great you are, when editors are looking to show the trends of the season, they are not going to be showing your clothes."[5]

Amanda Ross, former market director of Harpers Bazaar, looks for something original with a point of view, along with the presentation, where it's sold, and where the designer worked before.[6]

As Laird Borelli of Style.com says, "Celebrity angles do help. Tell them if Christina Ricci just bought or wore pieces. But don't call about non-important things. If Christina Ricci's publicist bought something for herself, it's not news."[7] Keep the celebrity angle relevant to the magazine. You wouldn't call *Nylon* to say that Mariah Carey just wore your dress, but you would tell them if Maggie Gyllenhaal did.

Don't try to fool the press. Know your strengths, and if you are better at Fall than Spring, be open about it. Separate aspirations from current, realistic goals. For example, if an editor asks whose collection your line should hang with at the store, say that you aspire to hang with Chanel but right now would fit best with Catherine Malandrino.

When to Approach

There are long-lead and short-lead publications. Newspapers, which come out daily or weekly, have short leads, meaning that the writers work very close to their print deadline. You can approach short-lead writers at any time to pitch a story. If it relates to a specific event, such as a fashion week, or a regular feature for which they plan in advance, you want to contact them at least a month in advance. On the other hand, if your story becomes suddenly relevant to their coverage of current events, you can contact them and potentially be included in a story that week. If a short-lead publication calls you for an interview or for photos, respond immediately, or you might miss the opportunity.

Monthly magazines are long-lead publications. They take longer to write and to print, and their stories are assigned several months in advance. Plan ahead and contact them four months in advance. If you call *Elle* in July about a great item for September, it's too late. The September and March issues of the

fashion magazines are the biggest, because they introduce Fall and Summer respectively, and new designers have a better chance of being included.

Whom to Approach and How

The writers and editors are all listed in the front of each publication on the masthead. First send the press kit to the fashion news or fashion features editor, not the fashion editor or director. Send a handwritten, personal note to attract the editor's attention. Exploit any personal connections to the editors, drop names, or get someone in the industry to call and introduce you. The news or features editors will review your work to see if it fits any of their upcoming stories. They may also pass it on to the market editor to consider for upcoming photo shoots.

If you don't succeed with the features editor, you may contact the market editor as well. But if two people at one magazine say no, it's not going to happen that season, and you shouldn't contact anyone else. If an editor says no, do not go to that person's boss. Editors confer as a group, and if you go over someone's head, you will annoy them all.

After you send a lookbook to an editor, call once to follow up. Ask if he received the package and tell him you would be happy to set up an appointment to show your samples in person. He will respond by confirming he received the lookbook and will either want to make the appointment or will tell you the collection doesn't fit the stories he is working on now. Once he says this, do not follow up again until you have a new collection or important news, such as a new order from a key store or a big name celebrity wearing your design. Don't be pushy or argumentative. The editor has specific story outlines created by the fashion director. If your product doesn't fit what the director needs at this moment, it may be perfect next season.

It's important to understand the position of the editors. They are generally overworked, terribly paid, and challenged to balance integrity with advertising. While they might like to be in your studio seeing the next hot thing, in reality, they don't have the time. In the end, the lookbook will work harder for you than anything else. Results might not be immediate, but editors will keep it in their files and pull it when they are looking for new sources.

Court the young editors who are looking for new talent. You can offer to go to the office and meet with a junior editor to get in the door. If the junior editor likes your work, most likely the more senior people will see it.

And always be nice to assistants. You never know who will be the next fashion director; it might be that assistant editor you snubbed four months ago.

If you land an appointment or a "desk-side," be sure to be prompt and prepared. Have your samples clean, ready, and easy to access. Get to the point with quick descriptions, answer questions, and be open to feedback and criticism. Present yourself passionately as you represent your line. Editors respond to engaging but sincere personalities. Tell them a brief story that they will remember and respond to emotionally.

The press release. A press release announces breaking news to editors in a concise, easy-to-digest format. Not everything is newsworthy. Releases are saved for specific timely announcements that set you apart and are of interest to the reader.

When writing a release, the headline is key to getting attention. It should strongly announce the focus of the announcement in an intriguing way that makes the reader want to hear more. The first paragraph should get straight to the point and provide the pertinent information. The following paragraphs should expand the story and include more detail. Keep the release short. One page is best; don't have more than two. Include your contact information in case the writer requires further information. Don't forget to spell-check. Templates for press releases at www.prwebdirect.com and www.publicityinsider.com can help you follow the correct the format.

Send the release via email or fax. Never send it on a Monday or Friday when writers are too busy or may forget about it over the weekend. Call to follow up on the release. Be polite and get to the point immediately. Explain why the news is important to them and ask if they need more information or photos to include in the publication. Again, if they can't cover your story now, don't harass them. Contact them the next time you have pertinent news.

Writers and editors are on deadline. Always return calls promptly and be prepared to provide photos, samples, and accurate information quickly.

Photos. Most publications provide guidelines regarding the format and quality required for photos or artwork. Generally, you should be ready to provide 4˝ × 6˝ digital images at 350 dpi for both Web and print. The editor can always size the images down but can't enlarge them or improve the quality. Send the images one or two at a time to avoid clogging the recipient's email in-box, especially if you email the writer directly rather than the photo editor or art department.

Befriend the stylists. Stylists are key to getting your clothes into the editorial photo shoots at magazines. They seek to pull clothes and accessories that fit into the trend story for the shoot, and the exposure can be extremely valuable. The stylists are also extremely connected. The Rodarte designers Kate and Laura Mulleavy sent a letter to Cameron Silver, the well-known Los Angeles stylist and owner of the vintage store Decades. He reviewed the collection, liked it, and became a mentor, introducing the designers to other key people in the industry.[8]

A key way to find stylists is to flip through magazines and look at the styling credits. You can also find them and their contact information in industry guides such as Le Book. Make sure you have the stylists on your mailing list and keep them up-to-date with current lookbooks and information on where the line sells. Invite them to your runway show and to the showroom to see the collection.

Samples. Samples are valuable, and while you want to have them out working for you with editors and stylists, taking some precautions will help you avoid damage or loss.

To borrow product, a magazine editor or stylist will first call to inform you that she wants to pull pieces for a particular shoot. She should fax a letter of responsibility that includes the dates of the shoots or bring it when she shows up and selects what she wants. After selection, she may leave and send a messenger for the product, or she may need to take it with her immediately. The designer should package the samples and create a content sheet or invoice with a description of each item the stylist is borrowing along with its dollar value. Clearly mark a due date by which the items must be returned and explain that if they are not, the borrower will be charged. Granted, you need to make sure the due date allows a reasonable amount of time to complete the shoot and return the items, especially if the editor is shooting in the Caribbean or Egypt. Include one copy of the content

sheet with the samples and keep a copy for yourself. The more professional you are with this process, the fewer problems you will experience.

Exclusives

The magazines are extremely competitive and want to be first. Therefore, a magazine might require an exclusive, meaning the designer must give it the interview or story and let it print the article before the designer shares it with any other publication. Be strategic with your exclusives. A high-end magazine is less likely to cover you as a new designer if you have already been covered by its competition. For example, if you really want to be in *Elle* and another magazine calls, you can call *Elle* and tell the editor that you have been approached but that you prefer to give the exclusive to *Elle* if the editor will commit to running it. However, be realistic and don't turn down good press in the hopes of something that might not happen. If *Elle* isn't interested, find out quickly and discretely get back to the other magazine before it moves on to someone else.

If you have an exciting announcement or news that will be interesting to several different news publications, try to entice your first-choice publication by offering it an exclusive. Once it prints the story, the press release can be sent out to all publications in hopes of further coverage. Keep in mind that stories can be delayed or cut because of space constraints or other late-breaking news. You are at the mercy of the news editor, and announcements can be published a week or more late because of these delays.

Be Ready for the Results

An item in *Lucky* magazine, *Daily Candy*, or on *The Oprah Winfrey Show* can result in a huge response. Adam Lippes, creative director of Adam Adam Lippes, had an eight-minute appearance on The Oprah Winfrey Show that resulted in $500,000 in sales in one week.[9]

When the phone starts ringing, you need to be ready with distribution and production, or else you risk disappointing your new customers. To predict results, ask the editor or producer about the response for previously featured products that are similar to yours. Make sure you know the exact date when the show will air or the issue will hit the newsstand. Then make arrangements

with the store or website that is listed as the source for your product to be prepared if it runs out of stock. After doing this preparation, its best to underestimate the amount of production that you need. It is possible to be featured in a major magazine and have absolutely no response. It is better to be sold out and in demand than have tons of excess.

Saying No

Some designers are selective about which magazines can borrow samples. They want to keep tight control on their image or control the rate at which they are "discovered" to stay "new" longer. If they put themselves out there too much too soon, they can become old news before being newsworthy. If you don't want to be included in a specific magazine because of its image or because you are holding out for an exclusive elsewhere, be tactful in turning down the publication. You can tell the editor the samples are already out or are back in production, or you can be honest and say the magazine doesn't currently fall into your press strategy. But don't be offensive or rude. The magazine could become important later, or the editor could become an important fashion director somewhere else. When deciding which magazines are important, keep in mind that many of the most prestigious or niche publications have small circulations. Magazines such as *Glamour* and *Cosmopolitan*, on the other hand, have huge national circulations with more than 2 million readers each.

Staying Power

Once you have been covered as a new designer by the magazines, it can be extremely difficult to get more coverage, and you need to develop new angles.

The press wants new designers, and as Sally Singer of *Vogue* explains, "You do the new designer story once and then you start thinking, 'well, if she is a female designer, does she have a nice house? Do they have children or dogs?' because you want to keep people's work in."[10]

A designer's second season is harder than the first, because the collection is not as new and there is now pressure and expectation based on the first season. The new collection each season is often not enough to warrant fresh coverage, so you need something fresh to attract attention.

Think about what you are doing that is new and has a press angle—raising money for a charity, creating political T-shirts, launching an accessories line, or dressing an A-list celebrity. *Vogue* covered Twinkle when the designer started designing her own prints. Shoe designer Holly Dunlap received a fresh wave of coverage when she launched her dress line. If you are entering a new geographic area with sales, you can target press coverage in that new market as well.

Designer Rebecca Taylor sponsored a competition, and two students from the Laboratory Institute of Merchandising (LIM), The College for the Business of Fashion, won the opportunity to design a holiday window display in her boutique. This created a new press-worthy angle and showed the designer's support for the fashion industry.

Themes and collaborations create buzz for the press. Andy Salzer of Yoko Devereux says "It's important to be more than just a T-shirt. Collaboration gives meaning and context to an unknown brand and reflects the wearer's lifestyle."[11] He designed T-shirts with numerous visual artists, created a bag for Bumble and Bumble, and customized shoes for Dr. Martens. Lutz & Patmos, known for their luxury cashmere sweaters, invited highly respected celebrity photographer Inez van Lamsweerde, director Sofia Coppola, and architect Richard Meier to act as guest designers for different seasons to bring attention and cachet to their collections.

Accessories designers often get valuable press exposure by collaborating with a newsworthy clothing designer. Bing Bang designer Anna Sheffield collaborated with ready-to-wear designer Phillip Lim for a new line of jewelry, called 88 Fine Jewelry, to be sold in his store. For a fashion week, ready-to-wear designers look for unique accessories for their runway shows. A designer can loan shoes, belts, or jewelry or design custom pieces for the show. Eugenia Kim has shown her hats with Michael Kors, DKNY, Ralph Lauren, Diane Von Furstenberg, and Catherine Malandrino.

Collaborations need to make sense for your brand. It's brilliant when Heatherette designs for Miss Piggy, but for your line, such opportunities may be absurd.

Is All Press Good Press?

Not all press coverage is flattering, and new designers are understandably mortified by a negative review. But realize, first, that it's not personal. Second, at

least you sparked a reaction and inspired feeling versus being ignored. Third, the feedback might actually help you grow and mature as a designer. It's doubtful that negative press will affect your sales, and there is always next season. Bad press today matters less because the system is more democratic. People can now view your collection on the Internet or via television coverage on *Videofashion* or *Full Frontal Fashion* and judge it for themselves. Of course, this also means that good reviews aren't as powerful as they used to be, either.

The most important thing is to move on and not take it too seriously. If you waste time and energy fuming over press coverage, your priorities are in the wrong place.

Dressing Celebrities
by Roger Padilha of MAO Public Relations

Garnering press for your collection and company is one of the most important aspects of keeping your name "hot" and in the public eye—a necessity if you plan on building a luxury brand. How many times have you walked into a store and justified spending a lot of money on a designer's work simply because of the "buzz" surrounding the company? The designer world is built on dreams, and the one way to sell yourself as a desirable, must-have designer is by having your collections worn by the right celebrities.

Celebrity dressing is an expensive, time-consuming chore and can often backfire, so make sure you think through your strategy. For example, if you make clothes for Upper East Side socialites, it does not make a lot of sense for your clothing to be seen on the latest sultry hip-hop star. Make sure that the people you target are men or women who inspire your customers and are people they try to emulate.

Most celebrities now employ stylists who choose their clothing for red carpet events and appearances. Do not send clothing to managers, PR people, venue managers, people who say they are friends of the celebrity, etc. Your clothing will most likely be "regifted" by these people to their friends, and the celebrity will never see your designs. Celebrities pay their stylists a lot of money, trust them, and really do wear what they present. Find out who these stylists are (it's not hard, because they are constantly on TV fashion programs and often credited in magazines). Send them your

lookbook, fashion show DVD, and press kits. Be persistent but not pushy. Stylists are always interested in seeing new work, but after many years of experience in the biz, they have a very good sense of what is right for their client and what isn't. They do not want to hear your opinion on why Ms. So-and-So would look so much better in your outfit than that Couture Chanel the stylist recently picked out for her!

A stylist might ask you to make something special for the celebrity that is not already included in your line. This is a great way to gain entry into that celebrity's closet! But stay true to yourself. If you specialize in tailored suits and a stylist asks you to make leather hot pants, you might want to suggest that a different designer handle the project. When you do accept an assignment, listen to what the stylist needs but feel free to put your own stamp on it.

Never, unless very specific arrangements are made prior, give your clothing away! Celebrities only wear things once and do not need to hold on to any clothing. You need the outfit back for other important editorial placements, especially after it's been worn by that hot celebrity. I have heard horror stories of items being placed on eBay or sold to resale shops by the celebrity's assistant! The only time this is acceptable is if it is for charity and you have cleared it first.

Networking

Fashion is a small industry, and often an invitation to a single party or a courageous "hello" can put you on track to potential suppliers, editorial coverage, or investment. Fashion is a social industry that thrives on people. As an entrepreneur, you need other people and connections to help you find solutions and expertise.

It is critical to talk to people. Make calls—ask to meet with people just to tell them about your company. Get out and attend events. Go to the runway shows, fashion week parties, and other industry events where fashion people meet and ask others to introduce you to buyers and editors. It may be intimidating but force yourself to go alone or take someone who is connected and can make introductions for you. At a Council of Fashion Designers of America (CFDA) Business of Fashion seminar, Kristina O'Neill, the fashion news features director for *Harper's Bazaar,* advised designers to ask editors who like a collection to use their connections to help you meet stylists and celebrities. She calls this the "honeycomb effect" of the industry. Editors and buyers know

everyone, from each other to finance and production contacts. And Peter Arnell, founder and CEO of The Arnell Group, advised designers to reach out to people who have money and influence. He says people are desperate to do good deeds, and big names in the industry want to help smaller names.[12]

Often, powerful people will be more responsive than you expect. When Lazaro Hernandez of Proenza Schouler saw Anna Wintour boarding the same flight as he was at Miami airport, he asked a flight attendant to pass her a napkin on which he'd written a note. Weeks later, he received a call from Michael Kors's studio stating that: "Anna Wintour says you should work here."[13] Rodnik designers Phillip Colbert and Richard Ascott saw Anna Wintour standing alone at the British Academy of Film and Television Arts (BAFTA) film awards in London and said hello. They told her about their label, and she invited them to the Vogue Anglomania Ball at the Met in New York.[14]

When you go out, wear your product (if it looks good on you) or take a beautiful person dressed in your clothes and get noticed. When Zac Posen started out, he was constantly seen with model and celebrity friends wearing his designs. He was building buzz for a year before he even launched the collection.

Many designers are naturally shy. But as an entrepreneur, it is important to schmooze, and the more you do, the easier it will become. You don't need to talk a lot. Introduce yourself and ask questions. Be sincere and really listen. People like to talk about themselves, and you can learn a lot. When you do talk, talk about things that you are passionate and excited about. You don't need to talk just about fashion and business, but don't be negative or gossip. If there are specific people you want to meet, find out something about them first and learn to be brief and move on so you do not take up too much of their time. After you meet someone, always follow up right away just to say it was nice to meet them, and try to include a personal detail about them or your conversation so they know you were paying attention and can quickly recall your meeting.

If you really struggle with networking, you may want to seek media training to help you in social situations. For better or worse, designers increasingly need to have personality. Editors are looking for someone interesting to write about, and buyers want someone who can come into the store and charm the customers.

Blogging

Blogging has become a legitimate PR strategy in itself. Designer Robert Geller says that blogs directly affect his retail sales. The customers are passionate and loyal, and it builds an "underground" desire for the product. The buzz grabs the attention of established fashion editors and buyers who are encouraged by the customer base and cool factor that is already there. For a designer who is trying to control his growth and stay "new" as long as possible, blogging can be the first step to being "discovered" multiple times.

Some designers create their own blogs to build buzz and create a stronger identity and relationships with their customers. Holly Dunlap from Hollywould told the New York Times that her website receives an average of 80,000 hits a day.[15] Designers Rafe, Sue Stemp, and Malcolm Harris of Mal Sirrah are just a few who keep their own blogs.

Give-Aways

Designers are often approached to donate product for publicity opportunities. But samples cost money, and you should weigh each opportunity carefully to make sure the expense is worth the potential benefit. Handle it delicately if you say no, especially when an editor wants product for free.

Placing product in gift bags for major events, such as the Golden Globe Awards, can be beneficial, especially when you don't have an advertising budget. There are no guarantees that the item will be seen with a celebrity, but if it is, the impact can be huge. Jess Alpert-Goldman of the handbag line World According to Jess gave 250 of her bags to be included in the official gift bag at the Oscars®. She said it was very worthwhile because the Oscars represent the pinnacle of gift bags, which are given to every Oscar presenter and winner. If you participate in a high-profile gift bag, you should publicize your involvement. Jess says, "I worked hard to let the world know that World According to Jess was the only bag designer included in the official Oscar gift bag that year. I was able to get placement on The Today Show, NYC WB11, US Weekly, InStyle.com, Grace, The Record, and The Boston Globe."[16]

Opportunities such as the Oscars are difficult for a new designer to land, but there are many small gift bag opportunities, which may or may not be

worthwhile. Confirm who will receive the bags and consider the scope of their influence with respect to your line. Weigh the potential opportunity against the cost. Gift bags for high-profile celebrities, fashion editors, and buyers can be very helpful, but be wary of unofficial gift bags and promotions that attach themselves to major events but are distributed to people who won't really help your business.

Gen Art

One of the most prominent organizations that supports emerging designers is Gen Art. In the past 15 years, Gen Art has provided the runway premiere for more than 400 new fashion designers, including Rebecca Taylor, Chaiken, Cloak, Sari Gueron, Twinkle by Wenlan, Louis Verdad, Shoshanna, and Zac Posen. CEO and founder Ian Gerard started the fashion program in 1995 because "at the time, unlike in art, music, or film, there was little industry-created support for new fashion designers."[17] Now Gen Art's high-profile fashion shows take place in New York, Los Angeles, Chicago, San Francisco, and Miami before hundreds of influential members of the fashion industry and press. Gen Art provides designers with additional support through competitions, business seminars, networking events, sales opportunities, and referrals to the industry. For information on how Gen Art can potentially help you, visit its website (www.genart.org).

Competitions and Industry Awards

Competitions and fashion awards can provide press exposure, money, industry attention, and validation. Designers who have won the Gen Art Styles Competition credit it with bringing many exciting opportunities, including investor interest, press exposure, new retail accounts, and future sponsorship. Fashion Group International has the Rising Star Award, Ecco Domani annually awards $25,000 each to five designers, and the CFDA/Vogue Fashion Fund provides $300,000 in grants to designers each year. Each year in France, the highly esteemed Hyeres International

Festival of Fashion and Photography awards large financial prizes, production support, guest design opportunities, and media exposure. Other, more obscure competitions are sponsored by fabrics and corporations. For example, The Australian Wool Innovation Protégé Project partners young designers with high-profile mentors, who have included Karl Lagerfeld, Donatella Versace, and Paul Smith, to design an Australian merino wool-based collection. The Swiss Textiles Award, now in its fourth year, offers a grand prize of 100,000 euros that comes in the form of assistance in developing an international fashion career and 10,000 euros in fabric vouchers.

It's important to explore opportunities and be open to what they can provide. Evaluate whether the effort is worth the potential award and keep your eye on the real prize of selling your collection and achieving your overall business goals. Don't let competitions and grants become distracting.

Who Should Handle PR?

The above information assumes that as a new designer, you are handling your own press. Obviously this approach will save you money. Nancy MacDonell, formerly of *Nylon*, says, "A designer should not be afraid to call the editors directly. It's their job to get new sources to keep their editor-in-chief happy."[18] In fact, some designers don't work with PR agencies because they say the editors who matter want to talk to the designers, not the PR people.

However, pitching and servicing the press is time consuming, and often it's even more difficult for designers to pick up the phone and handle their own PR than to handle sales. A PR representative with a strong reputation can open doors. That professional has personal contacts at magazines and television shows and knows what stories the writers are writing, and the editors and producers trust the rep's recommendations. A PR firm will work on your behalf to develop your press materials; pitch your story to the press; send samples to editors and stylists; and often handle press or even production of promotional events, parties, or runway shows. Most often, a press rep will house your collection in a showroom, and editors and stylists can go there to review or pull for shoots.

As with sales, your PR firm represents you and your brand. If your product is perfect for *Paper* magazine, don't go to a firm that is very *Town and Country*.

Before you hire, interview many representatives to find the one who believes in your product and understands your goals. Ask who else she represents and for how long, and call some of her other clients as references. Find out who represents the designers who receive the coverage you desire. Ask the reps if they have contacts at the magazines and press outlets appropriate for your line. Review their press files to see if they have landed features and items for other clients in these places.

The Cost of Representation

PR firms are usually hired on a monthly retainer, which can range from $1,500 per month (at a small or generous firm) to $10,000 per month. You can and should negotiate price, especially if your line is hot and will bring cachet to the firm's existing client list. It's not unheard of for a firm to take on a new line for free because of the potential to excite editors. PR firms usually charge for expenses on top of the retainer. Keep an eye on these and dispute anything that seems extreme. One designer was shocked to receive a bill for sushi and cheesecake ordered by her PR firm's interns.

When choosing a firm, consider whether it's better to be a small fish in a big pond versus a big fish is small pond. One designer left a very prestigious firm where she was paying $10,000 per month for a smaller firm that cost only $4,000 per month. While the bigger firm was well known and connected and brought legitimacy to her new label, her account was more important to the smaller firm, and she received more attention and service there.

Actively Communicate With the Rep

When working with a PR firm, it's up to the designer to regularly communicate her PR goals to the rep. Listen to the rep's advice and the feedback he receives from editors to make sure the goals are realistic. If he tells you that the exciting "news" you provide to him isn't interesting the press, brainstorm with him to find something else to pitch. Keep your press person up-to-date with accurate information and check in often. It's frustrating to pay a monthly fee if you aren't getting any coverage. Ask him for updates on whom he pitches and the response. You want to stay with a rep long enough to let him build momentum for you as his client, but be aware if he is burning out on you or is just not able to land meaningful coverage—it might be time for a change.

10

The Runway

The runway is the epitome of fashion glamour and intrigue—the world of Ralph, Oscar, and Karl with models, backstage frenzy, bright lights, cameras, and celebrities. Many new designers feel a fashion show is the apex of success—that moment in the spotlight that gives the sense of playing with the "big boys."

Fashion shows are powerful and can catapult a designer into the industry eye. If the right people attend and the collection is strong, the press will cover you, the stylists will pull clothes for magazines and celebrities, buyers will be intrigued, and the public will learn your name. Lindy and Kathryn of Palmer Jones hold runway shows to position themselves as a competitive luxury firm. They feel that it's even more important for small companies like theirs to have a show than the big brands, because they don't have money to advertise and a show, if done well, can provide important visibility.[1]

No one can blame a designer for wanting to get work out onto the catwalk, especially when he spends the rest of the year slaving away alone in the studio. Designer Louis Verdad confirms, "The 15 minutes on the runway is very rewarding after working for six months."[2]

To Show or Not to Show

The Financial Reality
Behind the glamour sits the harsh reality that shows often contribute to the financial ruin of good designers. Look at recent history: numerous designers

who showed during fashion week just last year are no longer in business. Perhaps if the resources spent on the show had been directed to a trade show booth or to paying suppliers, they would have survived another season. Menswear designer Robert Geller says the smart thing is to put the money you would spend on a show toward a year of much more effective PR.[3]

Staging a fashion show is extremely expensive. Emerging designers generally spend a minimum of $15,000 and as much as $120,000 on each show. The least expensive tent in Bryant Park during New York Fashion Week costs $28,000, and that only covers the space, staging, and a basic lighting package. The designer still needs to create, print, and mail invitations; secure models and hair and makeup teams; hire photographers and videographers; create and send press releases; and of course produce and accessorize a runway-worthy collection.

Some resourceful designers spend as little as $5,000 by finding donated space, sponsors to cover production costs, and friends to handle PR. Creativity can help you cut costs. I've seen designers light their runway with a spotlight held by a friend on a ladder. Just keep in mind that while inventiveness is admirable, the show is a direct reflection of your collection and positioning. It is not expected to look as polished as Carolina Herrera's, but if it looks amateurish, that reflects on your designs and may fuel concerns about your professionalism and ability to produce high-quality product that meets retail expectations. It may be better to wait to stage a show until you have the resources to do it right.

Will Anyone See It?

Sad but true: at a young designer's runway show, 80 percent of the audience is often friends and family. It's extremely difficult to get the right people to a new show. With more than 160 shows in New York each season and dozens more in London, Paris, Milan, Los Angeles, and other cities around the world, the schedule is extremely competitive, and many shows take place at exactly the same time. Editors must attend the shows of their advertisers, and buyers have to show up to see their biggest vendors. With travel and waiting time, each show requires at least an hour, and unknown names are the lowest priority.

Should Anyone See It?

Not all collections belong on the runway. Even if your cashmere sweater is a best seller at Henri Bendel, it's not necessarily right for the runway. The runway is for innovation and trend leaders. Don't waste time and money if you can get better results at a trade show, and don't waste the press's and buyers' time on something easily introduced online or best seen in the showroom.

Alternative Presentations

Editors and buyers rarely recommend that a new designer stage a runway show. In fact, I highly recommend forgoing the runway for an installation or presentation format. There are many ways to present a collection on models or mannequins in a showroom, in a hotel suite, or at a cocktail reception. A market director at *Harper's Bazaar* stated, "A great way to get noticed is to have a presentation. It's refreshing, new and different and it's a way to see the clothing close up. It's not always about a fashion show."[4]

When editors and buyers are trying to see as many things as possible during fashion week, a show requires them to be in a specific place at a specific time, essentially trapping them there for the show's duration. But if a designer can present the line at a convenient location, throughout a four- to five-hour window, press can stop in for 15 minutes between other shows, greatly increasing the likelihood that they will have the time. Many designers hold receptions and informal presentations at the Bryant Park Hotel across the street from the Mercedes Benz Fashion Week tents. It takes very little effort for editors to cross the street and review a collection quickly between shows.

Be creative, and you will stand out. Designers have held tea parties, hosted breakfasts, and used unique venues such as museums and gardens. As Four even staged a presentation with miniature versions of the collection on mechanical dolls. Just don't lose the purpose of the event in the antics. A simple set in a photo studio or showroom, with models in still poses or casually interacting, can be the most elegant and effective way to show a high-end collection.

© Patrick McMullan

A Gen Art installation showing the collection on live models.

Photo by Dan & Corina Lecca Courtesy of Gen Art.

An installation showing the Form New York collection.

Photo by Howard Wise / Gen Art

An installation during Los Angeles fashion week for the Mintee collection.

What Are the Benefits?

The allure of the runway is strong, but you need to check your ego and think about what you really achieve by walking down the runway with a parade of models behind you clapping. Simon Doonan, creative director of Barneys New York, has said, "The fashion system is doing a terrible disservice to students and young designers by making them think they can become the next Tom Ford by putting on a great fashion show."[5] Even designers who show say it's hard to measure what the runway does. It helps build brand awareness, but they are not sure how it cor-

relates to sales. Other designers feel their first or second show brought initial attention and press coverage, but after that, the results didn't justify the cost.

A runway show is distracting and emotionally exhausting. The planning requires significant time and energy and can leave you drained during the selling season when you need to be focused. Designers often say their show is the most stressful thing they do, and many experience a postshow depression because of the pressure.

The excitement and flurry created by the press and celebrities during fashion week can also be extremely distracting for designers who don't show, making them feel as though they are missing out. It is critical to stay focused on your overall business strategy, goals, and budget. Realize that often it is best to stay under the radar and away from the spotlight to let buyers and editors discover you in a more strategic way.

Solicit the opinion of others in the industry before you show. Ask buyers and editors, and be wary of show producers and public relations people who may be eager for you to show for their own personal profit.

Is This the Right Time?

If you want to show and it fits your business strategy, consider whether the time is right. First impressions last, and a show can negatively affect your reputation and image if you aren't ready. Designer Rebecca Taylor says, "We didn't do shows for a long time,"[6] and designer Nicole Miller said she was in business five to six years before ever having a fashion show.[7] Designer Michelle Smith from Milly says, "We didn't start doing runway until we were making money."[8]

Once you show for one or two seasons, it doesn't make sense to continue to show if you still don't have retail accounts. Editors cannot continue to cover a collection that isn't available to their readers, and the buyers will not return if you aren't serious about production.

Producing a Runway Show

When the time is right to show, first create a complete budget that takes into account each of the necessary elements outlined below. Once you know what

you can afford to spend, stay within those amounts. With any type of presentation, it is easy for costs to escalate out of control.

Location and Space

An interesting location can add depth and intrigue to the collection, but during fashion week, the primary concern is to make it as easy as possible for the press to attend. This is why many shows are staged in one location, such as the tents at Bryant Park in New York, the Louvre in Paris, and Smashbox Studios in Los Angeles.

These venues are financially out of reach for most new designers. In New York and in Los Angeles each season, alternative group show spaces created by showrooms, magazines, or event companies are less expensive and generally offer a basic show space, including lighting, sound, and staging. In New York each season, hair brand Bumble & Bumble sponsors Fashion Week at the House of Bumble, providing a selection of designers with a 6,500-square-foot loft space, along with production support, hair teams, and PR exposure. In Los Angeles, arts organization BoxEight provides an alternative show venue by hosting several days of fashion shows in a downtown location for a handful of chosen designers.

If you want to secure your own show space, consider distance and convenience relative to the major shows. If a buyer has to travel for half an hour from another show to get to your venue, she might not bother. But if your show follows Calvin Klein in the art gallery across the street, it's ideal. Space options can include raw lofts and warehouses, galleries, photo studios, restaurants, hotels, bars, alleyways, former churches and synagogues, embassies, and gardens. The venue should fit the image of your line. An edgy line could make sense in a tunnel, but a more sophisticated line is better suited to a high-end hotel. Nightclubs generally have a tacky reputation that can prevent a line from being taken seriously.

Designers have held "guerilla shows" on the street outside a well-known designer's show or in the street outside the tents. Again, image is everything, and there's a fine line between being perceived as innovative versus amateurish. The impact of a renegade show can be significant, but depending on the location, you can be shut down and arrested, resulting in a lot of stress for a little PR.

Group Shows

Group shows, such as those produced by Gen Art, benefit from having several designers in one show. Buyers and editors only have to travel to one space, at one time, to see several new talents. Partnering with other designers to create a group show lessens the financial burden for each designer, and you can leverage each other's connections, increasing the odds that influential people will attend.

Staging Considerations

When reviewing locations, consider the layout of the space and the staging. The cheapest route is to have the models walk directly on the floor with three rows of chairs for attendees, plus standing room in the back. If you have more than three rows of chairs, you should either raise the models by building a higher runway, raise the audience by putting the back rows of chairs on platforms, or use bleachers. A press area should be designated at the end of the runway where cameras can set up to get a clear, head-to-toe shot of each look. If you have a raised runway, the press needs to be on a riser at the same height.

The runway backdrop will appear in all of the photos and video from the show and, therefore, should be appropriate for the collection. A plain white wall featuring the designer's logo works well. It identifies the collection in photos while hiding the backstage line-up action from the audience. You don't need a backdrop if the show space is attractive and each model can enter the runway from a connecting room or hallway. Beware of using any shiny surface or material for your backdrop, logo, or runway. It may reflect the show lights and cause a glare that distorts photographs and hampers the view for the attendees.

Ideally you will be able to work with a production company that has experience with fashion shows; can handle your staging, lighting, and sound needs; and can help you address unexpected concerns. Venues often have production companies that they recommend and who have experience with the space, but you should definitely shop around for competitive pricing.

Plan to have ample space backstage to accommodate areas for dressing, as well as hair and makeup. The more models and staff, the more space you need. Check that the power capabilities at the space can accommodate several hair dryers, makeup lights, and steamers without blowing a fuse.

Think through the traffic flow and the number of attendees allowed in a space. If only one small elevator goes to a seventh-floor space, it will take a long time to get everyone into the room. You want attendees to remember the clothes, not the wait or cramped space. The fire code will limit the number of people allowed in the space, and if you exceed that number, you can be shut down before the show begins—especially in Los Angeles and Chicago, where the fire inspectors are strict. Ask the venue to give you a floor plan of the space or create one yourself and use it to map out your check-in area, runway, each individual seat at the show, and the backstage. This plan will be extremely useful in mapping out lighting, sound, and other items brought in by vendors. Non-traditional locations often demand flexibility. When designer Michelle Mason obtained a permit to show in the Second Street tunnel in Los Angeles, the tunnel had to remain open to emergency vehicles, and a fire truck drove through just before the show began.

When to Show

The international fashion week calendar kicks off in New York, with Spring in early September and Fall in early February. New York fashion week is followed immediately by fashion weeks in London, Milan, and Paris. Los Angeles, Toronto, Montreal, Brazil, Australia, India, and Iceland have their own fashion weeks, and many other cities, from Chicago and San Francisco to Berlin and Moscow, are jumping on the bandwagon.

The fashion weeks in New York, London, Paris, and Milan are the critical shows for the fashion industry to attend each season. The calendar is extremely crowded, and the challenge for a new designer is finding a time slot with the least conflict for your target audience. In New York, the designers call Ruth Finley at *The Fashion Calendar* to arrange a time slot and list their show on the schedule of upcoming fashion industry events. An annual subscription to the calendar costs $475 and includes several listings each year. A single issue for one season can be purchased for $95. Both options are accompanied with insightful advice from Ruth and her staff, who can recommend a time slot with the least amount of conflict. The Fashion Calendar is also a valuable resource to discover which locations and PR firms other designers use and when fashion events are

taking place that you should attend. In Los Angeles, you can list your event for free at *www.fashionweekla.com*. As the new kid, you have to be flexible with your time slot. If you choose 5:00 P.M. on Wednesday and Ralph Lauren wants the same time, you will need to move if you want to avoid the conflict.

If you are a new designer in New York, consider holding your first show or presentation outside of fashion week, when there is less competition and the press and retailers are more likely to attend. Showing a Spring collection in August or a Fall collection in late January when people are less busy gives you a jump on fashion week. Everyone wants to see collections as early as possible, when their editorial calendars are still open and their buying budgets are full. Many of the new fashion weeks around the globe are reaching out to emerging labels, inviting them to bring their collections to show. While it can be a great ego boost to be invited to Iceland, it is critical to evaluate whether the time and effort spent to show will truly help you meet your business goals. If you have a new store in Dubai and your potential customers there will be attending the show, it may be worth taking your collection. But if the event is not going to attract the editors, buyers, or customers who will impact your business, it is a distracting waste of valuable time.

Inviting the Right People

Fashion shows generally accommodate a minimum of 100 guests and as many as 1,000, with the average seating around 300. The size of a show is much less significant than the importance of the people who attend. It's better to show your collection to 5 of the right people than 50 people who really can't affect your business. If you show in the tents at New York Fashion Week, you'll be provided a press list of people who register to attend the shows. The list is a good place to start when deciding whom to invite, but you need to edit it carefully. Many of the writers and editors on this list are not appropriate for all collections and don't need to be at your show. If using this list, you also need to add writers and editors from alternative publications who don't register. Many designers build their own list from scratch, carefully researching the appropriate editors and buyers whom they want to attend.

Fashion shows really aren't about the buyers. They are not writing orders at the shows and often have already seen the collection in the showroom. But a fashion show is an ideal opportunity to attract the attention of buyers, and they should be invited. At the shows, the buyers also network with editors and share opinions on new designers, which can result in an appointment or at least a lookbook request. However, be sure to invite other people who can influence your success, including factory owners, potential investors and sponsors, fabric suppliers, and showroom owners.

The show invitation may be the first impression that many in the industry receive of you and your line. It should be creative, enticing, and representative of your brand but, most important, it should clearly communicate the pertinent information concerning when, where, and what you are showing and how to RSVP.

Invitations are costly when you add up the expense for designing, printing, and postage. However, it's not difficult to create a nice invitation on the cheap. Avoid oversized or square invitations, which add to the postage cost. You don't have to mail a printed invitation to everyone. A very small quantity can be printed for VIPs and then an email version used for others. Printing in one color is less expensive than using four, postcards are cheaper than folded invitations, and vellums and other specialty paper add significantly to the cost.

Although it happens in the big leagues, don't even think of banning an editor who wrote a bad review of your last show. It happened recently with some newer designers in Los Angeles, and it's not smart. When this happens, the designer is overestimating his importance and insulting a writer for doing her job, regardless of how much they disagree.

How Many to Invite

Unless there is considerable buzz about your line, up to 70 percent of your industry invitees will not respond. Of those who confirm, as many as 30 percent might not show up, especially if you are unknown or your show time conflicts with other shows. A designer should invite many more people than chairs—up to three times that number—to ensure having a full room at the show. It is unrealistic to expect the seats at your first show to be full of fashion directors and editors-in-chief. But realize that associate buyers have influence and edito-

rial assistants get promoted. Sending invitations alone will not succeed in getting the target people to your show. Call and follow up with important people who have not responded to confirm that they have the information. If they tell you they can't make it, ask if someone else from the store or publication could attend on their behalf and offer to send a lookbook or video after the show.

Seating Charts

The RSVPs are used to create a seating chart for the show. Ideally, a publicist or PR firm that understands how to prioritize attendees should handle the chart. In general, the most important people are seated in the front row, and then you work your way back. Try to keep rival publications and stores away from each other by seating them on opposite sides of the runway or placing others between them. Generally, it's acceptable to seat magazine editors together by publishing company and retailers by parent company. For example, *Vogue* can sit by *GQ* and *Allure* because they are both published by Conde Nast. If several people RSVP from a specific publication, such as *WWD*, call and ask which person is actually covering the show. Even if higher-ranked writers are coming, the covering writer should sit in the front row.

The challenging part of seating is that you don't know which people who RSVPed won't attend. Instead of assigning individual seats, assign just by section and row. This allows you to overbook the row and lessen the number of empty seats resulting from no-shows. When the show is about to start, the ushers should ask people to move forward and fill in the front rows to keep the room from looking empty to other attendees and in photographs. Once the seating chart is mapped out, everyone on the chart should be called to confirm their RSVP; remind them of the date, time, and location; and give them their seat assignment.

Celebrities

Celebrities attract photographers and press, but celebrity wrangling is very time consuming and there are no guarantees. It's best to try to work a connection to a celebrity who has worn your clothes or through a stylist who regularly pulls them. If you get a celebrity confirmation, fax a media alert to the press and have someone photograph the celebrity at the show for distribution after the fact.

Photography

Good photographs are often the most important result of a show. They are used for the lookbook, to remind press and buyers of the collection, and to show the collection to those who weren't there. A good photographer with fashion show experience is critical to getting the photographs you need. Photography ranges in price, but the prevalence of digital photography has helped to lessen the expense. Most designers spend a minimum of $600 on the photographer. Arrange to receive high-resolution photos after the show on CD to make prints and email them out as necessary. Some professional runway photographers work closely with magazines and may feed photos directly to them on your behalf. Give clear instructions to the photographer about the shots. Ideally, you want a head-to-toe shot of each look along with close-ups that show the details of the design. It's a good idea to take a few photographs of the hair and makeup action backstage, and don't forget the celebrities in the front row.

Photos by Dan & Corina Lecca.

A runway photographer should take full shots of each outfit as well as close ups of the details.

Photos by Georgia Nerheim.

Photos from the Vena Cava fashion week installation are ideal for the lookbook.

A videographer is necessary to shoot video of the entire show. The footage can be used to show the collection to buyers and editors and for television or Internet coverage. TV producers do not always have the budget to send a crew to shoot a young designer's show, but they may cover the show if the designer can provide high-quality footage. Bad video is useless. If the camera is moving or the focus is blurred, you have wasted your money. A good videographer generally costs $800 or more.

Another reason to videotape the show is for your own review. Watching the show reveals a great deal about the collection and the show production. Perhaps the models should pose in front of the backdrop, maybe the tempo should be faster, or next time you should remember to take the price tags off the bottom of the shoes. Pay attention to detail and take notes for next time.

Lighting

Good lighting is critical to show the clothes clearly, especially for photos and video. There are lighting options for any budget, and Gordon Link, president of Bernhard Link Theatrical, offers the following advice on what is most important: "Firstly, make sure your show has adequate, even, front light positioned just over the press riser, as low and/or flat as possible. What's best for your show depends on the location (indoor or outdoor), the time, (daytime or night), and the designer's vision. Backlight is the second most important because front light alone makes objects appear flat and two-dimensional. Backlight looks great in

pictures and allows audience members to view the back of the garment after the model has passed. Budget permitting, background or architectural lighting affects the overall look of the show. This can be achieved with color, intensity, pattern, silhouette, or special effects."[9]

When starting out, it's best to keep it simple and avoid too many effects or colors, which can distort the appearance of the clothes. It's key that you have enough light—either hung above the runway or set on goalposts at the ends and sides of the runway to flood the entire runway fully. Spotlights cast shadows and can result in dark or distorted photographs, so they should only be used as additional, not primary, lights. Before the show, the designer should test the lighting with a model on the runway and instruct the models on where to pose to achieve the best photographs and avoid shadows. Confirm that the space can meet the power requirements for the lighting. A few new designers have had power failures during their shows, leaving the audience uneasily waiting in the dark for the show to start again.

Music

Upbeat music keeps people awake, sets the pace for the models to walk, and gives energy and movement to the clothes. While moody or esoteric music sets a dramatic tone for an intellectual collection, it can put the audience to sleep or even annoy them. Don't forget preshow music to set the mood as audience enters the space and waits for the show to begin.

Basic sound equipment needs are speakers, a CD player, and someone to play the music. Bringing a stereo system from home will not suffice. The sound needs to fill the entire space and be clear and loud enough to cover any noise from the audience, the backstage, and the models stomping down the runway. If there is live music or a DJ spinning during the show, the equipment needs will increase. Ideally, the space will have a sound system, and your basic needs will be included in the rental. Remember to rent walkie-talkies or clear-com headsets to enable the sound and lighting technicians to communicate with the producer during the show.

Models

The models you choose are key to how your collection is perceived. Good models show the clothing at its best and lend personality to the collection. A fresh-faced, all-American blond will set a different tone than a broody or exotic brunette. Of course, during fashion week, models are extremely busy, and the designers are competing to book the best ones.

Start casting by contacting agencies and asking to speak to their runway agents. A press kit or lookbook can help convince them that you are a rising star worthy of their assistance. When you talk to the booker, describe the type of model you want in terms of pale or dark, thin or curvy, tall or petite, muscular or lean, grungy or clean-cut. The agency will generally send new, developmental models who need runway experience and initial exposure. If there is considerable buzz about your line, it will help you book more established models who attract press and make you appear influential.

Request cards for the available models and choose the models whom you would like to see. Make sure you request several more than you need. Arrange a casting time to see the models as soon as possible and send a call sheet with the casting time and location information to the booker to give to the models. Once you are certain that you want to book a particular model, confirm with the booker immediately, before they send the model to cast for a conflicting show. Set up a fitting time and confirm the backstage call time and date for your show with the booker. New designers have to be flexible during the madness of fashion week. Backstage call will be three hours before show time, but some models may come from other shows or fittings and have only minutes to be prepped for the runway. You may lose models to designers with a bigger budget or better name, even on the day of a show. If this happens, stay calm and work with the booker to replace the model quickly. Another option is to add a change to one of the other models in the show to cover the remaining outfit. If you need assistance, casting directors have connections and relationships at the agencies and can leverage their other shows to help you.

Be up front with the bookers about your ability to compensate the models. Generally, new models will walk in exchange for clothing, and it can be great PR for you if the model shows up at magazine castings wearing your designs.

The models can be given clothing immediately from the current collection, or you can order clothes for them from the collection you show. Each model should receive a complete outfit or significant item such as a coat or dress. A T-shirt is not adequate compensation! Communicate immediately with the booker or model following the show regarding compensation. If the booker has to chase you down for clothes, he may decide you aren't worth the trouble next season. If your clothing is extremely expensive, it may not make sense to use it to pay models. Instead, it might be cheaper to hire the models at their rate or find alternative compensation. Designers have persuaded show sponsors to provide product such as Olympus cameras for the models. Other designers have succeeded in having shoes donated for the show, rather than loaned, and given those to the models as payment. If you pay cash, realize that there is usually a 15 to 20 percent commission to the agency on top of the model's rate.

Fashion week is extremely stressful for models. They are running from castings to fittings to shows all day long and late into the night. People are constantly touching them, pulling on their hair, and dressing them in a multitude of uncomfortable clothes and shoes. Have some respect and patience during the casting, fitting, and backstage prep at the show. Provide water and food and don't make the models wait long or ask them to return repeatedly for fittings. A model can become a valuable advocate for your line, agreeing to work with you for photo shoots and in future shows.

The number of models you need is based on the number of looks on the runway. Generally, the models will walk more than once in a show, so you should book at least one model for every two looks and then book additional models to give yourself more time for changes or to wear more complicated looks. To ensure smooth changes, recruit skilled dressers and assign one to each model. At the fittings, take a Polaroid or digital photo of each model in the outfit, complete with shoes and accessories. These photos should be attached to a large sheet of paper or poster board in the order they will appear in the show and used backstage to communicate the looks to the dressers before the show.

Styling and Merchandising

A new designer's show should be short and sweet. Don't show 50 looks; 25 to 30 looks are ideal. Edit heavily and only present the best editorial looks to create buzz for the press and entice the buyers. The showroom is where the industry can see more, so all your options shouldn't be on the runway. The designer is often too close to the collection and should enlist a stylist to help merchandise a concise show.

Styling is important to the presentation. The accessories, hair, and makeup should all enhance the garments and communicate a consistent message. Working with a reputable stylist can also lend cachet to the show and draw press attention.

A stylist can help with accessories and important elements such as shoes. A loan from a prominent luxury line adds prestige to your collection, but the competition for high-end shoes and jewelry is great. A new shoe designer might love the publicity, but make sure she has enough samples. Buying new shoes is extremely expensive, but a designer can be creative with shoes from the Salvation Army. Spray paint, glue, ribbon, or cloth can go a long way. The typical female model wears a size 9 shoe, but you will probably need to accommodate a few models who are size 7 or 11. Slides, mules, and sandals are more flexible, but models may still have to share shoes during the show.

Photo(s) by Glenn Pasquariello (aka: 610-Glenn).

These run of show boards include photos of each outfit in the runway show for use by the dressers backstage

Hair and Makeup

There are a few options for securing hair and makeup services for your show. Hiring professionals is one, but the more affordable route is to find hair and makeup brands that will donate services to promote their stylists, salons, or products. These companies provide teams and, if you are fortunate, may even give financial support to the show.

When communicating inspiration or direction for the show, remember that hair and makeup artists are visual people. It's best to provide tear sheets from magazines or color sketches and be as clear as possible to avoid disappointments backstage. I recommend testing the hair and makeup looks before the show with the artist and a model to agree on the final look. Send copies of the model cards to the hair and makeup teams to help them plan accordingly for each model's hair and skin.

At the show, be organized and help the hair and makeup teams do their job. Provide plenty of space along with mirrors, lighting, power, and a list of models with the order in which they will walk in the show.

Run of Show

A run of show, which describes each runway look in the order of appearance, should be placed on every chair at the show. It can be printed on simple white paper and should include details about each look to help the writers describe it, editors remember it for shoots, and buyers place orders for it. The run of show should list the models; include credits for hair, makeup, styling, shoes, public relations, production, and accessories; and thank sponsors, bookers, front and backstage staff, and anyone else who helped with the show.

Gift Bags

Gift bags are often given to attendees at the shows. People do love free stuff, but it's really not necessary to have a gift bag. It takes time and money to obtain the bags and their contents and to assemble them. If a gift bag is important to your sponsors, ask them to donate the bag and the items inside. Whatever you do, don't fill the bag with junky brochures or paper handouts. Cosmetics, food, and toys are best. If you have something particularly fun or unique, it might end up in the press.

Staff

If you have a few extra thousand dollars, hiring a public relations firm or production company to help organize the show will make it much easier. Before hiring either, find out whether it has other shows on the same day or during the week and ensure that you will receive the attention you need. There are publicists who take on some production responsibility and producers who do PR. Clearly define responsibilities up front to make sure nothing is forgotten.

Staff at the show will need to manage arrivals, check-in, and seating and should have an RSVP list to check off the name of each person who attends. Appoint a backstage manager and someone else to guard the entrance to avoid overcrowding and to prevent thieves or spies from stealing or copying the clothing. Several designers have warned to watch out for strangers with cameras in the backstage taking close-up shots of the designs, probably to copy them.

Don't forget to have someone, ideally a producer or professional, to "call" the show. This person coordinates the lighting, sound, and model cues via headset to ensure that everything runs smoothly and looks professional. Most PR firms and production companies have people with experience who can call the show.

Rehearsal

Before the show, conduct a full rehearsal with models, lights, and sound to make sure everyone understands their roles and their cues and to make sure that you are happy with the show as a whole. Give direction to the models on how you want them to walk and what attitude they should project. Let them practice walking on the runway in the shoes to build their confidence.

The show's pacing should be energetic with a continual and even spacing of models on the runway. Ideally, there will always be at least two models on the runway at once, with a new model entering from backstage as soon as one turns at the end of the runway to walk back. However, if there are problems with changes during the show, the pacing can be adjusted gradually to provide more time for the activity backstage. If a model is not fully ready for the cue, send out one who is, even though the show order will be wrong. Slow pacing is boring, but there is nothing worse than an empty runway.

Start Time

Unfortunately, there is no such thing as a runway show that starts on time. It takes time for industry people to arrive and sit down, especially if they are coming from another show. Plan carefully to make your check-in and seating system run as quickly and smoothly as possible and don't start more than a half an hour late. Late arrivals may come from another show, but generally once 30 minutes has passed, there is no point in waiting for editors who have not yet arrived. If they were planning to come, by this time they will assume it's too late.

Because they were in other shows, sometimes models arrive late in hair and makeup that needs to be changed. Some changes can be managed quickly, and sometimes you need to compromise on the hair and makeup or decide to show without that model. If there are no late arrivals, there is no reason for the backstage to not be ready on time. I recently attended a show by a new designer that started an hour late despite being the first show of the day. Editors who had waited for 45 minutes had to leave before the show began. It was a waste of their time and showed a complete lack of respect on the part of the designer.

Fashiontainment

The runway is a stage, and designers do receive press for their runway antics. Galliano's models arrived on a steam train, McQueen's models were positioned on a giant chessboard, and Imitation of Christ staged a circus with models hanging from a trapeze. The runway offers an opportunity to be unique, but you don't want to appear absurd or gimmicky or let the performance overshadow the clothes. There was more buzz about the sheep falling off Miguel Adrover's runway than about the clothes. For a new designer who wants to be taken seriously, nothing is better than a solid, straightforward presentation.

Leveraging the Show

Alert the press in advance about anything particularly unique about your collection to try to land preshow coverage. Tell them about celebrities who will attend the show, models of note on the runway, or interesting facts about the inspiration or materials, such as the 500 yards of tulle used for one dress. Trade publications such as *WWD* and websites such as *Style.com* often run fashion week previews,

including sketches and inspiration statements on collections. Have a CD of clean, high-resolution images of the collection ready to email out for magazine and website coverage before the show. The photos can be simple. Even if you take them at the fitting in front of a plain white wall, you should have something ready to send out immediately to increase the chance of coverage. After the show, follow up with the press and buyers who attended as well as those who did not. Offer to send photos or video to be included in their fashion week coverage.

Sponsorship

A financial sponsor will certainly relieve the financial pressure of producing a runway show, and fortunately, more companies are looking for opportunities with new designers. Ian Gerard, CEO of Gen Art, says, "Many companies want to align with the glamour of fashion and position their brand and product as fashionable. Others want to align specifically with new designers as benefactors and supporters of new talent."[10]

Both Ecco Domani and Swarovski Crystal have been consistently sponsoring up-and-coming designers for their fashion week shows and presentations for several years. Finding sponsors is very competitive. Dozens of designers target the same companies, as well as other non-fashion-related events. Show producers and PR firms can often help secure sponsorship.

When seeking sponsorship, start early. Many corporations move slowly when reviewing and approving proposals, and they often allocate their funds up to one year in advance. Do not write a letter, send it out to marketing and sponsorship departments at dozens of companies, and then sit by the phone expecting calls. As with approaching stores and editors, the more targeted the outreach, the more the likelihood of success.

Think about your brand and which companies would be a good match. The obvious ones are hair and makeup companies, beverages, and fashionable consumer electronics such as MP3 players, cameras, and mobile phones. Look at magazine advertisements to find companies targeting fashion audiences and note their approaches. Companies with a new product or redesign usually have large budgets to launch and promote the product. Examine your collection and

themes. If you use large quantities of a particular fiber, such as cotton or jersey, contact the fiber manufacturer or trade organization. If your collection is cruise inspired, contact a cruise line. If the collection is washable, call Woolite. If your line is street or athletic inspired, call a sneaker company. Sometimes the trade commission of the country where you produce has promotional funds.

Once you have a targeted list of companies, call the marketing or public relations department and ask for the appropriate contact for fashion sponsorship. Introduce yourself and send a package that includes a few key press pieces, some intriguing photos of the line, and anything to make you appear to be the next hot thing. A company wants to believe that by aligning with you, it will receive press coverage, reach potential customers, and eventually increase the sales and image of its product.

Potential sponsors need a list of entitlements outlining what they receive by sponsoring your show. Generally, they want presence in exchange for their money. You can serve their champagne, wine, water, or chocolate at the show or backstage; put items in a gift bag on every chair; provide signage at the entrance to the show; or even park their car in front of the venue. Try to think of fun and creative ways to integrate their brand in a meaningful way. Gen Art's Ian Gerard says, "Companies look for integration with the designer. They may seek to have the designer create a customized product which they can take to the press to promote the partnership between you and their brand."[11] The sponsor should receive a number of seats at the show, as well as inclusion in the press release and on the run of show.

Of course, when working with sponsors, there are limits to what a designer can do without compromising integrity. You may or may not be comfortable putting a sponsor's product on the runway, but be nice about it and simply explain how it hurts the sponsor's integrity, too. Don't work with anyone in desperation. Even if you have already paid a deposit for the space, a show is all about image and PR. It might not be worth it to partner with a panty liner sponsor.

After the show, send copies of press, a list of key attendees, and photos of both the show and their presence to the sponsor. Emphasize the success of the event and make it a good experience in hopes that the sponsor will return next season.

Are You Selling Out?

Some designers and artists feel that working with corporate sponsors is selling out. They are afraid they might tarnish their image or artistic integrity by partnering with a large company. Granted, there are risks to image and integrity if the partnership isn't right, but in reality, corporate sponsors are the artistic patrons of today. During the Renaissance, artists and creators like Michelangelo were sponsored by the Catholic Church. As church support dwindled, artists received support from private patrons like the Medici family. The patrons of today are the corporations who have the money, and you can build valuable relationships with these entities that will support your business for years to come.

11

Copyrights and Knockoffs

Having a design copied is an extremely common and frustrating part of being a new designer, but before we delve into the issue, keep in mind the words of the late, great Diana Vreeland, "Don't look back. Just go ahead. Give ideas away. Under every idea there is a new idea waiting to be born."

 ### Fashion Design and the Copyright Laws
by Attorney Jason Gabbard

The fashion business is an exceedingly difficult one. Hordes of copycats are waiting in the gates to rip off the labor of your love, and the U.S. intellectual property laws provide scant protection for fashion designs.

A quick jaunt through a few blocks of lower Manhattan makes it strikingly apparent that "knocking off" fashion is big business. While designers toil to showcase the latest and greatest designs in fashion hotspots across the United States, street vendors offer imitations at a fraction of the cost. This practice is not confined to the streets of New York's Chinatown. Some companies have built big and legitimate businesses selling replicas of haute couture designs on the Web and in malls across the United States.

In most other industries, such blanket copycatting would be unfathomable. Countless courts across the country have enforced the right of the music industry to quash pirates of sound recordings and motion pictures, often levying huge criminal and pecuniary sanctions. Yet in the fashion industry, legal

protection remains largely elusive. At least once a month, a distraught designer will call me wanting to sue an alleged copycat. More often than not, my advice only further disappoints the designer—either no legal protection is available, or the designer simply cannot afford the expenses associated with a lawsuit.

Discouraged yet? Me too. Well, it is not quite that bad. Some legal protection is available. The following summary of the intellectual property laws is not, and should not be viewed as, a substitute for a good lawyer. However, hopefully with the information you glean from this chapter, you will position yourself to understand better what is and is not against the law and what you can do to protect yourself.

The Law

The laws in the United States that protect creative works and other intangible property are very complicated. Before discussing what the law does protect, let's first dispense with some commonly held misconceptions.

Simply because two products are similar, even very similar, in appearance or in composition, it does not necessarily follow that one is a copycat of the other or that illegal activity has taken place.

Copyright generally *does not* protect fashion designs.

Patent generally *does not* protect fashion designs.

Even if you have a right or legal entitlement, and even if the law protects it, getting a judgment (i.e., money damages from a court) is often the hardest part. It's expensive (often prohibitively so), time consuming, and uncertain.

With that information, you are already two steps ahead of the game. Half of the questions I take from young designers faced with an infringement situation involve one of those misconceptions.

So let's now take a look at what the law does say and what protections are available. A basic tenet of the law says that someone owns nearly everything. With real property (land, condominiums, etc.) and personal property (watches, books, appliances, etc.), that should be axiomatic. But with intangible property, such as ideas, inventions, and methods of creating, that notion is a bit less clear. The following discussion is structured around the three main areas of intellectual property law— copyright, trademark, and patent—and should shed light on these concepts.

Copyright. Copyright is a bundle of rights that provides legal protection for authors of nonuseful, original works, including literary, dramatic, artistic, and musical works. The copyright owner enjoys the right to use the works and to exclude others from using them. These rights can be quite broad (and confusing) but generally prove useless in protecting fashion designs. Despite the fact that unmeasurable time, energy, and aesthetic genius are devoted to today's couture, copyright has never protected clothing.

Under the U.S. Copyright Act, protection is denied to any article that has a utilitarian function—that is, a useful everyday purpose beyond artistic expression. Accordingly, courts of law typically deny copyright protection to clothing on the grounds that garment designs are intrinsically useful articles. It is worth noting, however, that some fashion accessories are copyrightable if they have a demonstrable nonutilitarian purpose. Basically, useful articles may receive very limited protection if the article has artistic elements—pictorial, graphic, sculptural—that exist independently of the utilitarian aspect of the article. For instance, I might copyright a belt buckle that contains an artistic rendering. Likewise, copyright would protect printed designs on fabric, as well as a designer's sketches of a garment. Pushing the envelope, you could argue for copyright protection (with a straight face) for a shirt with an embroidered drawing. It is not clear a court would buy this argument, but it is a possibility. In any event, the utility of such a copyright is dubious, as the copyright would only protect the schematic, not the actual garment.

Trademark. Trademarks are words, names, symbols, designs, and other distinctive items that tell a story to consumers about the origination, quality, and embodiment of goods (and services, too). If a handbag bears the "mark" of an upscale French fashion house, it means that you can be assured of the source and quality associated with that brand. The process through which trademarks are obtained is fairly time consuming but can in most circumstances be handled by a layperson.

Trademarks are established through use in commerce, or in business, or through filing a federal trademark application. Examples of types of trademarks include words, like Coca-Cola and KODAK; names, like Ford automobiles and Tommy Hilfiger designs; symbols and logos, such as the Nike swoosh; colors, scents, and

sounds; and perhaps most important to fashion, overall product image/configuration (known as "trade dress"), in which the design of a product is so widely recognized that it stands for the quality and origin of the product.

One obvious example of trademark infringement would be counterfeit Lacoste shirts bearing the signature alligator. Trademark law has been useful in protecting logos, names, and other emblems on garments. Another prevalent violation about which designers often inquire is cloning an entire garment. Trade dress might address such a situation and provide monetary remedies. Unfortunately, courts and lawmakers have been reluctant to see beyond the utilitarian function of a piece of clothing.

Patent. Patents protect novel and nonobvious inventions. Under almost every circumstance, a fashion design (garments and accessories) will not be considered an invention. Courts in the United States have repeatedly determined that garment designs do not meet the requirements for patent. Moreover, the reality of a design's life cycle, coupled with the time and financial demands of the process through which an inventor acquires a patent, mean that the patent system could never be a viable alternative for protecting clothing designs.

Preventative Measures

Now that you understand some of the facts and fictions, you need to continue to stay informed and be prepared to protect yourself and your designs. A few best-practice pointers will likely prove worthwhile. Take copious notes of your ideas, preserve your sketches, and always maintain organized records. An organized paper trail of your cognitive progression should behoove you in the event of a controversy. Also, when disclosing preliminary ideas, drawings, business plans, and the like to third parties, use a simple nondisclosure/confidentiality agreement. Forms of such contracts abound on the Internet. Also, do not hastily take your ideas to the public. Publishing concepts on the Internet or disclosing information to outsiders too early can nullify business and legal first-mover advantages. Additionally, it pays to be educated. Many free resources are available on the Web. Using these resources, along with this book, will help you understand the law and at the very least identify real issues. Just a few of many helpful websites include the following:

- U.S. Patent and Trademark Office *(www.uspto.gov)*. Time and expense permitting, you can probably obtain trademarks for your brands without the assistance of a lawyer.

- Association of Research Libraries *(www.arl.org)*

- Legal Information Institute, maintained by Cornell University *(www.law.cornell.edu)*

- Volunteer Lawyers for the Arts, maintained by a group of lawyers performing pro bono work for select clients in the arts *(www.vlany.org)*

Understanding the many nuances of intellectual property law typically requires the assistance of a legal counsel experienced in this field. However, without going to law school, you can reach a level of sophistication where you can spot a violation (an actionable one, at least) without a lawyer. The ability to spot a problem too big to handle alone is critical from both a legal and a pure business standpoint.

What Should You Do If Your Designs Are Knocked Off?

Call an attorney! Too many designers make matters worse by first trying to solve the problem alone. If you have reached the level of success where someone desires to copy your designs, then you most likely will have developed a relationship with a lawyer. No matter what, please do not start writing letters willy-nilly and threatening the counterfeiter.

After a violation of one of the intellectual property laws is established, the remedies available are usually swift and severe. An attorney should be able to tell you quickly if the problem is real and if the problem is viably actionable. After that, he can easily pen a cease-and-desist letter that will, in most cases, halt the infringing activity.

Then several reparative solutions should be available. An attorney can get the U.S. Marshals or some other law enforcement agency to confiscate and destroy the counterfeit goods. An action in a court of law could result in an award of both compensatory damages (i.e., to compensate you for actual lost income) and punitive damages (i.e., to punish the wrongdoer). Punitive damages can easily run into the millions of dollars.

But wait, I cannot finish the chapter without letting you down one more time. You may have detected a huge assumption in the preceding sentence—that financial resources are available to both parties in the dispute. Most attorneys charge by the hour and require hefty up-front retainers. I would never consider taking on such a

lawsuit without a retainer of at least $7,000 in addition to my standard hourly rate (never under $200, even for friends). Most young designers simply cannot afford such expenses. Perhaps more importantly, to collect on a damage award, the defendant (the source of the knockoffs) must have some assets in the United States—either property or cash. All too often, such party is destitute. Attorneys have coined a phrase to describe the peddlers in Chinatown and the copycat designers holed up in Brooklyn basements: "judgment proof," meaning broke. If the purveyor is not broke, she is likely to be located in Eastern Europe or Asia, far outside of the reach of U.S. jurisdiction.

A Parting Word

Clearly, our current legal regime falls short of providing designers with bulletproof remedies against knockoffs. Fashion, no less than painting, music, sculpture, and other conventional art forms, deserves legal protection. Unfortunately, our current system is not perfectly designed to protect fashion design, and the expensive realities of litigation typically make it impractical for all but a few designers to seek complete redress.

Many designers have complained to me that our laws discourage exclusivity and high fashion, lowering revenues, pressuring margins, and ultimately chilling creativity. Of course, the flip side contends that piracy actually encourages creativity and brings high fashion and awareness to the masses.

All debate aside, perhaps the key lesson from this chapter is the importance of being reasonably educated and having a good lawyer. Telephone calls and initial consultations are usually free. Find yourself a lawyer whom you can afford and who is interested in watching you realize your goals and dreams and willing to be a mentor and partner in your business. You will without doubt have to pay that person, but it will be well worth the expense. Consider it a cost of doing business. You can't make samples without fabric; you can't go to production without patterns and samples. If you couldn't afford the fabric, the patterns, and the cost of production, you wouldn't consider a line. Likewise, if you can't afford other essential elements of your business, such as good business and legal counsel, perhaps you should reconsider investing your time, energy, and money.

For the past two years, American designers, including Diane Von Fursten-berg, Narciso Rodriguez, and Nicole Miller, along with the Council of Fashion Designers of America, have lobbied in Washington, D.C., for copyright protection for fashion designs. Their efforts have resulted in the development of the Design Piracy Prohibition Act, which—backed by New York Senator Charles Schumer, among others—will be voted on by both the U.S. House and Senate in spring 2008. The Act would protect original fashion designs for three years once they are registered with the U.S. Copyright Office. While current trademark laws only address fashion counterfeits if they involve infringement of a registered trademark, logo, or brand name, under the new law, a designer could photograph the front and back of a garment and send those images to the copyright office, and the design would be registered for approximately $30. Designers would have six months after the first public appearance of the design (on the runway, in a showroom, at a tradeshow, etc.) to register it, allowing them time to choose which items to register based on sales.

Each year, technology and the ever-increasing speed of information flow enables the rapid growth of fashion design piracy. During fashion week, mass manufacturers and private label designers for major department and chains send photos and sketches of the runway looks directly from the shows or from websites such as *Style.com* to foreign factories with cheap labor and materials. There, product can be manufactured and distributed to the public in as little as four to six weeks—weeks or even months before the originals become available. Designers who receive store orders for their designs have had those orders canceled midproduction when the high-end store buyers see cheap versions flood the market.

Knockoffs are big business, with companies such as Allen B. Schwartz building an empire off inexpensive versions of Oscar gowns. Websites, such as *www.counterfeitchic.com* and *www.fashionista.com*, discuss or display photo examples of blatant fashion piracy. Up until this point, the only reason that designers such have Anna Sui have been able to bring lawsuits against companies such as Forever 21 is because her prints—not her designs—are protected under current law. Unfortunately, many mass chains find it cheaper to hire lawyers to handle lawsuits than to invest in a legitimate design team. However, Europe already has

tough laws in place that protect original fashion designs, and Yves Saint Laurent did successfully sue Polo Ralph Lauren for copying a tuxedo dress in 1994.

Some critics of the proposed law do not believe that fashion needs copyright protection. They believe that the creative process is organic and fashion and design have a life cycle that includes mass distribution. They believe fashion relies on consumers' tiring of a design or style by next season and moving on to the next. Cheap copies and mass distribution speed this cycle, as the fashion-forward won't wear a style that is now available to the masses. This theoretically brings more money to the overall industry, as more people spend money on new clothes more often, and it forces designers to innovate quickly and be more creative to meet customer demand. However, this same argument could be applied to other innovative and creative industries, such as software, music, or film, which are all currently protected by the law.

Some argue that copies don't really hurt the designer. If a designer creates a $2,000 dress of silk with the finest craftsmanship and it is copied in polyester with no lining and poor stitching, then it is not a copy, and it's definitely not appealing to the same customer. But unfortunately, it does prevent the designer from creating an authentic lower-priced version of the design himself, and it prevents customers from receiving an authentic designer product. For example, designer Erin Fetherston designed a high-end heart coat for her collection and then created a less expensive version for the Target Go International program. Designer Marc Bouwer intended to make an affordable version of the highly praised Oscar gown he designed for actress Marcia Cross, but it was knocked off and brought to market before he had the chance. Customers at any price point would prefer to have a real designer product, and copyright protection for fashion would also encourage more mass retailers like Kohls, Target, and H&M to continue to work with designers to create true designer collections for their stores.

Some worry that tough restrictions will make designers fearful of being sued, leading to fewer design offerings and less innovation. For example, if the trench coat had been copyrighted by the original designers, no one else would have taken that idea and developed it into the thousands of stylistic options that currently exist. However, the fear of being copied is already stifling creativity from designers, who are afraid to put their best ideas out to the market in case

they are immediately stolen. And the law will only protect the designs for three years; after that, the design will become public domain, and anyone can use it and it can develop as a trend for years to come. Three years gives the designer time to bring the high-end design to market, to benefit from its sales for one year, and then develop a more affordable version of the design and benefit from that for one more year before opening it up to the entire market.

Of course, there is the question of who is going to check all the copyrights and decide what is truly original versus inspired by someone else's design. The law will not cover commonplace designs such as jeans, T-shirts, trench coats, or anything in existence before the passing of the law. And fashion is often inspired, with well-known designers readily admitting that they are influenced by vintage, by Hollywood, by each other, and by conceptual designers such as Comme Des Garcons and Martin Margiela. But as CFDA Executive Director Steven Kolb states, "It's not a line by line, stitch by stitch protection, it's about protecting the DNA of the designer."[1] Despite challenges related to enforcement of the law, the existence of the law alone will deter dubious practices.

12

Expanding the Business

For designers with established retail accounts, press recognition, and annual sales of $1 to $4 million or more, the next step of growth can be elusive. The place between emerging and emerged is frustrating, and designers fear being pigeonholed as "young designers" for too long. Designer Alice Roi calls it "fashion puberty" and says, "No one in this place is anywhere firm."[1]

Some believe growth just takes time, and others believe it requires a cash infusion. At this stage more than ever, volume and finance become codependent. Increased volume causes costs to balloon, as the designer hires more employees and begins to outsource more work. The better department store accounts may require greater allowances or advertising co-op dollars before expanding your product into more doors. It becomes harder to protect your margin as your expenses increase.

This is where, if you don't have that business manager or partner on board, you need to find someone. It is critical for early-stage companies who have passed the initial start-up phase to focus on business strategy and to build a team with business acumen to find and evaluate opportunities and efficiencies to take the company to the next level. While many designers fear giving up any control, there is too much to do alone, and bringing in business expertise is often the only way to grow.

Designers often fear that the window of opportunity for growth is small, but beware of the desire to grow too quickly. Fast growth can suffocate a company that isn't ready, and while you expand, it is increasingly critical to

maintain tight control over quality and image. Build the business one step at a time, creating efficiencies before rushing to the next level.

Take time to map out each of your strategic options for growth with real time lines and numbers. This will help you effectively analyze your best and worst case scenarios and understand the cash flow and the potential profit or loss realities for each option.

As you seek to grow your business, the key is to remain focused and open at the same time. Currently, the trends are to break into the mass market, to offer product at a lower price point, and to partner for distribution. But these trends will change. The key is to stay focused as you look for new opportunities in the market, stay flexible in the face of change, and adapt with each evolution in a way which makes sense for your specific label.

Licensing

Licensing is the leasing of your brand name and product to a manufacturer for a specific purpose, for a specific length of time, and in a specific area in return for a "royalty," or percentage of sales. Generally, a licensee manufactures and distributes product under the designer's name and handles all the costs of production and sales. Licensees usually look to partner with known names that have cachet in the marketplace.

The main reason to license is to partner with someone who has expertise in an area that you do not. This can mean licensing to an expert in a new product category, such as eyewear or perfume. For the early-stage designer, however, it usually means partnering for production or distribution of their designs to enter a new market, such as Japan or China. While a designer may be able to develop a few accounts in a new market on her own, the differing laws, language, cultural issues and control of the sales and distribution channels may make building any sizable business difficult without a partner. Designers may also license to increase efficiency in their production. Designer Ria Brown started Mella in 2000 when she saw the opportunity to fill a void in the market for an upscale stylish flip-flop. She quickly grew the business to 800 accounts and established

strong brand awareness. After a few years, she decided to license her production to increase efficiency for the business.[2]

In addition to increasing income, licensing expands brand awareness with product categories and in markets outside the designer's specialty. Designer Alvin Valley is known as "The King of Pants," yet his jeanswear collection is licensed to a manufacturer that specializes in denim. Alvin Valley CEO Richard Rosenthal comments, "Licensing works best when a designer's name and designs add value to the manufacturer's expertise. The designer provides the designs, patterns, and the brand name; the manufacturer provides production expertise and economies of scale."[3]

Giving up the headaches of production, sales, and cash flow sounds ideal, but the risk is losing control. It's critical that you protect your image by requiring approval on all products and places of distribution and firmly set the quality standard for them. Require approval on any advertising and marketing that includes your name. An unethical licensing company could create product without your knowledge to make up its volume. In fact, a line from England had a licensing agreement for high-end clothing in Japan. When traveling there, the designers stopped at a convenience store and saw water bottle holders bearing their logo. They had not approved this type of product or this type of store. It's a good idea to attach an approved distribution list to your licensing agreements.

When choosing a licensee, ask for references and talk to some of its clients. Make sure the financial arrangement makes sense. Typically, the designer is paid a licensing fee based on a percentage of sales. It generally ranges from 3 to 6 percent. But if you have good sales connections that will open new doors for the licensee, you may be able to negotiate a higher percentage. Usually the licensor receives a guaranteed amount of royalty regardless of the product's performance.

Don't rush in to a deal. Jeffrey Tweedy, former executive vice president of Sean John, said because the company waited and built equity in its name and increased distribution first, it was able to get a better deal with a higher percentage and a high-end partner in Estee Lauder for its fragrance license.[4] Designers turn down deals for a multitude of reasons. Some agreements don't offer enough money, others want the designer to design a private label as part of the deal or pigeonhole the line in one specific design direction. Don't agree to a product unless it fits your

brand and helps to sell your other products. Beware of companies that may have a conflict of interest. For example, if you sign a licensing agreement with a retail store, it may be less motivated to distribute the product outside its stores.

A Second Line

Many designers feel they max out the market with their high-end line and can't keep growing the business exponentially. This can be common in the designer menswear category, where the market for high-end merchandise from new names is limited. A second line at a lower price point, or a line that focuses on a specialty item or new category, can increase awareness of your brand and open up another market and distribution channel. For example, designer Alicia Bell created Bell Epoque, a second line offering her signature shirts at multiple price points. Shoe label Loeffler Randall expanded its product offerings quickly. After two seasons of shoes, it added bags, and after two more seasons, it added apparel. The bags were a natural extension of shoes, and buyers were asking for them from the start. The apparel extension was inspired first by the addition of coats.[5]

A second line can take advantage of changes in the marketplace or the mind-set of a customer. For example, women's shoe designer Kristen Lee recently introduced a men's line of shoes called The Reform Party. She noticed the increasing number of fashion-forward menswear lines, including Trovata, Thom Browne, and Band of Outsiders, and saw an opportunity to create the shoes to accessorize them. She also added a simple, Italian-inspired attaché to accommodate the increasing amount of "stuff" that men now carry—mobile phones, wallets, iPods, keys, Blackberries, tickets, passports—which cannot be crammed into tight jean pockets.[6]

If a second line is created at a different quality level or focuses on a different market than your signature line, give it a different name to keep the cheaper goods from eroding the quality and image of the signature collection.

For example, designer Jeffrey Sebelia, who won season three of Project Runway, launched a new young contemporary line called "Jeffrey Sebelia," which targets a younger customer than his high-end, rocker label Cosa Nostra. The casual,

lower-priced collection still reflects his edgy aesthetic, but it will appeal to a wider audience, growing his reach and capitalizing on his Project Runway fame.

Remember that any brand extensions need to stay consistent with your signature product. The greater your consistency, the more easily you can reach even further into nonfashion lifestyle categories.

 ## The Council of Fashion Designers of America

The Council of Fashion Designers of America (CFDA) is a not-for-profit trade association whose membership consists of America's foremost fashion and accessory designers. The CFDA has several initiatives that are helpful to emerging designers, including the CFDA/Vogue Fashion Fund, the Swarovski Perry Ellis Awards, the Business Services Network (BSN), and the Business of Fashion seminar series with Gen Art.

The CFDA/Vogue Fashion Fund annually presents one emerging designer with a cash award of up to $200,000, two runners-up with $50,000 each, and business mentoring from a team of industry experts. This is one of the most coveted awards in fashion, and many designers say the true value of the award is the mentoring, not the money. An applicant must be in business for at least two consecutive years, have garnered recent editorial coverage, and have orders from key retailers. For consideration, designers complete a preliminary application with a biographical statement. These applications are narrowed down to a smaller group, who submit Phase II applications from which 10 finalists are selected. Past finalist designers who didn't even win say that going through the process and exercise of applying for the award changed their business strategies and brought them to a new level. They received valuable exposure to the industry and met potential business advisors and investors. The connections the award brings are extraordinary. Recent winners were given the opportunity to design white shirts for the Gap. And many of the finalists and winners have gone on to great new opportunities since being involved with the award. Alexandre Plokhov of Cloak is designing for Versace, Thakoon Panichgul for Hogan, Edmundo Castillo for Sergio Rossi, and Michael and Nicole Colovos of Habitual for Helmut Lang. Each year at the CFDA Fashion Awards, the Swarovski Perry Ellis Awards are presented to emerging design talent in women's ready-to-wear, menswear, and accessories. The award comes with considerable prestige and financial support.

Membership in the CFDA is by invitation, and each year, several new candidates are voted in by the board of directors. Members have the opportunity to attend numerous functions throughout the year, network with established designers, and make important fashion industry contacts. Members can also take advantage of the CFDA Business Services Network (BSN), which promotes "enterprise matchmaking" and offers designers discounted shipping, special services, and opportunities such as a free show booth at trade show Designers & Agents. A job network is being developed for the CFDA website (www.cfda.org), which will offer two tiers of industry jobs—one for members and another open to all.

Partnerships/Consulting

With the continued popularity and hype surrounding emerging designers, designers have increasing opportunity to extend their brand awareness, distribution, production abilities, and income through collaboration and partnership opportunities. Marc Beckman of Designers Management Agency (DMA) says there are opportunities in creative direction, licensing, product endorsement, sponsorship, and personal appearances.[7] His agency manages designers in a similar manner as talent agents handle actors and rock stars and helps them find alternative revenue streams.

It's no longer taboo or downscale to partner with mass-market retailers. Designer Isaac Mizrahi led the way with Target, followed by Karl Lagerfeld, Stella McCartney, and others partnering with mass retailers such as H & M, and then Simply Vera by Vera Wang for Kohls. During this evolution, mass retailers began showing an interest in bringing new emerging labels to their customers. Targets Go International Program gave the mass customer authentic but affordable designer wares from Luella Bartley, Libertine, Proenza Schouler, Keanan Duffty, Behnaz Sarafpour, Alice Temperley, Erin Fetherston, and more.

Through partnership with the CFDA/Vogue Fashion Fund, Gap launched its Design Editions program to introduce fledgling designers and Fashion Fund finalists, Doo-Ri, Rodarte, and Thakoon, to its broader audience through a series of limited-edition white shirt designs.

Photos by Dylan Griffin

Designs from the
Doo.Ri collection.

© Gap 2007 Inez & Vinoodh for Gap

Designer Doo-Ri with Model Stella
Tennant in one of Doo.Ri's designs
for Gap © Gap 2007 Photograph by
Inez van Lamsweerde and Vinoodh
Matadin for Gap.

The trend caught on, with Payless Shoes working with Lela Rose and Laura Poretsky of Abaete; Thakoon Panichgul creating footwear, gloves, and handbags for Nine West; and Uniqlo's collaboration with a series of eight designers. The Uniqlo program launched with designer Alice Roi, and the items, priced between $49.50 and $69.50, sold out of four styles almost immediately in New York. Phillip Lim, Alexander Plokhov of Cloak, and Lutz & Patmos are also creating collections for the chain.

It's not just the discount brands seeking collaboration with new talent. Brooks Brothers hired menswear designer Thom Browne as its first guest designer to create the higher-priced, edgy Black Fleece collection. And luxury company Tod's Group hired designer Thakoon Panichgul to work on a special collaborative project with Hogan.

Nonfashion partnerships and design opportunities abound as well and can be a great way to align with a large consumer brand and benefit from its advertising reach and customer base. Designer Luella Bartley is designing a suite at a resort owned by Sir Richard Branson, and New York designer Dana Buchman was commissioned to design the interior of a prototype Cadillac SRX. Other opportunities include collaborating with fabric companies; creating I-Pod cases; and designing uniforms and shopping bags and interiors for restaurants, bars, stores, and airlines.

All of these programs represent a key movement in marketing by larger, established brands. According to Marc Beckman, whose Designers Management Agency (DMA) arranges many of these deals, "traditional advertising doesn't connect with consumer in the same way anymore; you aren't going to buy a skirt because you saw it on a billboard or heard about it in a radio ad."[8] The larger companies instead use partnerships to bring the cachet and excitement of a new, buzz-worthy designer name to their brand as they try to respond to growing demand for designer name product at a different price point. The new, innovative product draws attention, which ultimately results in increased sales of their entire product range.

A partnership introduces the designer to a new and larger audience that doesn't otherwise buy that label. The designer benefits from the large distribution network of the partner and from the large marketing budgets that highlight the designer's name in advertising and PR campaigns.

A partnership also provides a unique opportunity to create designs at a lower price point without having to handle sourcing and production, and it can open new markets that a designer has previously been unable to crack. For example, the Alice Roi for Uniqlo designs were available at 900 Uniqlo stores in Asia.

Each deal comes with some financial support for the designer, though many say these deals are generally not that profitable. Compensation may include a flat design fee and a percentage of sales, which is generally between 2 and 6 per-

cent. According to *The New York Times Magazine*, people familiar with the Target Go International program say the designers have been paid approximately $250,000 for each collection.[9] Negotiating the details of the deal is important. Be very specific in defining your duties. Designing a bag could include sourcing the fabric and overseeing production or just providing sketches. The compensation should equal the time and effort put into the project as well as the use of your name. The agreements can last for one season or one product or include a multiyear contract for full collections or product lines.

Of course, you need to make sure you partner with the right brand. While the high-end brands bring enviable endorsement to the designer, a few designers have had their wholesale accounts drop their collections because the buyers were worried that their mass-brand partnership made the designer's product and name too accessible and not special enough for their high-end customers. If you are a new brand with high-end accounts and are offered a mass-market partnership, you may want to limit the partnership to just a few months rather than gamble on whether your brand can sustain a longer-term commitment at the low end.

Creative Direction

Beyond just a partnership or consulting opportunity, an independent designer may actually land a job as creative or design director for a large company. Investment companies that buy large fashion firms often seek a new designer who has buzz in the industry to renew and design the collections. For example, Bill Blass was acquired by NexCen Brands Inc., which hired Peter Som as its next creative chief. Halston was bought by Harvey Weinstein Co., which has been working with consultants and well-known stylists while looking for a designer. Other large brands will show their commitment to being fashion-forward as Gap did by hiring Patrick Robinson as executive vice president of design. European labels also tap new designers to revive a brand or replace a design talent as Tods brand did by hiring Derek Lam as creative director. Most of these designers continue to design their own labels while working with the larger brand (as Marc Jacobs does with Louis Vuitton).

Investors and Partners

Each growth step requires more money up front, and fortunately, as a business becomes more established, it becomes more attractive to investors. (See chapter 3, "The Money," for information on types of financing and finding and attracting investors.)

Investors ideally want a designer who has a history and track record but who is still interesting and fresh. In the past, the few investment companies interested in fashion were seeking designers with buzz regardless of their business acumen or profitability. They incorrectly assumed that if the talent was there, they could simply place high-level executives at the company and make it work. The new fashion investor realizes that the existing dynamic between people in a small business has to be strong, and big execs often don't understand the workings of a small business. Investors now look for companies that currently have a strong team that meshes well. They seek a designer and a businessperson who work in sync with each other and communicate and collaborate on a strategy to grow a brand. They want a company that is not just design talent but is already focused on a profitable business strategy, has at least $5 million in sales, and has significant potential for growth.

At any stage, designers are most likely to obtain funds from someone in the industry. Friends can be helpful if you have the right friends, such as David Geffen who helped his friend Calvin Klein in 1992. Think about the people with whom you conduct business. Approach factories, fabric suppliers, and retailers about potential partnership and support. You might find opportunities with distribution groups like Gibo, who distributes Victor and Rolf and Hussein Chalayan, and Diesel, who is supporting Martin Margiela. Be open about your desire and plans to grow and continue to get more involved in the fashion community at large.

Once you receive investment, the job is not done. Often, early-stage companies have several partners or need to go back to the market for a second round of investment. Proenza Schouler bought out its initial banking investor to open the door for Valentino Group, and Matthew Williamson has had investors from two different private equity groups.[10]

Acknowledgments

This book couldn't have been written if it weren't for all the designers who have taught me so much by sharing their triumphs, frustrations, and laughter during the past decade at Gen Art. There are too many to name, and while some are mentioned in this book, many more also have inspired me with their vision and drive.

Thank you to the many industry experts who have shared their valuable knowledge and perspective via interviews, emails, and casual conversations backstage. I'm particularly grateful to Sally Beers, Jason Gabbard, Steven Hahn, Melanie Jones, Charles Klein, Barbara Kramer, Tim Moore, Rachel Shectman, and Roger Padilha, who provided the thoughtful contributions in the book.

Gen Art has been my home for several years, and I'm truly thankful for the support and friendship of everyone there. Especially from Ian Gerard, who generously provided time and significant encouragement for this project.

Thank you to Shannon Berning, Joshua Martino and Dominique Polfliet, the editors at Kaplan who have worked so hard to help this second edition fall into place.

Thank you to my friends and colleagues Michelle Barge, Hope McGrath, Cator Sparks, Tali Sedgwick, Lee Trimble, and Linden Schaffer, who provided invaluable support and feedback. And to my parents: Eleanor Gehlhar, who sparked my love for fashion, and Len Gehlhar, who inspired me with the enthusiasm, humor, and business acumen of a successful entrepreneur.

Most of all, thank you to my wonderful husband, Mark Kiernan, for unending encouragement, brilliant insight, and so many evenings, Saturdays, and Sundays.

Notes

Chapter 1

1. "CFDA/Gen Art: The Business of Fashion," panel discussion, CUNY Graduate Center, New York, November 3, 2004.
2. Miles Socha, "The Luxury Hangover: Designers Struggling with Harsher Reality," *WWD*, July 1, 2002.
3. Teri Agins, "The Lessons of Isaac," *The Wall Street Journal*, February 7, 2005.
4. Discussion with author, October 12, 2004.
5. Discussion with author, October 1, 2004.
6. Discussion with author, December 2, 2004.
7. Discussion with author, September 24, 2004.
8. Discussion with author, December 12, 2004.
9. Discussion with author, January 27, 2005.
10. Discussion with author, November 12, 2004.
11. "CFDA/Gen Art: The Business of Fashion," panel discussion, CUNY Graduate Center, New York, November 3, 2004.
12. Correspondence with author, February 2005.
13. Stephanie D. Smith, "Start Them Young," *WWD Global*, October 2007.
14. *Vogue*, December 2003.
15. Discussion with author, December 22, 2004.
16. Discussion with author, December 15, 2004.
17. "CFDA/Gen Art: The Business of Fashion," panel discussion, CUNY Graduate Center, New York, November 3, 2004.
18. Discussion with author, January 2005.
19. Discussion with author, September 24, 2004.

Chapter 2

1. 1. Discussion with author, December 22, 2004.
2. 2. Discussion with author, November 30, 2004.
3. 3. Discussion with author, December 12, 2004.
4. "CFDA/Gen Art: The Business of Fashion," panel discussion, Kronish, Lieb, Weiner, &

Hellman, New York, July 13, 2000.

5. Discussion with author, November 1, 2007.

6. "CFDA/Gen Art: Business of Fashion" panel discussion, Saks Fifth Avenue, New York, August 8, 2007.

7. Julee Greenberg, "Adam Lippes Goes Forward Minus Eve," *WWD*, August 9, 2007.

8. "CFDA/Gen Art: Business of Fashion" panel discussion, Saks Fifth Avenue, New York, August 8, 2007.

9. Discussion with author, October 21, 2004.

10. Discussion with author, January 27, 2005.

11. Correspondence with author, October 2004.

12. "CFDA/Gen Art: Business of Fashion" panel discussion, Saks Fifth Avenue, New York, August 8, 2007.

Chapter 3

1. Discussion with author, November 11, 2004.

2. Miles Socha and Marc Karimzadeh, "Backing the Boys: Valentine Group Takes Stake in Proenza Schouler," *WWD*, July 11, 2007.

3. Josh Patner, "Fashion Darwinism: Surviving Until the Next Season," *The New York Times*, February 10, 2002.

4. Michael Spaulding (designer, Gunmetal), discussion with author, December 12, 2004.

5. Tracie Rozhon, "Applause Won't Buy Many Buttons," *The New York Times*, February 8, 2004.

6. Discussion with author, July 22, 2004.

7. "CFDA/Gen Art: Business of Fashion" panel discussion, Saks Fifth Avenue, New York, August 8, 2007.

8. Nike Ingwa Clausing and Tina Hernaiz Melero (designers, Ingwa; Melero), discussion with author, October 7, 2004.

9. Wenlan Chia (designer, Twinkle), discussion with author, October 26, 2004.

10. Michelle Smith (designer, Milly), discussion with author, October 21, 2004.

11. Eric Wilson, "The Cost of Starting Out," *WWD*, February 7, 2003.

12. Discussion with author, December 15, 2004.

13. Discussion with author, October 16, 2004.

14. Discussion with author, October 26, 2004.

15. Discussion with author, December 15, 2004.

16. Discussion with author, November 1, 2004.

17. 17 "CFDA/Gen Art: The Business of Fashion," panel discussion, Kronish, Lieb, Weiner, and Hellman, New York, July 13, 2000.

18. "CFDA/Gen Art: The Business of Fashion," panel discussion, CUNY Graduate Center, New York, July 13, 2004.

19. "Fashion Darwinism: Surviving Until the Next Season," *The New York Times*, February 10, 2002.

20. Discussion with author, September 24, 2007.

21. Correspondence with author, November 24, 2007.

22. Miles Socha and Marc Karimzadeh, "Backing the Boys: Valentine Group Takes Stake in Proenza Schouler," *WWD*, July 11, 2007.

23. Discussion with author, September 24, 2007.

24. Amy Larocca, "Mr. In-Between," *New York* Magazine, July 30, 2007.

25. Samatha Conti, "Richemont Backs Fashion Investment Fund," *WWD*, February 5, 2007.

26. Marc Karimzadeh, *WWD*, August 28, 2007.

27. Tom Braithwaite, "VC Fund Is Tailor-Made for Fashion," *Financial Times*, March 5, 2007.

28. David Moin, *WWD*, September 7, 2007.

29. Ibid.

30. "CFDA/Gen Art: The Business of Fashion," panel discussion, National Arts Club, New York, July 17, 2001.

Chapter 4

1. Discussion with author, October 26, 2004.

2. Discussion with author, November 1, 2007.

3. "CFDA/Gen Art: The Business of Fashion," panel discussion, CUNY Graduate Center, New York, February 22, 2005.

4. Discussion with author, October 19, 2007.

5. "CFDA/Gen Art: The Business of Fashion," panel discussion, CUNY Graduate Center, New York, November 3, 2004.

6. Discussion with author, November 30, 2004.

7. Discussion with author, October 26, 2007.

8. Discussion with author, November 30, 2004.

9. Discussion with author, October 29, 2007.

10. Discussion with author, October 21, 2004.

Chapter 5

1. Discussion with author, October 26, 2007.

2. Discussion with author, January 11, 2005.

3. "CFDA/Gen Art: The Business of Fashion," panel discussion, CUNY Graduate Center, New York, July 13, 2004.

4. Discussion with author, November 1, 2007.

5. Discussion with author, September 14, 2004.

6. Amy Larocca, "Mr. In-Between," *New York* Magazine, July 30, 2007.

7. Discussion with author, October 12, 2004.

8. Discussion with author, September 14, 2004.

Chapter 6

1. "New York's Premier Patternmaker Is Transforming American Fashion One Stitch at a Time," *Elle*, September 2007.

2. Correspondence with author, October 2004.

3. Discussion with author, November 4, 2004.

4. Discussion with author, December 12, 2004.

5. Hamish Bowles, "Hooray for Hollywould," *Vogue*, November 2004.

6. Discussion with author, August 2004.

7. Correspondence with author, January 2005.

8. April Y. Pennington, "Smarts: Snapshots Natalie Chanin & Enrico," *Entreprenuer*, February 2003.

9. "CFDA/Gen Art: The Business of Fashion," panel discussion, CUNY Graduate Center, New York, July 13, 2004.

10. Discussion with author, October 26, 2007.

11. Discussion with author, October 17, 2007.

12. Discussion with author, November 1, 2007.

13. Discussion with author, October 5, 2004.

14. Discussion with author, December 22, 2004.

15. Correspondence with author, January 2005.

16. Discussion with author, December 12, 2004.

17. Discussion with author, November 1, 2004.

Chapter 7

1. Jeff Bercovici, "Every Picture Tells a Story," *WWD*, May 24, 2004.

2. "CFDA/Gen Art: The Business of Fashion," panel discussion, CUNY Graduate Center, New York, November 3, 2004.

3. Discussion with author, January 25, 2005.

4. Discussion with author, December 3, 2004.

Chapter 8

1. Discussion with author, January 13, 2005.

2. "CFDA/Gen Art: The Business of Fashion," panel discussion, CUNY Graduate Center, New York, July 13, 2004.

3. Discussion with author, October 16, 2004.

4. Discussion with author, December 22, 2004.

5. Discussion with author, October 24, 2004.

6. Discussion with author, September 24, 2007.

7. Discussion with author, December 2, 2004.

8. Discussion with author, October 19, 2007

9. Discussion with author, November 1, 2004.

10. Marc Karimzadeh, "Rolling the Dice," *WWD*, November 14, 2007.

11. Discussion with author, October 19, 2007.

12. Discussion with author, December 15, 2004.

13. Discussion with author, November 1, 2004.

14. Hitha Prabakar, "Style Spotlight: Chloe Dao," Forbes.com, March, 5, 2007.

15. Discussion with author, January 11, 2005.

16. Discussion with author, November 9, 2004.

17. "CFDA/Gen Art: The Business of Fashion," panel discussion, CUNY Graduate Center, New York, November 3, 2004.

18. Discussion with author, November 30, 2004.

19. Discussion with author, November 4, 2004.

20. Discussion with author, October 2004.

21. Correspondence with author, March 2005.

22. Discussion with author, November 1, 2007.

23. "CFDA/Gen Art: The Business of Fashion," panel discussion, CUNY Graduate Center, New York, November 3, 2004.

24. Discussion with author, October 29, 2007.

25. "CFDA/Gen Art: The Future of Fashion," panel discussion, CUNY Graduate Center, New York, March 25, 2003.

26. Caitlin Lui, "The Brains Behind the Brand," Conde Nast Portfolio.com, December 6, 2007.

27. "CFDA/Gen Art: The Business of Fashion," panel discussion, CUNY Graduate Center, New York, November 3, 2004.

28. Discussion with author, November 30, 2004.

29. Correspondence with author, November 5, 2007.

30. "CFDA/Gen Art: The Business of Fashion," panel discussion, CUNY Graduate Center,

New York, November 3, 2004.

31. Discussion with author, December 7, 2004.

32. Discussion with author, January 2005.

33. Discussion with author, October 26, 2004.

34. Correspondence with author, January 2005.

35. "CFDA/Gen Art: The Business of Fashion," panel discussion, CUNY Graduate Center, New York, November 3, 2004.

36. Discussion with author, November 30, 2004.

37. "CFDA/Gen Art: The Business of Fashion," panel discussion, CUNY Graduate Center, New York, July 13, 2004.

38. Bonnie Bing, "Designers Sometimes Play Well Together," The Wichita Eagle, June 16, 2003.

39. Discussion with author, October 19, 2007.

40. Discussion with author, December 9, 2004.

41. Discussion with author, January 11, 2005.

42. Discussion with author, October 21, 2004.

43. Discussion with author, December 7, 2004.

44. "CFDA/Gen Art: The Business of Fashion," panel discussion, CUNY Graduate Center, New York, November 3, 2004.

45. Discussion with author, December 9, 2004.

46. Discussion with author, October 29, 2007.

Chapter 9

1. "CFDA/Gen Art: The Business of Fashion," panel discussion, CUNY Graduate Center, New York, July 13, 2004.

2. "CFDA/Gen Art: Business of Fashion," panel discussion, CUNY Graduate Center, New York, February 22, 2005.

3. Teri Agins, The End of Fashion: How Marketing Changed the Clothing Business Forever, William Morrow, 1999.

4. Discussion with author, October 2004.

5. 5. "CFDA/Gen Art: The Future of Fashion," panel discussion, CUNY Graduate Center, New York, March 25, 2003.

6. "CFDA/Gen Art: The Business of Fashion," panel discussion, CUNY Graduate Center, New York, November 3, 2004.

7. Discussion with author December 3, 2004.

8. "The Next Big Names in Fashion," The ShowBuzz.com, June 5, 2006.

9. Beth Wilson, "Adam Lippes Gets Boost From Oprah Appearance," WWD, October 16, 2007.

10. "CFDA/Gen Art: The Future of Fashion," panel discussion, CUNY Graduate Center, New York, March 25, 2003.

11. Discussion with author, November 11, 2004.

12. "CFDA/Gen Art: Business of Fashion" panel discussion, Saks Fifth Avenue, New York, August 8, 2007.

13. Jaime Huckbody, "Fashion & Style: Partners in Style," *The London Independent*, February 3, 2005.

14. Vanessa Friedman, "From Scarf to Finish," FT.com, July 14, 2006.

15. Susan Cernak, "Blog Is the New Black," *The New York Times* T: Women's Fashion Magazine, August 26, 2007.

16. Correspondence with author, November 2004.

17. Discussion with author, January 2005.

18. Discussion with author, December 17, 2004.

Chapter 10

1. Discussion with author, November 2, 2004.

2. Discussion with author, January 27, 2005.

3. Discussion with author, November 1, 2007.

4. "CFDA/Gen Art: The Business of Fashion," panel discussion, CUNY Graduate Center, New York, November 3, 2004.

5. David Lipke, "If I Only Knew Then What I Know Now," *DNR*, January 6, 2003.

6. "CFDA/Gen Art: The Future of Fashion," panel discussion, CUNY Graduate Center, New York, March 25, 2003.

7. "CFDA/Gen Art: The Business of Fashion," panel discussion, CUNY Graduate Center, New York, July 13, 2004.

8. Discussion with author, October 21, 2004.

9. Discussion with author, February 2005.

10. Discussion with author, January 2005.

11. Ibid.

Chapter 11

1. Discussion with author, October 3, 2007.

Chapter 12

1. Discussion with author, November 30, 2004.

2. Discussion with author, October 29, 2007.

3. Discussion with author, October 24, 2004.

4. "CFDA/Gen Art: The Business of Fashion," panel discussion, CUNY Graduate Center, New York, July 13, 2004.

5. Discussion with author, October 26, 2007.

6. Discussion with author, October 29, 2007.

7. Discussion with author, September 2, 2004.

8. Discussion with author, September 17, 2007.

9. Eric Wilson, "The Big Brand Theory," *The New York Times Magazine*, September 9, 2007.

10. Samantha Conti, "Bauger Banking on Growing Brands," *WWD*, August 28, 2007.

Business Resources

- Athena International (www.athenafoundation.org) Supports woman-owned businesses and sponsors the Athena Powerlink program, which matches woman entrepreneurs with a group of mentors and business advisors.

- The Business of Fashion (www.uberkid.typepad.com) Imran Amed advises emerging fashion designers, global fashion houses, and online fashion companies on strategy, business development, and investment issues, and some of his day-to-day learning is shared on The Business of Fashion, a blog that attracts an audience of senior-level fashion executives, fashion designers, industry insiders, equity analysts, and students and journalists of fashion and business from over 140 countries.

- Centre for Fashion Enterprise (CFE) in London, England (www.fashionenterprise.com) The CFE at London College of Fashion builds new high-fashion companies and global brands in London.

- Chicagoland Entrepreneurial Center (www.chicagolandec.org) Helps provide Chicago entrepreneurs with financial support and business advice. A sponsor of the Chicago Fashion Incubator.

- Columbia University Small Business Consulting Program (SBCP) (www0.gsb.columbia.edu/students/organizations/sbcp/) SBCP was founded by MBA students to provide pro bono consulting services to entrepreneurs, nonprofit organizations, and other local businesses.

- Counterfeitchic (www.counterfeitchic.com) Website and blog by law school professor Susan Scafidi extensively covers issues of fashion counterfeits.

- Designers Management Agency (DMA) (www.designersmanagement.com) This fashion "ecosystem" of designers, nonprofits including the CFDA, manufacturers, retailers, and consumer goods companies focuses on creating strategic retail partnerships. DMA provides talent representation services for luxury fashion designers, including creative director placement, licensing, cobranding, sponsorships of shows and events, and product endorsements. DMA is interested in working with designers who are currently maintaining top-tier distribution, have an ability to design beyond apparel into other product categories, and have some influential following and are open-minded to new business models.

- Entreprenuer's BizStartUp (www.entrepreneur.com/bizstartups) Covers all aspects of starting a business, from business plan and financing to market research and legal issues.

- Fashion Business Club (www.fashionbusinessclub.net) This London-based membership group was created on the basis of bringing bright-minded, fashion business professionals together six times a year at an informal venue to listen, learn, and do business together.

- Fashion Business Inc. (www.fashionbizinc.org) Business resource for fashion entrepreneurs in Los Angeles, California, offers classes, mentoring, referrals, and a resourceful website.

- Fashion Inc. (www.portfolio.com/views/blogs/fashion-inc/) This is an excellent blog by Lauren Goldstein Crowe of Condé Nast Portfolio on the fashion business.

- Fashion Institute of Technology (www.fitnyc.suny.edu) Offers business classes and computer software training programs.

- Global Purchasing Group (www.globalpurchasinggroup.com) This buying office conducts workshops, training, and production management seminars for emerging designers.

- Industrial Technology Assistance Corporation (ITAC) (www.itac.org) Offers multiple resources for small New York City businesses, including 12-week small business training sessions.

- Launch Collective (www.launchcollective.com) This boutique consulting firm specializes in providing business expertise to creative businesses in design and retail.

- My Own Business (www.myownbusiness.org) Offers a free online course for starting a business.

- Network Solutions (www.networksolutions.com) Checks availability for Internet domain names.

- New York Business Development Corporation (www.nybdc.com)

- New York City Economic Development Corporation (www.newyork biz.com)

- On the Runway (http://runway.blogs.nytimes.com) This is Cathy Horyn's excellent fashion blog for the New York Times.

- Parsons School of Design (www.parsons.edu) Offers continuing education on the business of fashion.

- Prosper (www.prosper.com) At America's first people-to-people lending marketplace, people list and bid on loans using an online auction platform.

- Service Corps of Retired Executives (www.score.org)

- Small Business Administration (www.sba.gov)

Fabrics and Production

- Alibaba (www.alibaba.com) Extensive and somewhat overwhelming directory lists global sources for materials and manufacturing for everything.

- The Alexander Report (www.thealexanderreport.com) This is a guide to hundreds of business resources and services, including fabrics, production, factors, and more.

- American Apparel Producers Network (www.aapnetwork.net/Content/114.htm) Directory lists American sources of production, fabric, and trim.

- Apparel Search (www.apparelsearch.com) Directory lists CMT factories and contractors.

- B&J Fabrics (www.bandjfabrics.com) 525 7th Avenue, New York, 212-354-8150

- Bergen Shippers (www.bergenshippers.com) Bergen is a leading warehouse and fulfillment center for the apparel industry.

- C&J Textiles Inc. (www.cjtextile.com)

- Duty and tariff rates (www.customs.gov/xp/cgov/import/duty_rates/determining.xml)

- E Source Apparel (www.esourceapparel.com/Home.asp) Directory lists international sources for textiles, production, factories, technology, legal advice, and shipping—all targeted to the apparel industry.
- Easysourcing (www.easysourcing.net) Gives apparel industry news and guides to find fabric and production vendors.
- Erich Soldat Textile Agency, New York, email: esoldat@peoplec.com
- Evans Group (http://evansgroupinternational.com) This fashion development and production house for independent and emerging designers has locations in Los Angeles and San Francisco. Specializes in high-end designs, making patterns and samples and filling small production orders.
- Fabric Link (www.fabriclink.com) Has education on fibers, burn tests, and care instruction.
- Fabrics.net (www.fabrics.net) Provides information on working on fabric and leather.
- Fabric Stock Exchange (www.fabricstockexchange.com/benefit.html)
- The Fashion Center (www.fashioncenter.com) Operates the information kiosk in the New York Fashion District. Provides lists of factories, fabrics, and services in the New York garment district.
- Fashiondex (www.fashiondex.com) Guide to fabric and contractors publishes The Small Design Company's Guide To Wholesale Fabrics.
- Fiber Source (www.fibersource.com)
- Garment Contractors Association of Southern California (www.gar mentcontractors. org) Lists services, minimums, and specialties.
- Garment Industry Development Corporation (www.gidc.org) Provides referrals to production resources in New York.
- Garment Manufacturers Index (www.klevenspub.com) Bilingual guide lists fabrics, contractors, trims, and services.
- The Handbag Resource (http://thehandbagresource.com/index.ptp) Sells handbag design software.
- Infomat (www.infomat.com) Guide lists suppliers, contractors, and industry calendar.
- Jasco Fabrics (www.jascofabrics.com)
- Los Angeles Fashion District (www.fashiondistrict.org)
- Mood Fabrics (www.moodfabrics.com)
- Nancy Whiskey and The Sewing Factory (www.thesewingfactory.com)
- Panjiva (www.panjiva.com) New York–based company helps fashion brands find and evaluate factories with a database of more than 40,000 apparel suppliers around the globe.
- Pattern Design (www.pattern-design.com)
- Patternmakers (www.tukaweb.com)
- Robert Kaufman Fabrics, Los Angeles, California (www.robertkaufman.com)
- S. Rimmon & Co. Los Angeles, California (www.rimmon.com/rimmon fabrics.htm)

- Style Source (www.style-source.com) Production and materials resource includes specific information geared to small companies.
- Textile and Apparel Traders (www.textileandappareltraders.com) Online community with forums, referrals, and trading opportunities to get rid of dead stock and partners to meet minimums and buy in bulk.
- Textile Association of Los Angeles (www.talausa.com)
- Textiles (www.textiles.com)
- "Threading Your Way through the Labeling Requirements under the Textile and Wool Acts" (www.ftc.gov)
- Uni Designers, London (www.unidesigners.com/company.php)
- Wear Canada (www.wearcanada.com) Provides services and directory that lists Canadian vendors and suppliers.

Organic and Eco-Friendly Organizations and Suppliers

- Aurora Silk (www.aurorasilk.com) This is Master Dyer Cheryl Kolander's source for natural dyes, fabrics, and fibers.
- Cotec (www.cotec-epo.com) Sells eco-friendly fabric, including PVC-free handbag linings.
- Earth Pledge (www.earthpledge.org) The Earth Pledge FutureFashion Initiative demonstrates that fashion can be sustainable. Working with the industry, promotes renewable, reusable, and nonpolluting materials and methods, while informing consumers of the impact of their choices.
- Eco Textile News (www.ecotextile.com)
- Jasco Fabrics (www.jascofabrics.com) Known for its high-end jersey and support of new designers, the new Jasco Eco line offers a stock service collection of certified organic wool and sustainable fabrics in vibrant colors created with eco-friendly dyes.
- Natural Fiber Mills (http://naturalfibermills.com/profile.html) Manufactures EcoShade yarn and fabric made from 100 percent organic cotton.
- Near Sea Naturals (www.nearseanaturals.com) Online source for natural and organic fabrics and notions.
- Organic Clothing (www.organic_clothing.com) Offers a wealth of information on organic fibers, suppliers, dyes and chemicals, fair trade, etc. plus useful "Facts about the Fiber" features on bamboo, hemp, cotton, wool, and more.
- Organic Cotton Directory (www.organiccottondirectory.net)
- Organic Exchange (www.organicexchange.org) Committed to organic agriculture, this organization's website includes a source guide for finding organic fibers and materials.
- Organic Trade Association (OTA) (www.theorganicpages.com) Guide lists organic products and resources.
- Sustainable Style Foundation (SSF) (www.sustainablestylefoundation.org) Includes an online fashion sourcebook.

Fashion Organizations

- Accessories Council (www.accessoriescouncil.org)
- BoxEight (www.boxeight.com) This Los Angeles arts organization sponsors a downtown fashion week venue for select designers.
- British Fashion Council (www.londonfashionweek.co.uk)
- Chicago Apparel Industry Board (www.aibi.com)
- Chicago Fashion Resource (www.chicagofashionresource.com) The City of Chicago's website includes a listing of local designers and boutiques and plans to include a directory of local job opportunities, manufacturers, stylists, and photographers.
- Council of Fashion Designers of America (CFDA) (www.cfda.com)
- Ecco Domani Fashion Foundation (www.style.com/eccodomani/fashion.html)
- Fashion Calendar (www.fashioncalendar.net) 212-289-0420
- Fashion Fringe (www.fashionfringe.co.uk) Offers a London funding opportunity for British designers.
- Fashion Group International (www.fgi.org)
- Fashion Quarters (www.fashionquarters.com) On this free networking website, designers can buy and sell excess inventory and materials and share information, news, events, services, and job opportunities.
- FashionWeekLA (www.fashionweekla.com) Free calendar lists all Los Angeles fashion events.
- Gen Art (www.genart.org) National organization showcases and supports emerging fashion talent through runway shows, business seminars, and shopping events.
- The Hyeres International Festival of Fashion and Photography Awards (www. villanoailles-hyeres.com/pdf_2008/h2008_mode.pdf)
- IMG Mercedes Benz Fashion Week (www.imgworld.com/entertainment/fashion/events.sps)
- Modem (www.modemonline.com/fashion) International reference lists fashion designers, showrooms, PR offices, and trade shows.
- San Francisco Fashion Industries (www.sffi.org)
- San Francisco Fashion Week (www.fashionweek-sf.com/fashion_week/2007/index.html)
- Swiss Textiles Award (www.swisstextiles.ch/en/index.cfm)
- YMA Fashion Scholarship Fund (http://the-yma.com) Nonprofit organization is dedicated to advancing the fashion industry through scholarships, mentoring, and internship programs.
- Zero Land, New Zealand (www.zeroland.co.nz/fashion_style.html)

Regional Markets

- Atlanta (www.americasmart.com)
- Chicago (www.merchandisemart.com)
- Dallas (www.dallasmarketcenter.com)
- Denver (www.denvermart.com)
- Los Angeles (www.carliforniamarketcenter.com)
- Los Angeles (www.newmart.net)
- San Francisco (www.fashionsanfrancisco.com)

Finance

- Accion New York (www.accionnewyork.org) Provides microloans to local microenterprise owners, mostly minorities and women.
- Brooklyn Economic Development Corporation (www.bedc.org)
- Dun and Bradstreet (D&B) (www.dnb.com) D&B provides a credit-checking service.
- Fashion Capital (www.fashioncapital.co.uk) London accounting firm has an informational website.
- Go Big Network (www.gobignetwork.com) Go Big Network is an angel investor network.
- Hilldun Corporation (www.hilldun.com) Offers accounts receivable, financing ,and factoring services; specializes in the needs of small business.
- Seed Co. Loans (www.seedco.org) National nonprofit organization works with local partners to create economic opportunities for neighborhood entrepreneurs in select cities and states, including New York, Atlanta, Baltimore, Memphis, and New Orleans.

Job Resources

- 24 Seven (www.24seveninc.com)
- Apparel Job Board (www.appareljobboard.com)
- DNR (www.dailynewsrecord.com) Offers classified ads.
- Fashion Career Center (www.fashioncareercenter.com)
- Fashion Career Expo (WWD) (www.fashioncareerexpo.com)
- Fashion Careers.com (www.fashioncareers.com) This is the online career center of WWD, DNR, and FN.
- Fashion Internships (www.fashioninternships.blogspot.com)
- Fashion Net (www.fashion.net/jobs/)
- Hint Fashion Magazine (www.hintmag.com) Offers classified ads.
- Style Careers (www.stylecareers.com)
- WWD (www.wwd.com) Offers classified ads.
- Vault (www.vault.com)

Legal Services

- Jason Gabbard is an entertainment and business attorney practicing in New York City. Mr. Gabbard's offices are in midtown Manhattan. Email: gabbard@gmail.com.
- Charles Klein is an attorney with the firm of Davidoff Malito & Hutcher LLP, a 35-lawyer midtown Manhattan law firm, where he specializes in the representation of fashion companies. Mr. Klein was the founding president of The Fashion Roundtable and of The Fashion Service Network, and he is the editor/publisher of Fashion & The Law. Contact at 646 428 3240 or ck@dmlegal.com
- Volunteer Lawyers for the Arts (www.vlany.org)

Sales Opportunities

- Henri Bendel Open Sees, 212-904-7992
- Saks Fifth Avenue Open Calls, 877-551-SAKS (7257)

Incubators and New Designer Markets

- Chicago Fashion Incubator at Macys (www.chicagolandec.org)
- Dallas Fashion Incubator (www.dallasfashionincubator.net)
- Dunedin Incubator, New Zealand (www.dfi.co.nz)
- I Heart Rummage, Seattle (www.iheartrummage.com)
- London Fashion East (www.fashioneast.co.uk)
- The Market NYC (www.themarketnyc.com)
- Melbourne Fashion & Design Incubator (www.mdfi.com.au)
- Portland Fashion News and Resource (www.ultrapdx.com)
- Toronto Fashion Incubator (www.fashionincubator.com)

Online Stores

- Active Endeavors (www.activeendeavors.com)
- Blue Bee (www.bluebee.com)
- Bluefly (www.bluefly.com)
- Intermix (www.intermixonline.com)
- La Garconne (www.lagarconne.com
- Le Train Bleu (www.letrainbleu.com)
- Miostile (www.miostile.com)
- Net A Porter (www.netaporter.com)
- Ravinstyle (www.ravinstyle.com)
- Refinery 29 Shops (www.refinery29shops.com)
- Revolve Clothing (www.revolveclothing.com)

- Shop Bop (www.shopbop.com)

Stylists, Photographers, Makeup, and Hair

- Fashion Book (www.fashionbook.com)
- Le book (www.lebook.com)
- Who Represents (www.whorepresents.com) Lists agents and representatives for celebrities.

Technology and Software

- Apparel Information Management System (AIMS) (www.aimshotline.com) A complete order and production processing system that manages fabric and trims, costing, sales and customer service, shipping, accounts receivable, returns processing, and EDI.
- Apparel Search (www.apparelsearch.com) Offers an extensive listing of apparel industry software companies and programs.
- Fashion GPS (www.fashiongps.com) This Web-based service streamlines the sample management process, tracking samples going to sales showrooms, to editorial, and to celebrities and stylists. It minimizes lost samples, sends email reminders, creates online lookbooks for editors and buyers to browse the looks online and place their requests, and tracks the resulting PR. Clients include Zac Posen, Peter Som, and Diane Von Furstenberg.
- Logon (www.logonsystems.com) Provides technology and software solutions specifically designed for the apparel and footwear industry. Has small-business, Web-based ERP solutions to manage the sales cycle, production control, and raw material management.
- Supply Chain Online (www.supplychainonline.com) Helps companies learn to create their own spreadsheets for production in Excel. Free downloads can help you understand what else you need to learn to maximize the efficiency of Excel.

Trade Shows

There are hundreds of other trade shows around the world in countries including Australia, Canada, China, Denmark, Hong Kong, Korea, Poland, Russia, and Sweden, and many shows focus on specific categories such as bridal, childrenswear, shoes, jewelry, and lingerie. This is just a selection of the primaryshows for smaller companies focusing on ready-to-wear and accessories.

Textile and Sourcing

- Direction New York (www.directionshow.com)
- Kingpin Sourcing and Textile Show, Los Angeles (www.olah.com) Invitation-only show focuses on premium denim. Created by New York–based garment and fabric agent Olah Inc.
- Linea Pelle, Italy (www.lineapelle-fair.it) This is the premiere exhibition dedicated to leather, accessories, components, and models for footwear and leather goods.
- Los Angeles International Textile Show (www.californiamarketcenter.com/markets/latextile_main.php)
- Première Vision Paris France (www.premierevision.fr)
- Première Vision Preview New York (www.europeanpreview.com)
- Sourcing at Magic, Las Vegas (www.fabricshow.com)
- Turkish Fashion Fabric Exhibition (TFFE), New York (http://turkishfabric.com)

Product Wholesale

United States

- Accessories Circuit, New York (www.enkshows.com) 212-759-8055
- Accessories the Show, New York and Las Vegas (www.accessoriestheshow.com)
- Capsule, New York, Menswear, accessories
- Clear, New York (www.enkshows.com) Luxury accessories
- Coterie, New York (www.enkshows.com) Womenswear, 212-759-8055
- Designers and Agents, New York and Los Angeles (www.designersandagents.com) better Designer and contemporary
- Intermezzo, New York (www.enkshows.com) 212-759-8055
- Lingerie Americas, New York (http://lingerie-americas.com)
- Londonedge, New York (www.lenylondonedge.com)
- Magic, Las Vegas (www.magiconline.com) Accessories, menswear, womenswear
- Pool, Las Vegas (www.pooltradeshow.com)
- Project Global Tradeshow, New York and Las Vegas (http://projectshow.com) Menswear, womenswear
- Sole Commerce, New York (www.enkshows.com) Shoes
- Swim Show Miami (www.swimshow.com)
- Trafik Tradeshow, Miami and Atlanta (www.trafiktradeshow.com)
- The Train, New York (www.thetrainnewyork.com) Women's ready-to-wear, accessories

Barcelona, Spain

- Bread and Butter (www.breadandbutter.com)

Berlin, Germany

- Fifth Floor (www.fifth-floor-berlin.de)
- Ideal, Berlin (www.ideal-berlin.com) Small innovative labels
- Premium (www.premiumexhibitions.com)

Italy

- Cloudnine, Milan (www.pittimmagine.com/it/fiere/touchneozonecloudnine) Women's accessories
- Mix Milano, Milan, (www.mix-milano.com) Young and emerging fashion talents
- Neozone, Milan (www.neozone.it) Women's ready-to-wear,
- Pitti Immagine and Pitti Uomo, Florence (www.pittimmagine.com) Menswear
- White, Milan (http://whiteshow.it) Womenswear

London, England

- Designers and Agents (www.designersandagents.com)
- Eye2eye (www.eye2eye-london.com) Accessories and footwear
- For Attention Of (www.forattentionof.com)
- Londonedge, London and New York (www.londonedge.com)
- Pure (www.purewomenswear.co.uk) Womenswear, accessories
- TBC-2BeConfirmed (www.2beconfirmed.com) Menswear

Paris, France

- 19 Vendome (www.xxb.fr)
- Atmosphere/Prêt à Porter (www.pretparis.com)
- Le Showroom (www.leshowroom.fr)
- Premiere Classe (www.premiere-classe.com) Accessories
- Rendez-Vous (www.rendez-vous-paris.com)
- Tranoi (www.tranoi.com) Menswear, womenswear
- Who's Next (www.whosnext.com)
- Workshop (www.workshopsalons.com) Womenswear

Tokyo, Japan

- Designers and Agents (www.designersandagents.com)
- Japan Creation (www.japancreation.com)
- International Fashion Fair (www.senken.co.jp)
- Livingroom (http://livingroomtokyo.com) Womenswear, accessories
- Rooms (www.roomsroom.com) Womenswear, menswear, accessories
- Workshop Tokyo (www.workshopsalons.com)

Wholesale Showrooms

- CD Network, New York (www.cdnetworkny.com)
- Cynthia O'Connor (www.cocandco.com)
- Denise Williamson, New York (www.dwshowroom.com)
- Findings, New York and Los Angeles (www.findingsinc.com)
- Greg Mills, New York (www.gregmillsltd.com)
- HASSON Mireles, New York 212-354-3272
- Laurie Hasson, Los Angeles, 213-229-8700
- L'Atelier Group, New York (www.l-ateliergroup.com)
- The News, New York and Los Angeles (www.495news.com)
- Opening Ceremony, New York and Los Angeles (www.openingceremony.us) 212-219-2688
- Peoples Revolution, New York and Los Angeles (www.peoplesrevolution.com)
- Seedhouse New York (www.seedinc.net)
- Showroom Seven New York (www.showroomsevern.com)
- Simon Showroom, New York (www.simonshowroom.com)
- Steven Alan, New York and Los Angeles (www.stevenalan.com)
- W29 Showroom, New York (www.w29showroom.com)

Who are they? Check out the designers interviewed for this book.

- Alice Roi (www.aliceroi.com)
- Alison Kelly (www.alisonkellyny.com)
- Alvin Valley (www.alvinvalley.com)
- Beckerman (www.beckermans.com)
- Bell by Alicia Bell (www.aliciabell.com)
- Binetti (www.ilovebinetti.com)
- Bliss Lau (www.blisslau.com)
- Brian Wood (www.brianwoodonline.com)
- Bruno Grizzo (www.brunogrizzo.com
- Built by Wendy (www.builtbywendy.com)
- Chrstine Alcalay (www.christinealcalay.com)
- Cloak (www.cloakdesign.com)
- Doo.Ri (www.doori-nyc.com)
- Duckie Brown (www.duckiebrown.com)
- Eve Alexander (www.evealexander.com)
- Form New York (www.formnewyork.com)
- Gary Graham (www.garyggraham.com)

- Geren Ford (www.gerenford.com)
- Grace Sun (www.gracesundesign.com)
- Gustavo Cadile (www.gustavocadile.com)
- Ingwa; Melero (www.ingwamelero.com)
- Kamkyl (www.kamkyl.com)
- Krelwear (www.krelwear.com)
- Kristen Lee (www.kristenlee.com)
- Lewis Cho (www.lewischo.com)
- Linda Loudermilk (www.lindaloudermilk.com)
- Linea Nervenkitt (www.lineanervenkitt.com)
- Loeffler Randall (www.loefflerrandall.com)
- Lost Art (www.lostartnyc.com)
- Mandula (www.mandula.com)
- Maria Marta Facchinelli (www.facchinelli.com)
- Mayle (www.mayleonline.com)
- Mella (www.mellausa.com)
- Milly (www.millyny.com)
- Mimi Turner (www.mimiturner.com)
- Nature vs. Future (www.naturevsfuture.com)
- Palmer Jones (www.palmer-jones.com)
- Patch NYC (www.patchnyc.com)
- Robert Geller (www.robertgeller-ny.com)
- Romain Kapadia (www.romainkapadia.com)
- Ruthie Davis (www.ruthiedavis.com)
- Slinky Vagabond (www.slinkyvagabond.com)
- Society for Rational Dress (www.societyforrationaldress.com)
- Subversive Jewelry (www.subversivejewelry.com)
- Sunshine and Shadow (www.sunshineandshadow.com)
- Tashkent by Cheyenne (www.tashkentnyc.com)
- The Reform Party (www.thereformparty.com)
- Tom Scott (www.tomscottnyc.com)
- Twinkle by Wenlan (www.twinklebywenlan.com)
- Vena Cava (www.venacavanyc.com)
- World According to Jess (www.worldaccordingtojess.com)
- Yarborough (www.yarboroughjewelry.com)
- Yoko Devereaux (www.yokodevereaux.com)

Index

A

Accounting, 27
Advisors, 23-25
Agents, 75
Agreement, 105-6, 190, 257-59
Angels, 50-51
Appointment, 159, 164-66
Assertiveness, 4
Atelier Fund, 53
Availability, 116

B

Background, 127, 128
Balance, 64-65
Balance sheet, 19
Bank loans, 44-45
Bankruptcy, 3
Biography, 134
Blogging, 215
Bookkeeping, 27
Boutiques, 145-47
Branding, 121-22
Budget, 71
Business of fashion, xiii-xviii, 2-10, 251-52
Business plan, 10-21
Business resources, 271-72
Buyer decisions/feedback, 165-66, 184-85

C

Cancellations, 141-42
Cash before delivery (CBD), 73
Cash flow, 35-37
Cash flow statement, 19
Cash on delivery (COD),
 73, 105, 177-78, 187, 196
Celebrities, 212-13, 229
Charge backs, 139-40
CIF (cost, insurance, freight), 73
Cold calling, 160-63
Collection, 64-65, 94, 134
Commerciality, 66-67
Communication, 89, 101
Company name, 22
Company overview, 15

Competition, 9, 216-17
Competitive analysis, 17-18
Connections, 7-8, 189
Consignment, 175
Consistency, 61, 165
Consulting, 256-59
Consumer direct sales, 150-53
Control, 55-56
Controlled distribution, 171
Converters, 75-76
Copyrights, 242-50
Corporation, 20
Cost considerations, 20, 71-74, 93, 101
Cost of goods sold (COGs), 93, 95, 143-45
Council of Fashion Designers of America
 (CFDA), ix, 6, 213, 216, 250, 255-56
Counsel, outside, 56
Creativity, xiii, xv, 70, 123, 259
Credibility, 104
Credit, 37, 177
Credit cards, 41-42, 178
Culture, 102
Custom clientele, 156
Customer service, xiv, 59-60,
 103-4, 153, 179-85
Cut and sew, 113-14
Cutting tickets, 112-13

D

Day job, 39
Dedication, xiii-xviii
Delivery, 103, 167-68, 179-81
Department stores, 145
Deposit, 178
Designers, 281-82
Design time, 4
Discipline, 4, 37-38
Discounts, 141
Domestic production, 99-100

E

Economic development organizations, 46
Editing, 64
Editorial wants, 204-5
Education, 29-30

Ego, 9-10
Electronic data interchange, 140
Employees, 27-28, 30-32
Employment, 6-10
Ethics, xiv
European Economic Community registration, 23
Exchange rates, 101
Exclusives, 79, 170-71, 209
Executive summary, 15
Exit strategy, 56-57
Expenses, 37
Exports, 147-49

F

Fabrics, 68-74, 76-83, 272-74
Factories, 52-53, 102-3, 106-7, 114-20
Factoring, 47-50
Fashion Enterprise Fund in England, 54
Fashion executives, 54-55
Fashion Institute of Technology, 27
Fashion organizations, 275
Fashiondex Inc., 77
Fashiontainment, 238
Federal Trade Commission, 76, 114
Finance resources, 276
Finances, 3, 7, 18-19, 33-46, 276
Fine print, 44
Flea markets, 154
FOB (free on board), 73
Focus, 65
Freelance work, 40, 107
Fulfillment centers, 119-20

G

Gen Art, 216, 222
Gift bags, 236
Give-aways, 215-16
Grading, size, 113
Green movement, 82-83, 274
Group shows, 225
Guaranteed sell-through, 140-41
Guests, 227-28

H

Hair, 236, 278
Handbag line, 5
Hanger appeal, 164
Harmonized Duty Tariff Code, 73-74
Hiring, 58
Holiday schedules, 101-2
Home Shopping Network, 155

I

Iceland's Bangur Banking, 54
Immediates, 176
Income statement, 18-19
Incubators, 155-56, 277
Indirect costs, 143
Industry awards, 216-17
In-house, 106-7, 192-93
Installation, 221-23
In-store appearances, 182-83
Insurance, 27
International sourcing, 77
Internet domain name, 23
Investment money, 57-58
Investors, 43-44, 50, 51-55, 260
Invitations, 228-29

J

Jobbers, 76
Job resources, 276

K

Knockoffs, 242-50
Knowledge, 7

L

Labels, 114
Labor costs, 38
Language, 101
LDP (landed duty paid), 73, 172
Lead time, 70-71, 102
Leftover merchandise, 185
Legal issues/services, 26, 277
Lenders, 43-44
Lending, online, 46
Letter of credit, 178
Leveraging show, 238-39
Licensing, 252-54
Lighting, 231-32
Limited liability corporation, 20, 21
Line of credit, 50
Line representation, 189
Lines, number of, 189
Line sales, 186-93
Line sheet, 132-33
Listening skills, 8-9
Location, 21, 224
Logos, 122
Lookbook, 122, 124, 126, 130-31

M

Maintenance, 20
Makeup, 236, 278
Manufacturers, 52
Markdown money, 140-41
Market, 1-2, 16-17, 71-72, 197, 277
Marketing, 16-17, 121-22, 134-37
Marking, 113
Materials, 68
Merchandizing, 235
Mills, 75
Minimums, 96-97
Minority loans, 46
Models, 126-27, 233-34
Music, 232

N

National chain stores, 147
Net terms, 178
Networking, 213-14
Nondisclosure agreement, 43-44
NRDC Equity Partners LLC, 54

O

Off-shore production, 100, 117-18
Online stores, 149-50, 277-78
Operations plan, 18
Order taking, 36, 166-74
Outside financings, 42-46
Outsourcing, 30-32
Overordering, 72
Overstock, 185

P

Packing, 119
Partnerships, 19, 23-25, 256-59, 260
Past due accounts, 179
Patent, 245
Patternmaking, 87-91
Pay premium, 70
Payment, 72-73, 105, 176-78, 191-92
Perfection, 92
Personal loans, 41
Personal savings, 39
Phone calls, 116
Photographer, 124, 278
Photography, 125, 208, 230-31
Postcards, 135, 136
Presentation, 130, 221-23
Press coverage, 134-35, 201-3
Press kits, 122-34

Press release, 207

Press release, 207
Pricing, 66, 72-73, 105, 142-45
Private clients, sales, 41
Private equity funds, 53-54
Product, 59, 74, 279-81
Production, 57, 80-81, 84-86, 94, 96-114, 272-74
Professionalism, 9
Professional services, 25-28
Promotional mailers, 135
Public relations, 203-12, 217-18
Purchase order financing, 50

Q

Quality control, 65-66, 81-82, 102, 108, 116-18
QuickBooks Pro, 27
QVC, 155

R

Referrals, 97-98
Regional markets, 276
Rehearsal, 237
Relationships, 8
Replacements, 80
Reputation, 8
Research, 156-57
Retailers, 52
Returns, 141-42
Run of show, 236
Runway, 219-21, 223-39

S

Sales, 17, 122-34, 138-45, 158, 179-92, 202-3, 277
Salespeople, 181-82
Salespeople information, 182
Samples, 69-70, 87-95, 137, 208-9, 210
Schedule, 108
Seating charts, 229
Secondary market, 76
Second line, 254-55
Selection, 168-69
Selling self, 186
Sell-through, 180, 184
Service approach, 189-90
Service Corps of Retired Executives (SCORE), 14, 54-55, 152
Services, 98-99
Set, 127
Sewn goods, 78
Shipping, 35, 73-74, 101, 119
Shopping events, 154-55

Showpieces, 66-67
Showrooms, 186-92, 198-200
Shows, 219
Signature, 60-62, 65
Small Business Administration, 2, 13-14, 45
Small collection, 64
Small orders, 168
Smart money, 51-52
Software, 278
Sole proprietorship, 19, 21
Space, 224
Special requests, 169-70
Specialty stores, 145-47
Sponsorship, 239-41
Staff, 237
Staging, 225-26
Start time, 238
Start-up period, 3-4
Staying power, 210-11
Stores, 151-53, 156-63, 181, 183-84
Styling, 128, 129, 208, 235, 278
Suppliers, 52-53
Sustainable fabrics, 82-83
Swap outs, 184

T

Target customer, 17
Tax liability, 20
Technology, 109-10, 278
Television, 155
Terms, 101, 191-92
Territory, 190
Timing, 101-2, 205-6, 226-27
Trademark, 22, 23, 244-45
Trade shows, 57-58, 74-75, 193-200, 244-45,
 278-79
Training, 101
Trends, 63-64
Trunk shows, 175
TSM Capital, 53-54

U

U.S. Patent and Trademark Office, 23-25
Unique selling proposition (USP), 17

V

Vanity investors, 55
Vertical manufacturing, 77-78

W

Website, 136-37, 150-51
Wholesale, 145-50
Women business owner loans, 46
Work schedule, 3